marie claire
seasonal
kitchen

acknowledgments

Once again I find myself wandering through the wonderful world of summery spoonfuls and wintery pots and for this I extend a huge thank you to Murdoch Books, and in particular Kay Scarlett and Juliet Rogers. A year in the kitchen is not only the subject of this book but could also describe the process of its creation. Books take time and someone needs to keep an eye on the details and the ticking clock. For this I thank the team at Murdoch and in particular Jacqueline Blanchard and Desney Shoemark who kept an eye on me and clicked their fingers when necessary. A big thank you goes also to Andrew De Sousa for all his hard work in the test kitchen. As well, a huge thank you goes to Katri Hilden for her keen eye, questioning mind and for editing this book with a series of cheerful emails.

Once again I am indebted to Marylouise Brammer for her gleeful enthusiasm and wonderful eye. I can't think of a nicer way to construct a book than spending a few sunny afternoons around your kitchen table looking at beautiful photos and talking about floating words. Thanks for all the hard work that follows such discussions.

Christine Rudolph has done an amazing job creating the seasonal variations of the kitchen out of the simplest gestures. Her beautiful styling and artful arrangements have turned my basic vision into wonderful images. Thank you for giving so much and travelling so far. For capturing those images in a gorgeous light, thanks go to Gorta Yuuki, for his calm, meditative approach to a very big book and for the beautiful photographs within. Thanks also to Geoff Lung and team for a great studio and environment to work in.

Once again Ross Dobson has brought his skills to the kitchen. This is our seventh book together and I thank him for all the good times, hard work, clever cooking and the amazing contribution he has made to the series. Thank you for turning a list of ingredients into a plate of yumminess.

This is a book about time spent in a kitchen, and my home kitchen gets a bit of a beating every time I start to write a book — as do the individuals who pass through it. To the boys in my life, Warwick, Ben and Sam, thank you for your understanding and patience in the face of odd dinners cobbled together out of leftovers, teetering piles of dishes in need of a scrub and my 'cooking' music being played over and over again!

First published in 2007 by Murdoch Books Pty Ltd.
This edition published in 2008 for WH Smith Retail Limited.
www.murdochbooks.com.au

Murdoch Books Australia
Pier 8/9
23 Hickson Road
Millers Point NSW 2000
Phone: +61 (0) 2 8220 2000
Fax: +61 (0) 2 8220 2558

Murdoch Books UK Limited
Erico House, 6th Floor
93–99 Upper Richmond Road
Putney, London SW15 2TG
Phone: +44 (0) 20 8785 5995
Fax: +44 (0) 20 8785 5985

Chief Executive: Juliet Rogers
Publishing Director: Kay Scarlett

Project managers: Jacqueline Blanchard and Desney Shoemark
Editor: Katri Hilden
Design concept and design: Marylouise Brammer
Stylist: Christine Rudolph
Photographers: Gorta Yuuki and Mikkel Vang
Food preparation: Ross Dobson
Production: Monique Layt

ISBN 978 1 74196 304 5

Printed by i-Book Printing Ltd in 2007. PRINTED IN CHINA.

IMPORTANT: Those who might be at risk from the effects of salmonella poisoning (the elderly, pregnant women, young children and those suffering from immune deficiency diseases) should consult their doctor with any concerns about eating raw eggs.

CONVERSION GUIDE: You may find cooking times vary depending on the oven you are using. For fan-forced ovens, as a general rule, set the oven temperature to 20°C (35°F) lower than indicated in the recipe. We have used 20 ml (4 teaspoon) tablespoon measures. If you are using a 15 ml (3 teaspoon) tablespoon, for most recipes the difference will not be noticeable. However, for recipes using baking powder, gelatine, bicarbonate of soda (baking soda), small amounts of flour and cornflour (cornstarch), add an extra teaspoon for each tablespoon specified.

marie claire

seasonal kitchen

michele cranston

photography by
gorta yuuki and mikkel vang

MURDOCH BOOKS

contents

introduction

Spring, summer, autumn, winter … nothing evokes
the passing of time more than the seasonal changes
within each year. And while most of us think of seasons
in terms of what is happening just beyond the front
door, those falling leaves or greying skies are also
vividly reflected in the changing moods of the kitchen.
Just think of the green and leafy celebration of spring,
the exuberant abundance of summer, the earthy
aromas of autumn and the warming richness of winter.
Not only are they illustrated by the varied shapes and
hues of the fruit piled into a bowl on the kitchen bench,
they are also evident in the staples that appear in the

cupboards and refrigerator. Note how the vinegars and olive oils of summer dressings are slowly replaced by the heavy spices and filling grains of winter, while summer's leafy salads are discarded in favour of the humble potato in all its varied forms. These changes reflect what is seasonal, what is available at the local farmers' market and what we crave and want to eat at different times of the year.

I must say that I love the whole seasonal nature of food. Who couldn't get excited by the changing seasons? After the richness of winter food, that first crunch of spring greens is a reminder that the long, blue-skied days of summer are just around the corner. Tropical summer fruits, salads and seafood can sometimes

make you feel like you are indulging in the food of the gods — and it's not hard to imagine forever whiling away your days in an idyllic world of blue skies. Yet with the passing of summer and the arrival of the golden hues of autumn, you find yourself suddenly remembering how good a warming bowl of soup can be or how the heavy, earthy flavours of a hearty winter stew can wrap you up in the foodie equivalent of a woolly winter blanket.

The modern supermarket may supply all foods at all times, but our own response to nature follows much more traditional lines. We crave freshness and a crisp crunch in summer and then delight in the comforting textures of wintery meals. This is how it should be.

We should revel in fruit and vegetables that are newly harvested as they hold the flavours that best suit each season. And when raw ingredients are freshly plucked from the earth and tree, they require very little work to turn them into great food. Just add a simple recipe, a few spices and a scattering of fresh herbs and turn the simply fresh into something wonderful.

This is a book that celebrates those changes with recipes that highlight the essential flavours of seasonal ingredients. To these simple recipes we've added quick and easy tips, fast food ideas and pages of simple favourites that are a must no matter what time of the year it is — be it spring, summer, autumn or winter.

spring

Spring is the season of rejuvenation. Even its name evokes a youthful energy — and who doesn't find an extra bounce to their step when soft, warm breezes arrive to herald the end of winter's gloomy chill. The days begin to lighten and so does the food. Abundant with verdant leafiness, curling tendrils and snappy baby vegetables, spring is all about leafy greens and the refreshing crunch of salads after the warming, robust dishes of winter. Make way for bright-green baby beans, new-season lamb, asparagus spears lightly drizzled with lemon and butter, grilled fish and an extravagance of herbs. Indeed, the tang of lemon and the deep green flavour of parsley, coriander (cilantro) and thyme are the predominant colours and taste of spring. So grab a handful of fresh herbs and celebrate the springtime abundance of all that is lush and fresh.

salads with crunch

asparagus

grilled fish artichoke papaya

crab and prawns spring onions

oranges mint

pineapples leafy mouthfuls

parsley seared lamb

strawberries snow peas

berries piled high with creamy desserts

buttery greens avocados

melons beans

spinach handful of herbs

mandarins peas watercress

bok choy zucchini

cakes with a citrus bite

fresh berries with honey-lime yoghurt

2 tablespoons honey
juice of 1 lime
generous pinch of ground cardamom
250 g (9 oz/1²/₃ cups) strawberries
310 g (11 oz/2 cups) blueberries
300 g (10¹/₂ oz/1¹/₄ scant cups) plain or Greek-style yoghurt

Put the honey, lime juice and cardamom in a small saucepan and warm over low heat. Stir until the lime and honey are well combined, then remove from the heat and allow to cool.

Hull the strawberries and slice them in half, or into quarters if large. Divide the strawberries and blueberries among four bowls. Top with a large dollop of yoghurt and drizzle the honey mixture over the yoghurt. Serves 4

coconut muesli

400 g (14 oz/4 cups) rolled (porridge) oats
125 g (4¹/₂ oz/1 cup) unsalted sunflower seeds
2 tablespoons sesame seeds
125 g (4¹/₂ oz/1 cup) slivered almonds
120 g (4¹/₄ oz/2 cups) shredded coconut
250 ml (9 fl oz/³/₄ cup) maple syrup
4 tablespoons vegetable oil
40 g (1¹/₂ oz/¹/₄ cup) finely sliced dried peaches
35 g (1¹/₄ oz/¹/₄ cup) finely sliced dried mango

Preheat the oven to 150°C (300°F/Gas 2). Put the oats in a large bowl with the sunflower seeds, sesame seeds, almonds and coconut and mix well.

Heat the maple syrup and vegetable oil in a small saucepan over low heat. Pour the warm mixture over the muesli and stir so that all the grains and seeds are well covered.

Spread the mixture over two baking trays and bake for 30 minutes, stirring occasionally, and swapping the trays around in the oven halfway through baking. Remove from the oven and allow to cool.

Transfer to a large bowl, add the peach and mango and toss well. The muesli can be stored in an airtight container for up to 1 month. Makes about 1.2 kg (2 lb 10 oz), enough for 12 serves

griddle cakes with maple-berry butter

maple-berry butter
200 g (7 oz) unsalted butter, softened
3 tablespoons maple syrup
100 g (3¹/₂ oz/about ³/₄ cup) dried cranberries

250 g (9 oz/2 cups) self-raising flour
2 heaped tablespoons soft brown sugar
400 ml (14 fl oz) buttermilk
2 eggs, separated
1 teaspoon natural vanilla extract
1–2 tablespoons butter, for greasing
fresh berries, to serve

To make the maple-berry butter, put the butter, maple syrup and cranberries in a food processor or blender and chop until well combined. Spoon onto a sheet of baking paper or plastic wrap and roll up to form a log. Refrigerate until ready to use.

Sift the flour and sugar into a bowl and make a well in the centre. Add the buttermilk, egg yolks and vanilla and stir to combine. In a separate bowl, whisk the egg whites until light and fluffy. Fold the egg whites into the buttermilk batter.

Heat a non-stick frying pan over medium heat and lightly grease with a little butter. Spoon the batter into the pan, in batches, to form pancakes that are 8–10 cm (3¹/₄–4 inches) in diameter. Cook until golden brown underneath, then flip the pancakes over and cook for a further minute or two. Transfer to a warm plate. Repeat with the remaining mixture, adding more butter to the pan as you need it.

Pile the warm griddle cakes onto serving plates. Serve with several slices of maple-berry butter and a scattering of berries. Serves 4

Start the day with fresh berries and a spicy sweet zing

opposite: fresh berries with honey-lime yoghurt
over: coconut muesli, and griddle cakes with
maple-berry butter

A bowl of crunchy grains and yoghurt on a crystal-clear morning

fried egg and aromatic rice

2 tablespoons butter
2 garlic cloves, crushed
1 red onion, finely diced
1 tablespoon finely chopped lemon grass, white part only
1 tablespoon finely chopped fresh ginger
370 g (13 oz/2 cups) cooked basmati rice
2 tablespoons olive oil
4 eggs
2 handfuls of coriander (cilantro) leaves, roughly chopped
a handful of parsley, roughly chopped
25 g (1 oz/1 bunch) chives, finely snipped
sweet chilli sauce (Favourites), to serve

Melt the butter in a large heavy-based saucepan or wok over medium heat. Add the garlic, onion, lemon grass and ginger and sauté for 5 minutes, or until the onion is soft and lightly golden. Add the rice and cook, stirring, for 5 minutes, or until all the ingredients are well combined and the rice is starting to stick to the pan. Remove from the heat and set aside.

Heat the olive oil in a large frying pan over medium-high heat and fry the eggs to your liking. Stir the coriander, parsley and chives through the rice and divide among four shallow bowls. Top each bowl with a fried egg and serve with a little bowl of sweet chilli sauce. Serves 4

corn fritters

125 g (4 1/2 oz/1 cup) plain (all-purpose) flour
1 teaspoon baking powder
1 teaspoon smoked paprika
1 tablespoon sugar
1 teaspoon sea salt
2 eggs
125 ml (4 fl oz/1/2 cup) milk
4 corn cobs
1/2 red capsicum (pepper), diced
4 spring onions (scallions), finely sliced
90 g (3 1/4 oz/1 bunch) coriander (cilantro), chopped
4 tablespoons vegetable oil

Sift the flour, baking powder and paprika into a large bowl, stir in the sugar and sea salt, then make a well in the centre. In a separate bowl, whisk together the eggs and milk. Gradually add the liquid ingredients to the dry, stirring to make a stiff, lump-free batter. Cover and refrigerate until ready to use.

Using a sharp knife, cut the corn kernels away from the cobs and put the kernels in a large bowl. Add the capsicum, spring onion and coriander. Toss to combine.

Just before serving, slowly work the batter into the fresh ingredients. Heat 2 tablespoons of the oil in a large non-stick frying pan over medium heat. Using 1 tablespoon at a time, drop spoonfuls of batter into the hot pan. Cook for a few minutes, or until golden underneath, then flip the fritters and cook for a further 2 minutes, or until quite crisp. Remove from the pan and keep warm while you cook the rest of the fritters, adding more oil as necessary — you should end up with around 30 small fritters. Delicious served with crisp bacon or fried eggs. Serves 6

breakfast bars

150 g (5 1/2 oz) butter
175 g (6 oz/1/2 cup) honey
200 g (7 oz/2 cups) rolled (porridge) oats
60 g (2 1/4 oz/1 cup) shredded coconut
1 teaspoon baking powder
3 tablespoons sesame seeds
200 g (7 oz/3/4 cup) pitted prunes, chopped
100 g (3 1/2 oz/2/3 cup) dried peaches, chopped
75 g (2 1/2 oz/1/2 cup) currants
3 eggs

Preheat the oven to 170°C (325°F/Gas 3). Line a 23 x 32 cm (9 x 12 3/4 inch) sandwich tin with baking paper.

Put the butter and honey in a small saucepan over medium heat and stir until the butter has melted.

Toss the oats, coconut, baking powder and sesame seeds together in a large bowl. Add the prunes, peaches and currants and mix well. Add the warm honey mixture and eggs and stir to combine, then spoon evenly into the sandwich tin.

Bake for 25–30 minutes, or until the mixture is cooked through and the top is golden brown. Remove from the oven and allow to cool in the tin before cutting into 12 bars. Makes 12

seasonal ideas
- Serve the aromatic rice with some roughly broken hot-smoked salmon or trout as a modern twist on kedgeree. It can also be served as a side dish to seared seafood and roast chicken.
- Add a scatter of baby rocket (arugula) leaves or finely chopped tomato to the aromatic rice and serve with seared lamb fillets.
- We've used a home-made sweet chilli sauce to accompany the fried egg and aromatic rice, but you could also use a bottled Thai sweet chilli sauce or an Asian-style chilli jam.

opposite: fried egg and aromatic rice
over: corn fritters, and breakfast bars

Sunshine, a cup of tea and a wholesome bar of nutty fruit

smoothies

Celebrate the new flavours of spring with healthy fruit drinks that are just bursting with energy.

fresh fruit whips

With a blender at hand and all the wonderful fruits of spring it's easy to whizz up fresh fruit whips. Here are some fantastic combinations to help you greet the morning with a zing.

- Orange juice, banana and passionfruit.
- Ruby grapefruit, mango and strawberry.
- Orange, ginger and rockmelon (or any other orange-fleshed melon).
- Orange, papaya and a splash of lime.
- Fresh pineapple, banana, passionfruit and mint.
- Honeydew melon, pineapple and lime.

banana smoothie

Put 1 roughly chopped banana, 185 g (6$^1/_2$ oz/$^3/_4$ cup) plain yoghurt, 1 tablespoon honey and 125 ml (4 fl oz/$^1/_2$ cup) milk in a blender with a pinch of nutmeg or ground cardamom and 8 ice cubes. Blend until smooth. Serves 2

strawberry lassi

Hull 250 g (9 oz) strawberries and put them in a blender with 250 g (9 oz/1 cup) plain yoghurt, 1 teaspoon honey and a pinch of ground cardamom. Blend until smooth. Serves 2

mango lassi

Put the chopped flesh of 1 ripe mango in a blender. Add 1 teaspoon honey, 1 teaspoon lime juice, 125 g (4$^1/_2$ oz/$^1/_2$ cup)

plain yoghurt and 6 ice cubes. Blend until smooth, pour into two chilled glasses and garnish with dried mint. Serves 2

pineapple, mango and coconut lassi

Put the roughly chopped flesh of 1 ripe mango in a blender with 125 g (4^1/$_2$ oz/^{3}/$_4$ cup) diced fresh pineapple, 250 g (9 oz/1 cup) plain yoghurt, 4 tablespoons coconut milk and 6 ice cubes. Blend until smooth, pour into two chilled glasses and garnish with a slice of fresh coconut. Serves 2

raspberry and honey lassi

Put a generous handful of frozen raspberries in a blender with 1 teaspoon honey, 250 g (9 oz/1 cup) plain yoghurt and 6 ice cubes. Blend until smooth. Serves 2

blackberry and vanilla milkshake

Put a generous handful of frozen blackberries in a blender with 1 teaspoon caster (superfine) sugar, 1 teaspoon natural vanilla extract and 600 ml (21 fl oz) cold milk. Blend until smooth. Serves 2

And for those afternoons when you feel like being indulged rather than virtuous …

strawberry sundae

Stir 125 g (4^1/$_2$ oz) hulled and mashed strawberries through 4 scoops of softened vanilla ice cream. Spoon into two chilled glasses. Pour chilled milk over the top and garnish with strawberries and a drizzle of maple syrup. Serves 2

crab and celeriac remoulade

1 egg yolk
1 tablespoon lemon juice
1/2 teaspoon finely grated lemon zest
1 teaspoon mustard
125 ml (4 fl oz/1/2 cup) light olive oil
1 large celeriac, about 350 g (12 oz), peeled and julienned
1 tablespoon finely chopped parsley
150 g (51/2 oz/about 1 cup) fresh crabmeat
1/4 teaspoon paprika
crispbread, to serve

Put the egg yolk, lemon juice, lemon zest and mustard in a large bowl and whisk to combine. Slowly whisk in the olive oil a little at a time until a thick mayonnaise forms. Add the celeriac, parsley and crabmeat and toss to combine.

Spoon into four small ramekins, pressing the mixture down lightly, then turn each remoulade out onto a serving plate. Sprinkle paprika over the top and serve with crispbread. Serves 4 as a starter

fried zucchini flowers

16 zucchini (courgette) flowers
70 g (21/2 oz) soft goat's cheese
2 eggs
a generous pinch of nutmeg
125 g (41/2 oz/1/2 cup) plain (all-purpose) flour
vegetable oil, for pan-frying
lemon cheeks, to serve

Open out the petals of the zucchini flowers and remove the stamens. Spoon 1/2 teaspoon of goat's cheese into the centre of each flower, then close the petals back around the cheese, pressing them gently together.

Crack the eggs into a shallow bowl and beat with the nutmeg and a generous sprinkle of sea salt and freshly ground black pepper. Put the flour on a plate.

Pour enough vegetable oil into a frying pan to fill it to about 1 cm (1/2 inch) and heat over medium–high heat. Dip one of the flowers into the flour and gently toss to ensure it is well coated. Shake off any loose flour, then dip into the beaten eggs. Allow any excess egg to drip off, then gently drop the flower into the hot oil. Cook on both sides for 1 minute, or until golden brown. Remove and drain on paper towels. Repeat with the remaining flowers.

Serve hot with a lemon cheek. Serves 4 as a starter

warm salad of roast tomato and buffalo mozzarella

4 vine-ripened tomatoes
1 red onion
1 teaspoon caster (superfine) sugar
4 slices of prosciutto
1 buffalo mozzarella cheese
6 radicchio leaves, roughly torn
1 tablespoon balsamic vinegar
2 tablespoons extra virgin olive oil

Preheat the oven to 150°C (300°F/Gas 2). Line a baking tray with baking paper.

Slice the tomatoes in half crossways and sit them on the baking tray, cut side up. Peel the onion and cut it in half, then slice into half-moons and add to the baking tray. Season the tomatoes and onion with the sugar and a generous sprinkle of sea salt and freshly ground black pepper. Bake for 30 minutes, or until the tomatoes are beginning to soften around the edges.

Slice the cheese into four thick rounds and wrap each one in a prosciutto slice. Add the mozzarella parcels to the baking tray and bake for a further 20 minutes.

Divide the tomatoes and onion among four serving plates. Scatter with the torn radicchio and sit the mozzarella parcels on top. Whisk the vinegar and olive oil together and drizzle over the salad. Serves 4 as a starter

seasonal ideas

- The velvety, milky texture of buffalo mozzarella is superb with the wonderful flavours of fig, prosciutto, roast tomato, olives and salami. It's also perfect with sliced ripe peaches, basil leaves and a drizzle of sweet balsamic vinegar.

- Soft and milky, mozzarella and bocconcini (fresh baby mozzarella cheese) work well with the fresh, herby flavours of spring. Finely slice and serve with butter lettuce, leg ham, cherry tomatoes, basil and wholegrain mustard.

- Toss cherry bocconcini through a salad of sugar snap peas, smoked salmon and roughly chopped parsley, and drizzle with a peppery lemon vinaigrette (Favourites). Or toss through a warm pasta flavoured with generous quantities of parmesan cheese, garlic and fresh herbs.

- Make a salad of finely sliced pear and radicchio and toss with a simple vinaigrette flavoured with dijon mustard. Serve the salad on top of individual slices of buffalo mozzarella, season with sea salt and cracked pepper and lightly drizzle with honey.

opposite: crab and celeriac remoulade
over: fried zucchini flowers, and
warm salad of roast tomato and buffalo mozzarella

spinach and coconut soup

1 kg (2 lb 4 oz/2 bunches) English spinach
4 tablespoons olive oil
2 onions, finely sliced
2 garlic cloves, finely chopped
1/2 teaspoon ground cumin
500 ml (17 fl oz/2 cups) vegetable stock (Favourites)
400 ml (14 fl oz) tin coconut milk

Rinse the spinach under cold running water, then drain and roughly chop. Heat the olive oil in a large saucepan over medium heat. Add the onion, garlic and cumin and sauté for 5 minutes, or until the onion is soft and translucent.

Add the spinach, cover and cook for 2–3 minutes, then toss the spinach about a little so that it cooks evenly. When all the spinach has sweated down to a dark green colour, take the pan off the heat.

Put the spinach in a blender with half the stock. Blend until smooth, then return to the saucepan. Stir in the coconut milk and remaining stock and warm the soup over medium heat. Season to taste with sea salt and ground white pepper. Serves 6 as a starter

bocconcini salad

1 tablespoon white wine vinegar
4 tablespoons extra virgin olive oil
20 mint leaves, roughly chopped
a handful of flat-leaf (Italian) parsley, roughly chopped
350 g (12 oz/2 bunches) thin asparagus, trimmed
200 g (7 oz) bocconcini (fresh baby mozzarella cheese), cut in half
2 avocados

Put the vinegar, olive oil, mint and parsley in a large bowl.

Bring a saucepan of water to the boil. Add the asparagus spears and blanch for 1 minute, or until they begin to turn emerald green. Rinse the spears under cold running water, then cut them into 4 cm (1 1/2 inch) lengths. Add them to the mint and parsley, along with the bocconcini.

Slice the avocados in half and remove the stones. Cut the flesh into bite-sized chunks or wedges and add them to the salad. Season with sea salt and freshly ground black pepper, then gently toss. Serves 4 as a side dish

artichoke and avocado salad

3 lemons, cut in half
4 artichokes
3 tablespoons extra virgin olive oil
8 mint leaves, finely chopped
a handful of flat-leaf (Italian) parsley, roughly chopped
1 garlic clove, crushed
2 avocados, diced
1 fennel bulb, shaved

Bring a large saucepan of salted water to the boil. Fill a large bowl with cold water and add the juice of one of the lemons.

Taking one artichoke at a time, trim the artichoke stalks to within 2 cm (3/4 inch) of the artichoke head, then keep pulling away and discarding the outer leaves until you reach leaves with a base that looks yellow and crisp. Using a sharp knife, slice away the top third of the artichoke, then rub the artichoke with the cut side of a lemon. Place it in the bowl of lemon water and trim the remaining artichokes. Working with one artichoke at a time, remove the artichokes from the water, scrape out the central choke and pull out any spiky inner leaves. Return to the lemon water until ready to use.

Add the artichokes to the boiling water, weigh them down with a plate and simmer for 20 minutes. Test that the artichokes are done by pushing the tip of a knife into each one just above the stem — they should feel tender. Drain the artichokes upside down for a minute, then slice in half lengthways.

Put the artichokes in a large dish with the olive oil, herbs, garlic and juice from the remaining lemon halves. Season with a little sea salt and freshly ground black pepper and toss to ensure that the artichokes are well coated in the marinade. Allow to cool, then arrange on a serving platter with the avocado and shaved fennel. Drizzle with some of the artichoke marinade and season with sea salt and freshly ground black pepper. Serves 4–6 as a side dish

seasonal ideas

- If you're cooking fresh artichokes, always cook a few extra and marinate them in olive oil, lemon juice, chopped mint and parsley. Serve as part of an antipasto platter, by themselves with some shaved pecorino cheese, or with a salad of rocket (arugula) leaves, roasted red capsicum (pepper) (Favourites) and a spoonful of soft goat's cheese. You can also serve fresh artichokes with grilled white fish and a garlicky aïoli (Favourites).

- If you don't have time to cook fresh artichokes, buy freshly marinated artichokes from good delicatessens — you'll find them less acidic than the bottled varieties.

opposite: spinach and coconut soup
over: bocconcini salad, and artichoke and avocado salad

roast pork with a pineapple glaze

500 ml (17 fl oz/2 cups) pineapple juice
3 tablespoons maple syrup
2 garlic cloves, finely chopped
4 star anise
2 cinnamon sticks
3 large red chillies, seeded and cut into large pieces
1 kg (2 lb 4 oz) pork loin, skin cut off and reserved
2 tablespoons balsamic vinegar
12 thin pineapple slices, skin and core removed
green salad, to serve

Make a marinade by mixing the pineapple juice and maple syrup together in a large bowl with the garlic, star anise, cinnamon sticks and chilli. Using a sharp knife, cut 5 mm (1/4 inch) deep slashes into the pork, 4–5 cm (1 1/2–2 inches) apart. Sit the pork in the marinade, roll it around until well coated, then cover and marinate in the refrigerator overnight.

Heat the oven to 200°C (400°F/Gas 6). Lift the pork into a roasting tin, pour the marinade all over and around the pork, then cover with foil and roast for 40 minutes.

Meanwhile, make the crackling. Score the pork skin lightly using a very sharp knife, then cut it into several strips. Put the strips in a roasting tin, brush them with water, sprinkle with sea salt and roast for 20 minutes, or until golden brown and crackly. Drain off any fat.

Take the foil off the pork and baste the meat with the pan juices. Roast, uncovered, for a further 30–35 minutes, or until the juices run clear when a skewer is inserted into the thickest part of the meat. Remove from the oven, loosely cover with foil and allow to rest for 10 minutes. Meanwhile, stir the vinegar into the pan juices.

Carve the pork and serve on the pineapple slices with a spoonful of pan juices, a green salad and some bits of crackling. Serves 6 as a starter or light meal

prawn and rocket salad

1 large red chilli, seeded and finely chopped
3 garlic cloves, crushed
4 tablespoons olive oil
20 raw king prawns (shrimp), peeled and deveined
150 g (5 1/2 oz/1 bunch) rocket (arugula), stalks trimmed
2 avocados, diced
2 tablespoons butter
4 tablespoons lemon juice

Put the chilli, garlic and olive oil in a bowl, add the prawns and toss to coat. Cover and refrigerate for a few hours.

Arrange the rocket leaves on four serving plates and scatter the avocado over the top.

Heat the butter in a large wok over high heat. When the butter begins to sizzle and turn brown, add the prawns — in batches if necessary — and cook for a few minutes on each side, or until they turn pink and begin to curl up. Divide the prawns among the plates.

Add the lemon juice to the pan and cook for 1 minute. Spoon the juices over the salad. Serves 4 as a starter or light meal

squid and fennel salad

8 small squid (about 750 g/1 lb 10 oz in total), cleaned (reserve the tentacles)
2 garlic cloves, crushed
1/2 teaspoon ground white pepper
3 tablespoons olive oil
3 tablespoons lemon juice
2 fennel bulbs
16 kalamata olives, pitted and roughly chopped
a handful of parsley, roughly chopped
1 tablespoon finely chopped mint
3 tablespoons unsalted butter

Rinse the squid under cold running water and pat dry with paper towels. Cut the tubes along one side and open them out into a flat piece. Using a sharp knife, lightly score the inside surface with crisscross lines — don't cut too deeply, just enough to mark the flesh. Slice into 3 cm (1 1/4 inch) wide strips and put the strips and tentacles in a non metallic bowl. Add the garlic, white pepper, olive oil and lemon juice, then toss well to coat. Cover and refrigerate for 1 hour.

Very finely slice the fennel and place in a bowl with the olives, parsley and mint. Season lightly with sea salt and freshly ground black pepper.

Drain the squid, reserving the marinating liquid. Heat 1 tablespoon of the butter in a non-stick frying pan over medium heat and add the squid a few pieces at a time. Cook for 2 1/2 minutes on each side, or until the flesh is opaque, then add the squid to the fennel. Cook the remaining squid in two more batches, adding more butter as needed.

When all the squid is cooked, add the marinating liquid and any remaining butter to the pan and simmer over medium heat until the butter has melted. Pour the pan juices over the salad and toss well. Serves 4 as a starter or light meal

opposite: roast pork with a pineapple glaze
over: prawn and rocket salad, and squid and fennel salad

spicy prawn salad

20 cooked prawns (shrimp), peeled and deveined
1 large red chilli, seeded and finely chopped
1/2 teaspoon cayenne pepper
1/2 teaspoon ground cumin
1 tablespoon finely grated fresh ginger
2 spring onions (scallions), finely sliced
2 tablespoons lime juice
4 tablespoons olive oil
a handful of coriander (cilantro) leaves
2 small avocados, diced
steamed couscous (Favourites), to serve

Put the prawns in a bowl with the chilli, cayenne pepper, cumin, ginger, spring onion, lime juice and olive oil. Toss to coat the prawns well, then add the coriander and avocado and season to taste. Lightly toss again and serve on a bed of steamed couscous. Serves 4

prawn and chicken salad

350 g (12 oz) small cooked prawns (shrimp)
1 teaspoon ground cumin
2 teaspoons fish sauce
4 tablespoons lime juice
4 tablespoons olive oil
1 tablespoon sesame oil
15 mint leaves, finely sliced
1 teaspoon sugar
2 cooked boneless, skinless chicken breasts, shredded
1 carrot, grated
100 g (3 1/2 oz) snow pea (mangetout) sprouts
1 telegraph (long) cucumber, peeled, seeded and diced
2 spring onions (scallions), finely sliced
1 baby cos (romaine) lettuce, finely sliced
1–2 tablespoons sesame seeds, toasted

Peel the prawns and put them in a large bowl.

In a small bowl, combine the cumin, fish sauce, lime juice, olive oil, sesame oil, mint and sugar. Stir until the sugar has dissolved, then pour the mixture over the prawns and toss until the prawns are well coated.

Add the chicken, carrot, snow pea sprouts, cucumber, spring onion and lettuce. Lightly toss together, then pile onto a serving platter or into individual bowls and sprinkle with the sesame seeds. Serves 4–6

crab omelettes

3 eggs
1 tablespoon mirin
1/2 teaspoon soy sauce
250 g (9 oz/about 1 1/2 cups) fresh crabmeat, shredded
1 teaspoon lemon juice
1 teaspoon olive oil
90 g (3 1/4 oz/1 cup) bean sprouts, trimmed
a large handful of coriander (cilantro) leaves
2 teaspoons vegetable oil
2 spring onions (scallions), sliced on the diagonal
1 large red chilli, seeded and very finely sliced

Whisk together the eggs, mirin and soy sauce in a small bowl. Season with ground white pepper and sea salt.

In a separate bowl, combine the crabmeat, lemon juice and olive oil. Add the bean sprouts and coriander, season to taste, then toss to combine.

Heat a small non-stick frying pan over medium heat and add 1/2 teaspoon of the vegetable oil. Ladle in one-quarter of the egg mixture and swirl it around so the egg thinly coats the base of the pan. When the egg is cooked, slide the omelette out onto a warmed plate. Repeat with the remaining mixture, adding oil to the pan as needed, to make four thin omelettes.

Place each omelette on a warmed serving plate. Spoon one-quarter of the crab mixture over one half of each omelette, then fold the omelettes back over the filling. Sprinkle with the spring onion and chilli and serve immediately. Serves 4

seasonal ideas

- Prawns (shrimp) always feel a little special, but they don't necessarily need special treatment. Pan-fry small peeled raw prawns in lots of garlic and butter. Split open a rosetta or soft sourdough roll, spoon the cooked prawns into the centre and drizzle with the garlicky butter.

- Marinate large prawns in olive oil, lime juice and grated fresh ginger. Pan-fry and serve with a salsa of chopped coriander (cilantro) leaves, finely chopped preserved lemon rind and roughly chopped roasted red capsicum (pepper) (Favourites). Serve with couscous.

- Wrap large raw prawns in thin strips of prosciutto and chargrill or barbecue until cooked. Serve with a rocket (arugula) salad and a dollop of mayonnaise.

- Lightly pan-fry chopped prawn meat with some finely chopped bacon. Remove from the heat and add some chopped garlic chives. Roll the mixture in spring roll wrappers and deep-fry. Serve as a starter.

opposite: spicy prawn salad
over: prawn and chicken salad, and crab omelettes

A scrumptious seaside salad of tangy flavours

seafood

Whether it's baked, pan-fried, barbecued or steamed, seafood needs only the simplest additions to make a flavourful and fuss-free meal. All you need is a quick sauce, a fresh salad and some wedges of fresh lemon or lime. It's that easy. Here are a few suggestions for classic seafood sauces that have stood the test of time.

salsa verde
Roughly chop a handful of flat-leaf (Italian) parsley with 10 mint leaves, 1 garlic clove, 3 anchovy fillets and 3 tablespoons capers. Tip into a bowl and mix with 1 teaspoon dijon mustard, 1 tablespoon lemon juice and 4 tablespoons extra virgin olive oil. For an extra kick, add a little chopped preserved lemon rind to the mix. Ideal to serve with most fish types, prawns (shrimp) and steamed mussels.

ginger and spring onion
Finely slice 2 spring onions (scallions) on the diagonal and place in a metal bowl. Add 2 tablespoons shaoxing rice wine or dry sherry, 2 tablespoons finely julienned ginger, 1 1/2 tablespoons light soy sauce, 1 teaspoon sugar and 1/2 teaspoon sesame oil. Heat 2 tablespoons peanut oil in a small frying pan until it starts to shimmer and smoke. Remove from the heat and quickly pour the hot oil over the dressing. Spoon the sauce over steamed fish or scallops and top with some fresh coriander (cilantro).

buerre blanc

Very finely chop 2 French shallots and place in a small saucepan with 2 tablespoons white wine vinegar, 4 tablespoons dry white wine and 4 tablespoons water. Simmer over low heat until the liquid has reduced to about 2 tablespoons. Dice 200 g (7 oz) butter and slowly add it cube by cube, whisking as you go, until the sauce is thick and creamy. Season to taste with sea salt, ground white pepper and lemon juice. If you wish to make the sauce in advance, keep it warm by storing in a heatproof bowl over a pot of gently simmering water. Spoon warm over baked scallops, steamed mussels and steamed or baked white fish.

rouille

Tear 1 thick slice of sourdough bread into pieces and put it in a bowl. Put a pinch of saffron threads and 3 tablespoons water in a small saucepan and bring to the boil. Reduce the heat, simmer for 1 minute, then pour the hot saffron water over the bread. Put the bread in a food processor or blender with the flesh of 1 roasted red capsicum (pepper) (Favourites), 1/4 teaspoon paprika and 2 garlic cloves. Blend to a smooth paste, then add 125 ml (4 fl oz/1/2 cup) light olive oil in a thin stream until it forms a thick consistency. Season with sea salt to taste. Serve with steamed mussels or spooned over baked salmon.

crab and lemon pasta

350 g (12 oz/about 2¹/₄ cups) fresh crabmeat
2 large red chillies, seeded and finely chopped
grated zest and juice of 1 lemon
4 tablespoons extra virgin olive oil
a handful of flat-leaf (Italian) parsley, roughly chopped
300 g (10¹/₂ oz/2 bunches) rocket (arugula), stalks trimmed,
   leaves finely sliced
400 g (14 oz) spaghettini

Put the crabmeat in a large bowl and roughly flake it with a fork. Add the chilli, lemon zest, lemon juice and olive oil. Season generously with sea salt and freshly ground black pepper and stir to combine. Pile the parsley and rocket over the top.

Bring a large pot of salted water to the boil and add the spaghettini. Cook the pasta until *al dente*, then drain and add to the crab mixture. Toss well until the rocket has wilted, then divide among four warmed pasta bowls. Serves 4

seared snapper with buttered greens

200 g (7 oz) sugar snap peas, trimmed
350 g (12 oz/2 bunches) asparagus, trimmed
2 tablespoons olive oil
4 x 150 g (5¹/₂ oz) snapper fillets, skin on
80 g (2³/₄ oz) butter
4 tablespoons lemon juice
2 fresh thyme sprigs, roughly chopped
12 mint leaves

Preheat the oven to 200°C (400°F/Gas 2–3).

Blanch the sugar snap peas and asparagus spears in a pot of boiling water for 2 minutes, or until they turn emerald green. Drain and rinse under cold running water.

Put the olive oil in a large frying pan over high heat. Rinse the snapper fillets in cold water and pat dry with paper towels. Season the fillets generously with sea salt and put them skin side down in the hot pan. Sear for 1–2 minutes, or until the skin is crisp and golden underneath, then turn the fillets over and briefly sear the other side. Transfer the fillets to a baking tray and bake for 8 minutes.

Return the frying pan to low heat and add the butter. When it has melted, add the lemon juice and thyme sprigs and swirl around. When the sauce begins to thicken, add the mint, asparagus and peas. Swirl the greens in the butter sauce a few times, then remove from the heat.

Arrange the greens on warmed plates, sit the snapper fillets on top and drizzle with any remaining pan juices. Serves 4

seared tuna with chilli dressing

2 tablespoons bottled Thai sweet chilli sauce
1 teaspoon finely grated fresh ginger
1 tablespoon lime juice
¹/₂ teaspoon worcestershire sauce
4 x 150 g (5¹/₂ oz) tuna fillets
1 teaspoon olive oil
steamed white rice (Favourites), to serve
a handful of mint
a handful of coriander (cilantro) leaves

Put the sweet chilli sauce, ginger, lime juice and worcestershire sauce in a small bowl. Stir to make a dressing.

Heat a large non-stick frying pan or chargrill pan over high heat. Rub the tuna fillets on both sides with the olive oil, then sear them on one side for 1 minute. Turn the fillets over, reduce the heat to medium and cook for a further 3 minutes.

Serve the tuna steaks on warmed plates on a bed of steamed white rice. Stir the dressing one more time and spoon it over the tuna. Scatter with mint and coriander. Serves 4

seasonal ideas
- The crab and lemon pasta recipe is an old favourite. I've tossed the crab mixture through pasta, but you can serve it on thin, crisp toasts as a great starter. Or spoon into soup bowls and ladle in a broth tinged with lemon grass and fresh ginger, or wrap in just-cooked large sheets of pasta and serve with a lemon butter sauce or buerre blanc (page 49).

- Make a quick sauce of olive oil and finely chopped chilli, tomato and coriander (cilantro) leaves. Toss through warm pasta with some finely sliced raw tuna and lemon juice.

- Top grilled tuna with chopped tomatoes, small olives, basil and a drizzle of balsamic vinegar and extra virgin olive oil.

- In a small bowl mix together some tapenade (page 79) and mayonnaise. Chargrill small pieces of tuna and serve them with a rocket (arugula) salad, a dollop of the olive mayonnaise and steamed green beans.

opposite: crab and lemon pasta
over: seared snapper with buttered greens,
and seared tuna with chilli dressing

lime pickle spatchcock

500 g (1 lb 2 oz) boiling potatoes, scrubbed
4 spatchcocks (poussin), butterflied
4 tablespoons lime pickle, finely chopped
2 tablespoons olive oil
steamed green beans, to serve

Preheat the oven to 200°C (400°F/Gas 2–3). Line a baking tray with baking paper.

Bring a pot of salted water to the boil. Thinly slice the potatoes and blanch them in the boiling water for 1 minute. Drain, then arrange the slices over the baking tray.

Rinse the spatchcocks under cold running water, then pat dry with paper towels. Rub the lime pickle over the spatchcocks and sit them on the potatoes. Drizzle with the olive oil, then bake for 30 minutes. Remove from the oven, cover loosely with foil and allow to rest for a few minutes.

Cut the spatchcocks in half and place on four warmed plates, with a pile of potatoes to one side. Serve with steamed green beans. Serves 4

aromatic roast chicken breasts

1 vanilla bean
2 tablespoons soy sauce
2 tablespoons grated palm sugar (jaggery) or soft brown sugar
2 tablespoons grated lemon zest
4 boneless chicken breasts, skin on
juice of 4 lemons
4 tablespoons olive oil
50 g (1³/4 oz) snow pea (mangetout) shoots
lemon couscous (page 255), to serve

Preheat the oven to 200°C (400°F/Gas 6). Using the tip of a small sharp knife, slice the vanilla bean in half along its length and scrape the seeds into a bowl (reserve the vanilla pod for another use). Add the soy sauce, sugar and lemon zest and stir to dissolve the sugar.

Using a sharp knife, cut several long incisions into the skin of each chicken breast, then rub the soy mixture into the skin. Pour the lemon juice and olive oil into a baking dish and add the chicken breasts, skin side up. Roast for 15 minutes, or until the chicken is cooked through.

Carve each chicken breast into several thick slices. Serve with the snow pea shoots on a bed of lemon couscous, with the roasting juices spooned over the top. Serves 4

crab and green bean salad

50 g (1³/4 oz/¹/3 cup) peanuts
2 tablespoons grated palm sugar (jaggery) or soft brown sugar
2 tablespoons fish sauce
4 tablespoons lime juice
2 spring onions (scallions), thinly sliced
2 large red chillies, seeded and finely sliced
1 tablespoon finely chopped lemon grass, white part only
200 g (7 oz) green beans, trimmed, blanched and sliced on the diagonal
150 g (5¹/2 oz/1²/3 cups) bean sprouts, trimmed
150 g (5¹/2 oz/about 1 cup) fresh crabmeat
a handful of coriander (cilantro), roughly chopped
10 mint leaves, roughly chopped

Put the peanuts in a small saucepan over medium heat and dry-fry for 2–3 minutes, or until they turn golden brown. Take them off the heat to cool a little, then put them in a blender or food processor and pulse until finely chopped.

Put the sugar, fish sauce and lime juice in a large bowl and stir until the sugar has dissolved. Add all the remaining ingredients, including the peanuts, and toss well. Serves 4

seasonal ideas

It's a great idea to always have a jar of both lime pickle and preserved lemons in the cupboard. They add an instant flavour punch to many dishes and can turn a few sad ingredients into an exciting meal.

- Add preserved lemon rind to a bread stuffing and let the exotic aromas infuse a roast chicken, or rub the salty flesh of the lemons over chicken before roasting or grilling.

- Finely chop some preserved lemon rind and scatter through salads, or fold through mayonnaise and serve with chargrilled salmon or chicken, or fold through an equal amount of chopped parsley and serve with braised lamb shanks or rich meaty stews as a spicy twist to gremolata.

- For a quick and tasty lunchtime pasta, toss some finely chopped preserved lemon rind through a warm pasta with tinned tuna, rocket (arugula) and roughly chopped tomato.

- Add finely chopped lime pickle to steamed couscous (Favourites) with a scattering of toasted almonds, currants and coriander (cilantro), or finely chop and rub over salmon fillets before baking.

- Finely chop 1 or 2 tablespoons of lime pickle and add it to brown rice with roughly chopped parsley and finely diced cucumber. Serve with roast chicken or grilled sausages.

opposite: lime pickle spatchcock
over: aromatic roast chicken breasts, and
crab and green bean salad

4 in a leaf

salmon carpaccio

300 g (10$^{1}/_{2}$ oz) piece of sashimi-grade salmon
2 small Lebanese (short) cucumbers, very finely sliced
$^{1}/_{2}$ teaspoon sea salt
1 teaspoon finely chopped mint
1 teaspoon finely chopped dill
1 teaspoon sugar
juice of 1 lemon
2 tablespoons sour cream
1 teaspoon grated fresh horseradish or horseradish cream
    (Favourites)
4 dill sprigs

Remove any small bones from the salmon, then wrap it
in plastic wrap and freeze for 30 minutes. Meanwhile, in a
non-metallic bowl, toss together the cucumber, sea salt, mint,
dill, sugar and lemon juice. Cover and refrigerate for 1 hour.

Using a very sharp knife, cut the chilled fish into thin slices.
Divide among four small plates and spoon the cucumber
salad over the top, reserving any liquid left in the bowl.

Combine the sour cream and horseradish, then stir in enough
cucumber liquid to make a thin dressing. Drizzle over the
salad and garnish with a dill sprig. Serves 4 as a starter

ma hor on betel leaves

2 garlic cloves, roughly chopped
a handful of coriander (cilantro) leaves
$^{1}/_{2}$ teaspoon drained green peppercorns in brine
1 teaspoon finely grated fresh ginger
2 spring onions (scallions), finely chopped
2 tablespoons peanut oil
150 g (5$^{1}/_{2}$ oz) minced (ground) pork
75 g (2$^{1}/_{2}$ oz/1 cup) prawn (shrimp) meat
2 makrut (kaffir lime) leaves, finely sliced
1$^{1}/_{2}$ tablespoons grated palm sugar (jaggery) or soft brown sugar
1$^{1}/_{2}$ tablespoons fish sauce
20 fresh betel leaves

Put the garlic, coriander, peppercorns, ginger, spring onion
and peanut oil in a blender or food processor and blend to a
smooth paste.

Heat a frying pan over medium heat, add the herb paste and
cook for 2 minutes. Add the pork and prawn meat and cook,
stirring, for 5 minutes, or until the meat has coloured. Add the
lime leaves, sugar and fish sauce, then reduce the heat and
cook for 2–3 minutes, or until slightly sticky. Allow to cool,
then spoon onto the betel leaves, about 1 tablespoon at a
time. Makes 20

san choy bau

2 iceberg lettuces
2 tablespoons peanut oil
2 teaspoons sesame oil
500 g (1 lb 2 oz) minced (ground) pork
2 tablespoons grated fresh ginger
8 spring onions (scallions), finely sliced
2 tablespoons soy sauce
2 tablespoons hoisin sauce
200 g (7 oz/1$^{1}/_{4}$ cups) chopped water chestnuts
a handful of coriander (cilantro) leaves

Remove the core and all the dark outer leaves from each
lettuce. Carefully uncurl the inner leaves, keeping them in
neat cups, then rinse in a large bowl of cold water and drain.

Heat the peanut and sesame oil in a large non-stick frying pan
over medium–high heat. Add the pork and sauté for 8 minutes,
or until lightly golden. Stir in the ginger, spring onion, soy sauce,
hoisin sauce and water chestnuts. Cook for 2 minutes, then
stir in the coriander. Serve in a warmed bowl, with the lettuce
leaf cups on a side plate. To eat, simply spoon the meat
mixture into the lettuce cups. Serves 4 as a starter

sweet pickled ocean trout

300 g (10$^{1}/_{2}$ oz) piece of fresh ocean trout
1 tablespoon grated fresh ginger
juice of 4 limes
10 finely chopped mint leaves
1 tablespoon soy sauce
1 tablespoon sesame oil
1 tablespoon finely chopped pickled ginger, plus 4 tablespoons
    of the pickling liquid
100 g (3$^{1}/_{2}$ oz/2$^{1}/_{4}$ cups) baby English spinach leaves
3–4 tablespoons freshly grated daikon
black sesame seeds, to serve

Remove any small bones and skin from the trout, then wrap
it in plastic wrap and freeze for 30 minutes. Meanwhile, put
the ginger in a non-metallic bowl with the lime juice, mint,
soy sauce and sesame oil. Add the pickled ginger, and the
pickling liquid. Mix well.

Using a very sharp knife, cut the chilled fish into thin slices,
put them in a non-metallic dish and add the ginger mixture.
Cover and refrigerate for 1 hour.

Divide the spinach leaves among four small bowls and scatter
with the daikon. Top with the pickled trout, sprinkle with
sesame seeds and drizzle with the pickled ginger juices.
Serves 4 as a starter

chicken and pine nut salad

1 tablespoon sea salt
2 boneless, skinless chicken breasts
1 egg yolk
zest and juice of 1 lemon
125 ml (4 fl oz/1/2 cup) light olive oil
2 anchovy fillets, finely chopped
3 tablespoons small salted capers, rinsed and drained
3 tablespoons pine nuts, toasted
3 tablespoons currants
a very large handful of flat-leaf (Italian) parsley, roughly chopped
warm crusty bread, to serve

Put a large pot of water over high heat, add the sea salt and bring to the boil. Add the chicken breasts, then cover with a tightly fitting lid and remove from the heat. Allow to sit, covered, for 40 minutes — during this time the residual heat will gently poach the chicken. Lift the chicken out of the water and allow to cool before shredding the meat.

In a small bowl, whisk together the egg yolk and lemon juice. Slowly add the olive oil, whisking until a thick, creamy mayonnaise forms. Fold the anchovies through and season with sea salt and freshly ground black pepper.

Toss the shredded chicken in a large bowl with the lemon zest, capers, pine nuts, currants and parsley. Mix the anchovy mayonnaise through the salad, then spoon into four bowls and serve with warm crusty bread. Serves 4

pickled swordfish salad

4 tablespoons olive oil
2 red onions, thinly sliced
2 green chillies, seeded and finely sliced
2 garlic cloves, finely chopped
1 teaspoon ground cumin
2 tablespoons finely chopped lemon grass, white part only
500 g (1 lb 2 oz) cherry tomatoes, cut in half, or into quarters
    if large
600 g (1 lb 5 oz) swordfish, cut into 1.5 cm (5/8 inch) cubes
a handful of coriander (cilantro) leaves
15 mint leaves, roughly torn
250 ml (9 fl oz/1 cup) lemon juice
baby leaf salad, to serve

Heat the olive oil in a heavy-based frying pan over medium heat and add the onion, chilli, garlic, cumin and lemon grass. Sauté for 5 minutes, or until the onion is translucent, then add the cherry tomatoes and cook for 1 minute, or until they are just starting to soften. Take the pan off the heat and allow the tomato mixture to cool completely.

Arrange the raw swordfish in a single layer in a wide, non-metallic dish. Spread the tomato mixture over the top, then sprinkle with the coriander and mint. Pour the lemon juice over the top, then cover and marinate overnight in the refrigerator. Bring to room temperature and serve with a baby leaf salad. Serves 4

poached chicken salad

90 g (3 1/4 oz/1 bunch) coriander (cilantro)
4 spring onions (scallions)
1 tablespoon sea salt
2 boneless, skinless chicken breasts
2–3 roasted red capsicums (peppers) (Favourites), torn into strips
4 tablespoons olive oil
1 tablespoon balsamic vinegar
1/2 teaspoon smoked paprika
1 telegraph (long) cucumber, peeled and diced
steamed couscous (Favourites), to serve

Put a large pot of water over high heat. Add some coriander sprigs, two whole spring onions and the sea salt and bring to the boil. Add the chicken breasts, then cover with a tightly fitting lid and remove from the heat. Allow to sit, covered, for 40 minutes — during this time the residual heat will gently poach the chicken.

Meanwhile, put the capsicum strips in a bowl with the olive oil, vinegar and paprika. Season generously with sea salt and freshly ground black pepper and toss until well combined. Pick the coriander leaves from the remaining sprigs and add a good handful to the capsicum. Roughly chop the remaining spring onions and add them to the salad, along with the cucumber.

Remove the warm chicken from the poaching liquid and finely slice against the grain. Add to the salad and toss to combine. Serve with steamed couscous. Serves 4

opposite: chicken and pine nut salad
over: pickled swordfish salad, and poached chicken salad

sliced leg ham with a burghul salad

10 bulb spring onions (scallions)
1 tablespoon balsamic vinegar
1 tablespoon olive oil
1 tablespoon caster (superfine) sugar
500 g (1 lb 2 oz) cherry tomatoes
90 g (3¼ oz/½ cup) burghul (bulgur)
1 teaspoon ground cumin
grated zest and juice of 1 lemon
2 tablespoons extra virgin olive oil
2 handfuls of flat-leaf (Italian) parsley, roughly chopped
8–12 slices leg ham, off the bone

Preheat the oven to 180°C (350°F/Gas 4). Trim the spring onions and slice them in half lengthways. Toss them in a bowl with the vinegar, olive oil and sugar until all the onions are thoroughly coated. Spread on a baking tray lined with foil and bake for 25 minutes, or until golden brown. Add the cherry tomatoes and roast for a further 5–10 minutes, or until the skins are starting to split. Remove from the oven.

Meanwhile, put the burghul and cumin in a bowl and cover with 125 ml (4 fl oz/½ cup) boiling water. Leave for 10 minutes, to allow the grains to soak up the water.

Add the roasted onion and tomatoes to the burghul, along with the lemon zest, lemon juice, extra virgin olive oil and parsley. Season to taste with sea salt and freshly ground black pepper and toss to combine. Divide the ham among four plates and spoon the salad over the top. Serves 4

roast pork with mango chutney

mango chutney
1 tablespoon olive oil
1 red onion, finely diced
1 tablespoon finely grated fresh ginger
2 tablespoons finely chopped lemon grass, white part only
2 tablespoons tamarind purée
125 ml (4 fl oz/½ cup) white wine vinegar
115 g (4 oz/½ cup) dark brown sugar
1 large red chilli, seeded and finely chopped
2 just-ripe mangoes, peeled, seeded and diced

1.5 kg (3 lb 5 oz) pork shoulder, skin scored
   (ask your butcher to do this)
green salad, to serve

To make the mango chutney, heat the olive oil in a saucepan over medium heat and add the onion, ginger and lemon grass. Cook, stirring, for 10–12 minutes, or until the onion is slightly caramelized. Stir in the remaining ingredients, bring to the boil, then reduce the heat and simmer for 20 minutes. Set aside.

Meanwhile, preheat the oven to 220°C (425°F/Gas 7). Pat the pork dry with paper towels and rub the scored skin with a generous amount of salt. Season with freshly ground black pepper. Sit the pork in a roasting tin, skin side up, and roast for 25 minutes, then turn the oven temperature down to 180°C (350°F/Gas 4) and cook for a further 1 hour. To test if the meat is done, insert a sharp knife or skewer into the centre — the juices should run clear.

Transfer the pork to a warm serving platter, then cover loosely with foil and leave to rest for 15 minutes. If the skin isn't quite crunchy and needs further cooking, slice it off using a sharp knife, put it back in the roasting tin and roast on the top shelf of the oven for a few minutes. Carve the pork and serve with the mango chutney and a green salad. Serves 6

crispy-skinned chicken

1 teaspoon Chinese five-spice
1 teaspoon finely grated fresh ginger
1 teaspoon sea salt
¼ teaspoon freshly ground black pepper
1 tablespoon soft brown sugar
4 boneless chicken breasts, skin on
1 tablespoon vegetable oil
350 g (12 oz/2 bunches) asparagus, trimmed
1 bunch of Chinese greens, trimmed and rinsed
2 tablespoons kecap manis
steamed white rice (Favourites), to serve

In a small bowl, mix together the five-spice, ginger, sea salt, black pepper and sugar.

Run your finger under the skin of each chicken breast to create a pocket, then spoon a teaspoon of the spice mixture between the flesh and skin of each breast. Massage the spice mixture over the flesh so that it forms a thin, even layer, being careful not to break the edges of the skin.

Heat a deep heavy-based frying pan over high heat and add the vegetable oil. Sear the chicken breasts, skin side down, for 4 minutes, or until golden brown underneath. Turn the chicken over, then cover and reduce the heat to low. Cook for 10 minutes.

Meanwhile, blanch the asparagus and Chinese greens in a pot of boiling water for 2 minutes, or until they turn emerald green. Drain, then rinse under cold running water and arrange over a serving platter. Drizzle with the kecap manis.

Thickly slice each chicken breast across the grain and arrange over the greens. Serve with steamed white rice. Serves 4

opposite: sliced leg ham with a burghul salad
over: roast pork with mango chutney, and
crispy-skinned chicken

spring greens

Now's the time when market gardens are bursting with nature's abundance, so here are some quick, fresh ideas to help you make the most of it …

- For a simple starter, sprinkle grated parmesan cheese and a few capers over blanched asparagus spears. Melt 80 g (2¾ oz) butter in a small frying pan, cook until it begins to brown, then spoon over the asparagus. Serve with a wedge of lemon. Or serve steamed asparagus soldiers with a soft-boiled egg and crisp pancetta.

- Blanch some trimmed beans until emerald green, dress with lemon juice and walnut oil and season to taste.

- Make a salad of rocket (arugula) leaves, blanched sugar snap peas and marinated artichoke hearts. Scatter with chopped parsley and dress with a lemon vinaigrette (Favourites).

- Toss finely sliced snow peas (mangetout) through a salad.

- Lightly toast slivered almonds and scatter them over steamed broccoli. Drizzle with kecap manis and serve.

- Pan-fry 3 chopped zucchini (courgettes) in 3 tablespoons butter until soft and golden. Remove. Add 1 tablespoon lemon juice and 1 teaspoon chopped capers to the pan, swirl together, then spoon over the zucchini.

- Chargrill thickly sliced zucchini (courgettes) and serve with a scattering of parsley and shaved parmesan cheese, and a drizzle of balsamic vinegar and extra virgin olive oil.

- Put 1 tablespoon butter in a pan with finely chopped garlic and red chilli. Cook for 1 minute, then add 3 tablespoons oyster sauce. Spoon over steamed bok choy (pak choy) and sprinkle with toasted sesame seeds.

- Rinse 1 tablespoon Chinese salted black beans and place in a bowl with 2 tablespoons orange juice, 1 finely chopped garlic clove, 2 tablespoons shaoxing rice wine or dry sherry, 1 tablespoon light soy sauce,1 teaspoon

sesame oil, 1 teaspoon soft brown sugar and 1 teaspoon finely grated fresh ginger. Stir until the sugar has dissolved. Spoon over steamed Asian greens.

- Keep frozen green peas and broad (fava) beans at hand for quick and easy risottos, soups and side dishes.

- Make a salad of blanched and peeled broad (fava) beans, blanched asparagus and crumbled goat's cheese. Scatter with parsley and dress with a lemon vinaigrette (Favourites).

- Melt gruyère cheese on thick wholemeal (whole-wheat) toast and top with baby rocket (arugula) and marinated artichoke.

pork cutlets with chestnuts and asparagus

350 g (12 oz/2 bunches) asparagus, trimmed
2 tablespoons butter
4 x 150 g (5½ oz) pork cutlets
4 tablespoons grapefruit juice
100 g (3½ oz/1½ cups) tinned chestnuts, drained
2 thyme sprigs
creamy mashed potato (Favourites), to serve

Blanch the asparagus spears in a pot of boiling water for 2 minutes, or until they turn emerald green. Drain and rinse under cold running water.

Cut the asparagus spears in half and set aside. Heat the butter in a large frying pan over medium heat until it has melted and begins to bubble. Add the pork cutlets and cook for 3 minutes. Turn them over, reduce the heat to low and cook for a further 4 minutes. Transfer the cutlets to a warm plate, sprinkle with sea salt, cover with foil and leave to rest.

Add the grapefruit juice, chestnuts and thyme sprigs to the frying pan and simmer for a few minutes, until the sauce begins to thicken. Add the asparagus and toss a few times to warm through. Arrange the cutlets on four warmed plates and spoon the chestnuts, asparagus and sauce over the top. Serve with creamy mashed potato. Serves 4

salmon wrapped in vine leaves

4 x 150 g (5½ oz) salmon fillets, pin bones and skin removed
16 preserved vine leaves
250 g (9 oz) cherry tomatoes
185 g (6½ oz/1 cup) instant couscous
1 tablespoon butter
a handful of flat-leaf (Italian) parsley, roughly chopped
2 spring onions (scallions), finely sliced
olive oil, to serve
lemon wedges, to serve

Preheat the oven to 200°C (400°F/Gas 6). Rinse the salmon fillets and pat dry with paper towels. Rinse the vine leaves several times to remove some of the saltiness, but leave them slightly wet to make them easier to work with.

Lay four vine leaves on a clean surface with their edges generously overlapping. Lay a salmon fillet in the middle, then wrap the leaves around the fish. Repeat with the remaining vine leaves and salmon fillets to make four parcels. Put them on a baking tray with the whole cherry tomatoes and bake for 15 minutes.

Meanwhile, put the couscous and butter in a large bowl and pour 250 ml (9 fl oz/1 cup) boiling water over the top. Cover and allow to sit for 5 minutes, then fluff up the grains with a fork. Cover again and leave for a further 5 minutes. When the couscous has absorbed all the water, rub the grains with your fingertips to remove any lumps.

Remove the salmon from the oven. Add the roasted cherry tomatoes to the couscous along with the parsley and spring onion. Lightly toss together. Divide the salmon parcels among four warmed plates and peel the vine leaves open. Spoon the couscous over the middle of the salmon and serve with a drizzle of olive oil and lemon wedges. Serves 4

caramelized chicken breasts

3 tablespoons vegetable oil
4 boneless chicken breasts, skin on
3 French or red Asian shallots, finely chopped
3 tablespoons caster (superfine) sugar
3 tablespoons fish sauce
1 tablespoon finely grated fresh ginger
¼ teaspoon ground white pepper
2 small Lebanese (short) cucumbers, finely sliced
2 witlof (chicory/Belgian endive), leaves separated
25 g (1 oz/1 bunch) chives, finely snipped
20 mint leaves
1 tablespoon lime juice
steamed white rice (Favourites), to serve

Heat the oil in a large heavy-based frying pan over medium–high heat. Add the chicken breasts, skin side down, and cook for 3 minutes, or until golden brown. Turn and cook the other side for 2 minutes, then remove the chicken from the pan.

Add the shallots to the pan and cook for 1 minute over medium heat. Add the sugar and cook for a further 2 minutes, or until the shallots are golden brown. Stir in the fish sauce, ginger and white pepper and cook for 1 minute.

Put the chicken back in the pan, skin side up. Cover, reduce the heat to low and cook for 12–15 minutes, or until the chicken is cooked through. Take the pan off the heat and keep the chicken warm while preparing the salad.

In a bowl, toss together the cucumber, witlof, chives, mint and lime juice. Season with sea salt.

Thickly slice each chicken breast across the grain. Pile the salad over bowls of steamed white rice and arrange the chicken slices over the top. Spoon the caramelized shallots and pan juices over the chicken just before serving. Serves 4

opposite: pork cutlets with chestnuts and asparagus
over: salmon wrapped in vine leaves,
and caramelized chicken breasts

71

Sweet ginger and mint give chicken a springtime twist

soy-baked salmon fillet with sesame salad

2 tablespoons soy sauce
2 tablespoons lemon juice
2 tablespoons mirin
1 red chilli, seeded and finely chopped
4 x 200 g (7 oz) salmon fillets, pin bones and skin removed
200 g (7 oz/1½ cups) peeled and julienned daikon
1 red capsicum (pepper), julienned
a handful of mint
a handful of mizuna leaves
2 tablespoons sesame seeds

Preheat the oven to 160°C (315°F/Gas 2–3).

Put the soy sauce, lemon juice, mirin and chilli in a small bowl and stir to make a dressing. Line a small baking dish with baking paper and add the salmon fillets. Pour the dressing over the fish and bake for 20 minutes.

Toss together the daikon, capsicum, mint and mizuna and divide among four plates.

Carefully remove the cooked salmon fillets from the baking dish using a wide spatula and place beside the salads.

Heat a small frying pan over medium heat and fry the sesame seeds until they begin to brown. Sprinkle over the salads and drizzle with the salmon cooking juices. Serves 4

spring greens risotto

1 litre (35 fl oz/4 cups) vegetable or chicken stock (Favourites)
2 tablespoons butter
2 garlic cloves, finely chopped
2 leeks, white part only, rinsed and finely chopped
330 g (11½ oz/1½ cups) risotto rice
125 ml (4 fl oz/½ cup) white wine
100 g (3½ oz/⅔ cup) freshly podded peas
50 g (¾ oz/½ cup) grated parmesan cheese
350 g (12 oz/2 bunches) thin asparagus, trimmed and cut
    into 2 cm (¾ inch) lengths
a handful of small basil leaves
extra virgin olive oil, to serve

Bring the stock to the boil in a saucepan, then reduce the heat and keep at a low simmer.

Heat a large saucepan over medium heat. Add the butter, garlic and leek and sauté for 5 minutes, or until the leek is soft and transparent. Add the rice and stir for 1 minute, or until the rice is well coated and the grains are glossy. Stir in the wine.

Ladle 250 ml (9 fl oz/1 cup) of the hot stock into the pan and simmer, stirring occasionally, until it has been completely absorbed. Add another 250 ml (9 fl oz/1 cup) stock and the peas. Cook, stirring, for a further few minutes until the stock has been completely absorbed, then add another 250 ml (4 fl oz/1 cup) stock. Cook, stirring occasionally, until all the liquid has been absorbed, then test the rice to see if it is *al dente*. If it needs more cooking, add the remaining stock.

Fold half the parmesan and all the asparagus through the risotto. Simmer for 2 minutes, then spoon into four warmed pasta bowls. Sprinkle with the remaining parmesan, scatter with the basil, drizzle with a little olive oil and serve. Serves 4

roast lamb with fresh mint aïoli

30 g (1 oz/1 bunch) fresh rosemary
1.5 kg (3 lb 5 oz) leg of lamb
2 tablespoons olive oil
boiled potatoes, to serve

fresh mint aïoli
1 egg yolk
1 garlic clove, roughly chopped
1 tablespoon white wine vinegar
125 ml (4 fl oz/½ cup) olive oil
30 mint leaves, finely chopped

Preheat the oven to 200°C (400°F/Gas 6).

Scatter the rosemary sprigs into a roasting tin, then sit the leg of lamb on top. Rub the lamb with a little olive oil, then rub sea salt and freshly ground black pepper into the skin. Roast for 30 minutes, then remove from the oven and spoon some of the roasting juices over the meat. Roast for a further 40 minutes, then transfer the lamb to a warmed serving plate and cover loosely with foil. Allow to rest for 15 minutes before carving.

While the lamb is resting, make the fresh mint aïoli. In a small bowl, whisk together the egg yolk, garlic and vinegar. Slowly whisk in the olive oil until a thick mayonnaise forms. Stir in the mint and enough warm water to make a thin sauce.

Carve the lamb and serve with the fresh mint aïoli and boiled potatoes. Serves 6

opposite: soy-baked salmon fillet with sesame salad
over: spring greens risotto, and roast lamb with fresh mint aïoli

4 spooned sauces

green sauce

a large handful of coriander (cilantro) leaves
10 mint leaves
1 tablespoon small salted capers, rinsed and drained
1 garlic clove, crushed
1 long green chilli, seeded and roughly chopped
1 tablespoon lime juice
1 teaspoon fish sauce
4 tablespoons olive oil

Pile the coriander onto a chopping board with the mint, capers, garlic and chilli. Using a sharp knife, chop all the ingredients together to form a rough paste.

Put the paste in a bowl and add the lime juice, fish sauce and olive oil. Mix together and spoon over baked or steamed white fish such as blue-eye cod, snapper or john dory. Makes about 75 g (2 1/2 oz/1/2 cup)

roast tomato sauce

500 g (1 lb 2 oz) roma (plum) tomatoes, cut into quarters
1 teaspoon sugar
1 teaspoon salt
1 tablespoon pomegranate molasses
10 basil leaves
1 garlic clove, roughly chopped
1 teaspoon ground cumin

Preheat the oven to 180°C (350°F/Gas 4). Line a baking tray with baking paper and sit the tomatoes on top. Sprinkle with the sugar and salt, then roast for 40 minutes, or until the tomatoes are beginning to blacken at the edges.

Put the tomatoes in a food processor or blender with the pomegranate molasses, basil, garlic and cumin and blend to a smooth sauce. Season well with sea salt and freshly ground black pepper. Serve with chargrilled lamb, beef or seared fresh tuna.

This sauce will keep in an airtight container in the refrigerator for several weeks. Makes about 250 ml (9 fl oz/1 cup)

preserved lemon and mint sauce

2 large handfuls of flat-leaf (Italian) parsley
30 mint leaves
1 tablespoon finely chopped preserved lemon rind
3 teaspoons lemon juice
125 ml (4 fl oz/1/2 cup) olive oil

Put the parsley, mint, preserved lemon rind, lemon juice and olive oil in a food processor or blender and blend to a smooth sauce. Serve with roast chicken, chargrilled blue-eye cod or baked salmon.

This sauce will keep in an airtight container in the refrigerator for several weeks. Makes about 250 ml (9 fl oz/1 cup)

tapenade

80 g (2 3/4 oz/1/2 cup) pitted kalamata olives
1 garlic clove, roughly chopped
a handful of flat-leaf (Italian) parsley, roughly chopped
10 basil leaves
2 anchovy fillets
1 teaspoon salted capers, rinsed and drained
3 tablespoons extra virgin olive oil

Put all the ingredients in a blender or food processor and blend to a rough paste. Season to taste with freshly ground black pepper. Serve with seared lamb or beef.

The tapenade will keep in an airtight container in the refrigerator for several weeks. Makes about 300 g (10 1/2 oz/1 cup)

opposite: preserved lemon and mint sauce

beef carpaccio

300 g (10¹/₂ oz) piece of beef sirloin
1 egg yolk
1 tablespoon mustard
1 tablespoon lemon juice
150 ml (5 fl oz) light olive oil
2 tablespoons red wine
1 tablespoon salted capers, rinsed, drained and finely chopped
2 tablespoons finely chopped parsley
1 celery stalk, finely sliced
4 tablespoons dried Asian fried shallots

Trim the beef of all fat and sinew. Cover with plastic wrap and freeze for 30 minutes.

Meanwhile, whisk the egg yolk with the mustard and lemon juice. Slowly whisk in the olive oil to form a mayonnaise. Thin it down with the wine and stir the capers through.

Using a very sharp knife, carefully cut the chilled beef into paper-thin slices and arrange on four serving plates. Drizzle lightly with the mayonnaise, then garnish with the parsley, celery and dried shallots. Any leftover mayonnaise can be stored in the refrigerator for 1–2 weeks. Serves 4 as a starter

lamb backstraps with puy lentils, broad beans and feta

150 g (5¹/₂ oz/²/₃ cup) puy lentils or tiny blue-green lentils
2 tablespoons lemon juice
2 tablespoons olive oil
250 g (9 oz/1²/₃ cups) frozen broad (fava) beans
2 lamb backstraps or loin fillets (about 500 g/1 lb 2 oz in total), trimmed
150 g (5¹/₂ oz) feta cheese
10 mint leaves, torn

Put the lentils in a saucepan and cover with 500 ml (17 fl oz/ 2 cups) water. Bring to the boil and simmer for 30 minutes, or until the lentils are soft. Drain and place in a bowl with the lemon juice and olive oil. Season generously with sea salt and freshly ground black pepper.

Bring a pot of salted water to the boil and add the frozen broad beans. Cook for 5 minutes, then drain and rinse under cold running water. Peel away the outer layer of the pods, then stir the broad beans through the lentils.

Heat a large, heavy-based frying pan over high heat. Add the lamb and sear until the uncooked side begins to look a little bloody. Turn the lamb over, reduce the heat and cook for a further 5 minutes. Transfer to a warm plate, cover loosely with foil and allow to rest for 5 minutes.

Crumble the feta into the lentils along with the mint. Thickly slice the lamb across the grain and add any meat juices to the lentils. Lightly toss the lentil salad, then spoon onto four plates and top with the warm lamb slices. Serves 4

moroccan lamb

125 ml (4 fl oz/¹/₂ cup) lemon juice
3 tablespoons olive oil
1 teaspoon ground cinnamon
3 garlic cloves, finely chopped
1 teaspoon ground cumin
finely grated zest of 1 orange
8 lamb loin fillets, trimmed
a handful of flat-leaf (Italian) parsley
20 oregano leaves
2 vine-ripened tomatoes, roughly chopped
400 g (14 oz) tin chickpeas, drained and rinsed
steamed couscous (Favourites), to serve

Put the lemon juice, olive oil, cinnamon, garlic, cumin and orange zest in a non-metallic bowl and stir to combine. Add the lamb fillets, toss to coat, then cover and marinate in the refrigerator for 3 hours, or overnight.

Heat a large heavy-based frying pan over high heat. Remove the lamb from the marinade, add to the pan and sear until the uncooked side begins to look a little bloody. Turn the lamb over, reduce the heat and cook for a further 3–5 minutes. Transfer to a warm plate, cover with foil and allow to rest for 5 minutes.

Toss the herbs, tomato and chickpeas together in a bowl, then divide among four plates. Slice the lamb fillets in half on the diagonal and arrange over the chickpeas. Serve with steamed couscous. Serves 4

opposite: beef carpaccio
over: lamb backstraps with puy lentils, broad beans
and feta, and moroccan lamb   81

A classic spring dish of minty greens and pink lamb

chocolate and cinnamon breadcrumbs with berries

4 slices of stale sourdough bread
50 g (1³/4 oz/¹/2 cup) ground almonds
1 tablespoon soft brown sugar
1 tablespoon dark unsweetened cocoa powder
1 teaspoon ground cinnamon
1 tablespoon unsalted butter
250 g (9 oz/1²/3 cups) blueberries
250 g (9 oz/2 cups) raspberries
400 g (14 oz) plain or vanilla yoghurt

Preheat the oven to 160°C (315°F/Gas 2–3). Remove the crusts from the bread, then tear the bread into small pieces and place in a food processor with the ground almonds, sugar, cocoa and cinnamon. Chop to form fine breadcrumbs, then add the butter and blend for a few more seconds.

Spread the chocolate crumbs on a baking tray and bake for 10 minutes, or until they feel crisp. Remove from the oven and allow to cool completely.

Arrange the berries and yoghurt in a bowl and sprinkle with the chocolate crumbs. Serves 4

black sticky rice with fresh papaya

200 g (7 oz/1 cup) black rice
4 tablespoons grated palm sugar (jaggery) or soft brown sugar
1 teaspoon natural vanilla extract
125 ml (4 fl oz/¹/2 cup) coconut milk
fresh papaya or banana slices, to serve
coconut milk, extra, to serve

Soak the rice in plenty of cold water for 1 hour. Drain, rinse, then drain again. Place in a saucepan with 500 ml (17 fl oz/2 cups) water. Bring to the boil, stirring occasionally, then reduce the heat to low. Cover and simmer for 35 minutes.

Stir in the sugar, vanilla, coconut milk and a pinch of sea salt. Simmer over low heat, uncovered, for a further 10 minutes, then take the rice off the heat and allow to cool. Serve with slices of fresh papaya or banana and a drizzle of coconut milk. Serves 4

pear and jasmine tea sorbet

3 tablespoons lemon juice
4 ya or nashi pears
375 ml (13 fl oz/1¹/2 cups) jasmine tea, made using 1 heaped tablespoon of tea leaves
80 g (2³/4 oz/¹/3 cup) caster (superfine) sugar
fresh longans or lychees, to serve

Pour the lemon juice into a non-metallic bowl. Peel and chop the pears, adding them to the lemon juice as you go so they don't discolour.

Put the pears, jasmine tea, sugar and 2 tablespoons of the lemon juice in a saucepan over medium heat. Simmer for 15 minutes, or until the pears have become opaque and soft. Set aside to cool.

Blend the pears and juice to a fine purée in a food processor or blender, then pour through a fine sieve into a plastic container. Allow to cool, then cover and freeze for 3 hours, or overnight

Remove the sorbet from the freezer and scoop into a food processor or blender. Blend to a smooth consistency, then return to the freezer until ready to serve.

Serve scooped into bowls with fresh longans or lychees. Serves 4

A seductive bowl of creamy berries and crunchy chocolate

opposite: chocolate and cinnamon breadcrumbs with berries
over: black sticky rice with fresh papaya, and
pear and jasmine tea sorbet

citrus delights

Sometimes the sweet tang of all things citrus is just exactly what you need to refresh a jaded palate.

- Fold citrus curd (page 101) through mascarpone cheese and serve in small individual bowls with almond bread or biscotti.

- For a simple dessert, slice or segment oranges and drizzle with a little honey. Cover with orange juice and some long strips of orange zest and chill for 30 minutes. Serve with a scatter of toasted flaked almonds and a dollop of sweet mascarpone (Favourites) or some caramel ice cream.

- While mandarins are perfect to eat just as they are, they also impart a wonderfully perfumed citrus flavour, so use mandarin juice instead of orange juice for a delightful twist when making a citrus glaze for cakes and cupcakes.

- To make mandarin syrup, put 125 ml (4 fl oz/$1/2$ cup) fresh mandarin juice and 55 g (2 oz/$1/4$ cup) caster (superfine) sugar in a saucepan. Bring to the boil, reduce the heat and simmer for 5 minutes, or until reduced by half. Allow to cool, then drizzle over a salad of ruby grapefruit, lime, lemon and orange segments. Serve with scoops of lemon sorbet.

- Using a small sharp knife, slice a vanilla bean all the way down the centre and scrape the seeds into a small bowl. Add the finely grated zest of 2 lemons and 1 orange. Fold through a classic butter cake mixture (Favourites) for a simple citrus cake. When baked, cover with lemon icing or drizzle with mandarin syrup (page 88).

- A squeeze of lime juice will bring the flavours of a ripe papaya to life. Serve with orange or mango sorbet.

- For a light dessert after a rich meal, serve lemon sorbet with a salad of ruby grapefruit segments, raspberries and blueberries, dusted with icing (confectioners') sugar.

- Serve a refreshing drink of chilled orange juice topped with freshly strained pomegranate juice.

- Make some home-made lemonade. Remove strips of lemon skin from 2 organic lemons using a sharp knife, then juice the lemons. Put the lemon strips in a small saucepan with 220 g (7¾ oz/1 cup) sugar and 125 ml (4 fl oz/½ cup) water and bring to the boil over high heat. Reduce the heat and simmer for a few minutes, then remove from the heat and allow to cool. Discard the lemon strips and stir in the lemon juice. (For an exotic touch, also stir in ½ teaspoon orange flower water.) Serve diluted to taste with chilled sparkling mineral water.

custard with nectarines and blueberries

custard
250 ml (9 fl oz/1 cup) milk
250 ml (9 fl oz/1 cup) pouring (whipping) cream
1 vanilla bean
4 egg yolks
4 tablespoons caster (superfine) sugar

2 tablespoons caster (superfine) sugar
4 nectarines, sliced
150 g (5 1/2 oz/1 cup) blueberries

To make the custard, pour the milk and cream into a heavy-based saucepan. Lightly rub the vanilla bean between your fingertips to soften it. Using the tip of a small sharp knife, split the bean in half along its length and add it to the milk. Put the saucepan over medium heat and bring the mixture just to simmering point, then remove the pan from the heat.

In a large bowl, whisk the egg yolks with the sugar until light and creamy. Whisk a little of the warm milk mixture into the eggs before adding the remaining liquid. Remove the vanilla bean and set aside, then whisk to combine.

Rinse and dry the saucepan, then return the custard mixture to the clean saucepan. Scrape the inside of the vanilla bean to remove the last of the seeds and add to the custard. Cook over medium heat, stirring constantly with a wooden spoon, until the custard thickens and coats the back of the spoon. If a line remains after you have dragged your finger across the spoon, the custard is ready. Quickly remove to a chilled bowl and continue to whisk until it has slightly cooled. If serving the custard cold, allow to cool completely before covering and chilling in the refrigerator.

Just before serving, prepare the fruit. Put the sugar in a deep frying pan with 1 tablespoon of water. Heat over low heat, swirling the mixture a little so that the sugar dissolves. Add the nectarine slices, swirl once, then cover with a lid. Cook over low heat for 4 minutes. Remove the lid and add the blueberries. Swirl a few more times until all the blueberries are glossy. Remove from the heat and divide among four bowls. Serve with the custard. Serves 4

ginger panna cotta

400 ml (14 fl oz) pouring (whipping) cream
grated zest and juice of 1 lemon
1 tablespoon finely grated fresh ginger
50 g (1 3/4 oz/scant 1/4 cup) caster (superfine) sugar
1 scant teaspoon powdered gelatine*
1 tablespoon Grand Marnier or orange-flavoured liqueur
cardamom almond bread (Favourites) or pistachio biscotti
    (page 278), to serve

Whip 150 ml (5 fl oz) of the cream in a bowl, cover with plastic wrap and refrigerate until needed.

Put the remaining cream in a saucepan with the lemon zest, lemon juice, ginger and sugar. Warm gently over low heat for 10 minutes, or until slightly thickened — do not let the cream come to the boil. Strain into a bowl.

In a small bowl, dissolve the gelatine powder in 2 tablespoons of boiling water. Stir well, until the gelatine crystals have completely dissolved, then stir into the warm cream mixture along with the Grand Marnier. Leave for about 40 minutes to cool, then fold through the whipped cream.

Spoon the panna cotta into four small bowls, then cover and refrigerate for 3 hours, or overnight. Serve with cardamom almond bread or pistachio biscotti. Serves 4

* When using powdered gelatine, always check the manufacturer's instructions.

honey-spiced parfait with fresh berries

5 egg yolks
100 g (3 1/2 oz/scant 1/2 cup) caster (superfine) sugar
2 tablespoons honey
1/4 teaspoon ground cardamom
500 ml (17 fl oz/2 cups) crème fraîche or sour cream
fresh berries, such as raspberries, blackberries or
    strawberries, to serve

Using a whisk or electric beaters, whisk the egg yolks, sugar and honey in a large bowl until thick and pale.

Gently fold the cardamom and crème fraîche through, then spoon into an 8 x 22 cm (3 1/4 x 8 1/2 inch) loaf (bar) tin lined with baking paper. Freeze overnight, or until firm.

Cut the parfait into six thick slices and serve with fresh berries. Serves 6

opposite: custard with nectarines and blueberries
over: ginger panna cotta, and
honey-spiced parfait with fresh berries

coconut and passionfruit bavarois

250 ml (9 fl oz/1 cup) pouring (whipping) cream
300 ml (10¹/2 fl oz) milk
45 g (1¹/2 oz/¹/2 cup) desiccated coconut
125 g (4¹/2 oz/heaped ¹/2 cup) caster (superfine) sugar
4 egg yolks
1 teaspoon powdered gelatine*
4 passionfruit
cardamom almond bread (Favourites) or pistachio biscotti
    (page 278), to serve

Whip the cream in a bowl, cover with plastic wrap and
refrigerate until needed.

Put the milk in a heavy-based saucepan over very low heat
and stir in the coconut and sugar. Allow the milk to just
simmer for 15 minutes, or until reduced and thick, then
strain into a bowl through a fine sieve. Using the back of
a large spoon, press as much liquid as possible out of the
coconut, into the bowl.

Whisk the egg yolks in a separate bowl, then whisk in the
warm milk. Pour into a clean saucepan and stir over medium
heat for 8–10 minutes, or until the mixture coats the back of
the spoon. Pour into a clean bowl.

In a small bowl, dissolve the gelatine powder in 2 tablespoons
of boiling water. Stir well, until the gelatine crystals have
completely dissolved. Pour the dissolved gelatine into the
warm milk and stir until thoroughly blended. Leave for about
45 minutes, or until cool.

Fold the whipped cream through the mixture and spoon
into four serving glasses. Cover with plastic wrap and
refrigerate for 3 hours, or overnight. Just before serving,
slice the passionfruit in half, scoop out the seeds and
spoon them over the top. Serve with cardamom almond
bread or pistachio biscotti. Serves 4

* When using powdered gelatine, always check the
manufacturer's instructions.

strawberry and tarragon jelly

500 g (1 lb 2 oz/3¹/3 cups) strawberries
175 g (6 oz/³/4 cup) caster (superfine) sugar
1 tablespoon finely chopped tarragon
30 g (1 oz/2 heaped tablespoons) powdered gelatine*
crème anglais or pouring (whipping) cream, to serve
chopped strawberries, to serve

Hull the strawberries, then slice them into a bowl. Add the
sugar and tarragon and stir a few times until well combined.
Cover and leave to macerate for 30 minutes.

Blend the strawberries in a food processor or blender with
125 ml (4 fl oz/¹/2 cup) water, then strain into a large
measuring container.

Sprinkle the gelatine over a cup of hot water and stir for a
minute or two to ensure that it has thoroughly dissolved. Stir
it into the strawberry juice, then add just enough warm water
to make 1 litre (35 fl oz/4 cups) of liquid. Leave to cool.

Pour the liquid into a large bowl and cover with plastic wrap.
Refrigerate for several hours to set the jelly, or overnight. To
serve, spoon the jelly into tall glasses and drizzle with crème
anglais or pouring cream. Scatter with chopped strawberries.
Serves 4–6

* When using powdered gelatine, always check the
manufacturer's instructions.

vanilla and almond cake

225 g (8 oz/1 cup) caster (superfine) sugar
200 g (7 oz/1¹/3 cups) blanched almonds
¹/2 vanilla bean, finely chopped
250 g (9 oz) unsalted butter, softened and cut into cubes
4 eggs
100 g (3¹/2 oz/heaped ³/4 cup) plain (all-purpose) flour
2 teaspoons baking powder
mixed berries, to serve
icing (confectioners') sugar, to serve
pouring (whipping) cream or vanilla ice cream, to serve

Preheat the oven to 180°C (350°F/Gas 4). Generously
grease a 27 cm (10³/4 inch) bundt or ring tin.

Put the sugar and almonds in a food processor with the
chopped vanilla bean. Process until the vanilla bean has
completely broken down and the almonds look like coarse
breadcrumbs. Add the butter and process until the mixture is
soft and creamy, then add the eggs, flour and baking powder
and process to a smooth batter.

Spoon the batter into the prepared cake tin and bake for
40 minutes, or until a skewer inserted into the centre of the
cake comes out clean. If the cake is browning too quickly,
cover it loosely with foil. Remove the cake from the oven and
allow to cool in the tin.

Turn the cooled cake out onto a serving plate. Fill the centre
with mixed berries and sprinkle with icing sugar. Serve with
whipped cream or vanilla ice cream. Serves 8–10

opposite: coconut and passionfruit bavarois
over: strawberry and tarragon jelly, and
vanilla and almond cake

summertime pavlova

3 egg whites
4 tablespoons caster (superfine) sugar
1/2 teaspoon white wine vinegar
1/4 teaspoon cream of tartar
1 teaspoon cornflour (cornstarch)
1 teaspoon natural vanilla extract
3 peaches, peeled and finely sliced
pulp of 3 passionfruit
whipped cream, to serve

Preheat the oven to 150°C (300°F/Gas 2). Line a baking tray with baking paper. Beat the egg whites until soft peaks form. Gradually add the sugar, then the vinegar, cream of tartar, cornflour and vanilla and beat until stiff, glossy peaks form.

Spoon the meringue onto the baking paper to form a 20 cm (8 inch) circle. Bake for 15 minutes, then reduce the oven temperature to 120°C (235°F/Gas 1/2) and bake for a further 1 hour. Turn the oven off and allow the pavlova to cool in the oven with the door slightly ajar. Serve topped with sliced peaches, passionfruit pulp and whipped cream. Serves 6

very vanilla peach meringues

4 egg whites
230 g (8 oz/1 cup) caster (superfine) sugar
2 vanilla beans, split
1/2 teaspoon natural vanilla extract
6 peaches, stones removed, cut in half
250 ml (9 fl oz/1 cup) dessert wine
3 tablespoons raw caster (superfine) sugar
300 ml (10 1/2 fl oz) crème fraîche or thick (double/heavy) cream

Preheat the oven to 110°C (225°F/Gas 1/2). Line two large baking trays with baking paper. Beat the egg whites until soft peaks form. Gradually beat in half the sugar until very shiny, then add the remaining sugar and beat until stiff, glossy peaks form. Scrape out the seeds from one vanilla bean and stir them into the egg whites, along with the vanilla extract.

Spoon the mixture onto the baking trays to form six 10–12 cm (4–4 1/2 inch) rounds. Bake for 1 1/2 hours, or until crisp and golden. Turn the oven off, open the door slightly and leave the meringues until cool enough to handle. Peel them off the baking paper and put them on a rack to cool.

Turn the oven temperature up to 210°C (415°F/Gas 6–7). Put the peaches, cut side up, in a single layer in a baking dish. Pour the wine over and sprinkle with the raw sugar. Cut the remaining vanilla bean into thirds and add to the baking dish. Bake for 15 minutes, or until the peaches are soft and slightly caramelized on top. Remove from the oven and allow to cool.

Divide the meringues among six serving plates and top with a dollop of crème fraîche or cream. Add two peach halves to each plate and drizzle with the syrup from the baking dish. Garnish with the vanilla bean pieces. Serves 6

rosewater pavlova with berries

4 egg whites
250 g (9 oz/1 heaped cup) caster (superfine) sugar
1 teaspoon cream of tartar
1 teaspoon rosewater
300 ml (10 1/2 fl oz) pouring (whipping) cream, whipped
750 g (1 lb 10 oz/3 cups) mixed fresh berries
icing (confectioners') sugar, to serve

Preheat the oven to 150°C (300°F/Gas 2). Line a baking tray with baking paper. Beat the egg whites using electric beaters until soft peaks form, then slowly add the sugar and continue to beat until stiff, glossy peaks form. Add the cream of tartar and rosewater and beat for a further minute.

Spoon the meringue onto the baking tray to form a 20 cm (8 inch) circle with a dip in the centre. Bake for 50 minutes, then reduce the oven temperature to 120°C (235°F/Gas 1/2) and cook for a further 15 minutes. Turn the oven off and allow the pavlova to cool in the oven with the door slightly ajar.

Transfer the meringue to a serving plate and top with the whipped cream and berries. Dust the berries lightly with icing sugar and serve. Serves 6–8

coconut pavlova with banana and passionfruit

4 egg whites
150 g (5 1/2 oz/1 1/4 cups) icing (confectioners') sugar, sifted
1 teaspoon white wine vinegar
1 teaspoon natural vanilla extract
25 g (1 oz/1/4 cup) desiccated coconut
300 ml (10 1/2 fl oz) pouring (whipping) cream, whipped
3 bananas, sliced
pulp of 6 passionfruit

Preheat the oven to 150°C (300°F/Gas 2). Line a baking tray with baking paper. Using electric beaters, beat the egg whites with a pinch of salt until soft peaks form. Gradually beat in the icing sugar until the meringue is stiff and glossy. Fold in the vinegar, vanilla and coconut.

Spoon the meringue onto the baking paper to form a 20 cm (8 inch) circle. Using a spoon, make a slight dip in the centre and pull the edges up into soft peaks. Bake for 40 minutes, then reduce the oven temperature to 120°C (235°F/Gas 1/2) and cook for a further 30 minutes. Turn the oven off and allow the pavlova to completely cool in the oven with the door slightly ajar. Store in an airtight container until ready to serve.

Transfer the meringue to a serving plate. Pile the whipped cream in the middle of the pavlova and top with the banana slices and passionfruit pulp. Serves 6

raspberry coconut cake

125 g (4¹/₂ oz) butter, softened
275 g (9³/₄ oz/1¹/₄ cups) sugar
2 eggs
125 ml (4 fl oz/¹/₂ cup) milk
185 g (3¹/₄ oz/1¹/₂ cups) plain (all-purpose) flour, sifted
2 teaspoons baking powder
70 g (2¹/₂ oz/1¹/₄ cups) shredded coconut
200 g (7 oz/2 cups) frozen raspberries
icing (confectioners') sugar, to serve

Preheat the oven to 180°C (350°F/Gas 4). Grease and line a 20 cm (8 inch) spring-form cake tin.

Beat the butter and sugar using electric beaters until pale and creamy, then beat in the eggs and milk. Fold the flour, baking powder, coconut and frozen raspberries through the cake batter.

Spoon the batter into the prepared cake tin and bake for 1¹/₂ hours, or until a skewer inserted into the centre of the cake comes out clean. Allow the cake to cool before removing from the tin. Serve dusted with icing sugar. Serves 8–10

lemon tart

23 cm (9 inch) pre-baked sweet shortcrust tart case (Favourites)
6 lemons
3 eggs
3 egg yolks
175 g (6 oz/³/₄ cup) caster (superfine) sugar
250 ml (9 fl oz/1 cup) pouring (whipping) cream
icing (confectioners') sugar, to serve
whipped cream, to serve

Preheat the oven to 150°C (300°F/Gas 2). Place the tart case on a baking tray.

Finely grate the zest of two lemons into a large bowl. Juice all the lemons: you should have about 185 ml (6 fl oz/³/₄ cup) juice. Add it to the lemon zest along with the eggs, egg yolks and sugar. Whisk to combine, then add the cream and whisk once more. Pour the mixture into the tart case.

Carefully transfer the tart case to the oven and bake for 35–40 minutes. The filling should be set, but still a little wobbly in the centre. Remove the tart from the oven and allow to cool. Serve dusted with icing sugar, with a good dollop of whipped cream. Serves 8

citrus curd

2 large lemons
1 mandarin
100 g (3¹/₂ oz) unsalted butter
175 g (6 oz/heaped ³/₄ cup) sugar
3 egg yolks, beaten
brioche, sourdough, sponge cake or pre-baked sweet shortcrust tartlet cases (Favourites), to serve
whipped cream, to serve

Finely grate the zest of both lemons and the mandarin, then juice them and pass the liquid through a strainer. You should end up with 170 ml (5¹/₂ fl oz/²/₃ cup) juice.

Pour the juice into a heavy-based saucepan and add the butter, sugar and grated citrus zest. Stir constantly over medium heat until the sugar has dissolved. Remove the pan from the heat and whisk in the egg yolks. Return to the heat and lightly whisk until the curd has begun to thicken, being careful not to let it come to the boil.

Pour the hot curd into a 300 ml (10¹/₂ fl oz) sterilized jar and allow to cool. Seal with a lid and refrigerate until ready to use. The curd will keep for several weeks in the refrigerator.

Serve with warm brioche, toasted sourdough or spooned over a sponge cake or tartlet cases and topped with whipped cream. Makes approximately 250 ml (9 fl oz/1 cup)

seasonal ideas

- Citrus or lemon curd is a handy treat to have on hand. Serve spooned over toasted brioche for breakfast with a twist.

- Dollop the curd into little ready-made tart cases and top with meringue (Favourites), or serve with freshly baked scones (Favourites) for an afternoon tea treat.

- Layer between thin layers of baked filo pastry and drizzle with passionfruit syrup (Favourites) for a cheat's mille feuille-style dessert.

- Or in memory of great aunts, spread it thinly over sponge cake, top with whipped cream and eat with glee.

opposite: raspberry coconut cake
over: lemon tart, and citrus curd

Who can resist this classic tart of tangy sweetness?

summer

Sugar and ice and everything nice ... that's what summer days are all about. Fruit bursting with sunny sweet ripeness, ruby-red tomatoes, rosy-cheeked stonefruit, sunset-hued mangoes, masses of berries and fantastic salad produce. With such wonders available, this is also the season to put up your feet and enjoy the crystal skies, twinkling seas and hot, hot days. With weather like this, the body craves healthy fresh foods, so why deprive yourself? Line the benchtop with bowls of ripening fruits, fill the crisper with crunchy vegetables and plan to eat *alfresco* — bare feet, outdoor tables, big bowls piled with salads and the barbecue at the ready. There doesn't need to be any fuss and bother since Mother Nature has provided the setting and a magnificent array of ingredients. Quality summer produce needs little more than a scattering of herbs, a splash of citrus, a swirl of dressing, or a sprinkle of sugar!

cucumbers salad leaves

smoked salmon plates of carpaccio

radishes crunch zucchini

noodles and broths tomatoes

drizzle capsicums

seared fish basil

sweetcorn coconut milk

flavoured butters

sizzle berries apricots

rinse and drain

fruit salads passionfruit

peaches marinate plums

mangoes icy treats nectarines

cherries lychees grapes

citrus cake fresh fruit tarts

The sunny blush of a perfectly poached peach

vanilla peaches

2 vanilla beans
220 g (7³/4 oz/1 cup) sugar
6 large peaches
plain yoghurt or muesli, to serve

Lightly rub the vanilla beans between your fingertips to soften them. Using the tip of a small sharp knife, split them in half along their length and place in a large heavy-based saucepan with the sugar and 1 litre (35 fl oz/4 cups) water. Bring to the boil, stirring until the sugar has dissolved. Reduce the heat to a simmer.

Lightly score the peaches along their natural groove. Lower the peaches into the syrup and cover with a piece of crumpled baking paper. Simmer for 5 minutes, rolling the peaches over halfway through cooking if they are not completely covered by the water. Test if the fruit is ready by inserting a skewer into the flesh — it should give, but not be too soft. Remove the peaches with a slotted spoon.

Bring the syrup to the boil and allow to reduce by one third. Peel the skin off the peaches, then place the fruit in six bowls. Pour the syrup over and serve with yoghurt or muesli. Serves 6

apricot and rhubarb with ginger-spiced yoghurt

4 cm (1¹/2 inch) knob of fresh ginger
3 cardamom pods, split
¹/2 teaspoon honey
4 tablespoons caster (superfine) sugar
400 g (14 oz/1 bunch) rhubarb
4 apricots
250 g (9 oz/1 cup) plain yoghurt

Preheat the oven to 200°C (400°F/Gas 6). Line a baking tray with baking paper. Peel the ginger and slice into four rounds. Pour 150 ml (5 fl oz) water into a saucepan and add the ginger, cardamom pods, honey and 2 tablespoons of the sugar. Heat over medium heat until the liquid forms a syrup, then remove from the heat and set aside.

Trim the rhubarb and cut it into 8 cm (3¹/4 inch) lengths. Rinse under cold running water, then put the rhubarb in a bowl. Add the remaining sugar and toss until the rhubarb is well coated. Spread the rhubarb on the baking tray, reserving the sugary juices in the bowl.

Cut the apricots in half, remove the stones and add the apricots to the rhubarb. Swirl a tablespoon of water into the sugar remaining in the bowl and drizzle it over the fruit. Cover with a sheet of baking paper, then top with a larger sheet of foil to hold it in place. Bake for 15 minutes, or until the rhubarb is soft. Remove from the oven and allow to cool.

Strain the syrup over the yoghurt and lightly fold together, then serve with the baked fruit. Serves 4

berry breakfast trifle

200 g (7 oz/2 cups) rolled (porridge) oats
250 ml (9 fl oz/1 cup) apple juice
500 g (1 lb 2 oz/3¹/3 cups) strawberries, hulled
3 teaspoons honey
125 g (4¹/2 oz/¹/2 cup) plain yoghurt
150 g (5¹/2 oz/1 cup) blueberries

Put the oats and apple juice in a bowl. Mix well, then cover with plastic wrap and refrigerate for at least 1 hour or overnight, to allow the oats to soak.

Mash half the strawberries with the honey, then mix them through the soaked oats along with the yoghurt. Slice the remaining strawberries.

Spoon half the oat mixture into four serving glasses, then top with half the strawberries and blueberries. Cover with the remaining oat mixture, then the remaining berries. Serves 4

seasonal ideas

Poached peaches are one of life's little treats and can be enjoyed at both the beginning and end of the day.

- In the morning they are the perfect fruit to eat with muesli or with a dollop of plain or ginger-spiced yoghurt.

- In the evening, serve them with raspberry coulis (Favourites) and vanilla ice cream, or topped with mascarpone cheese and a crumbled amaretti biscuit (cookie).

opposite: vanilla peaches
over: apricot and rhubarb with ginger-spiced yoghurt, and berry breakfast trifle

tropical fruit with rosewater syrup

rosewater syrup
3 tablespoons sugar
2 tablespoons lime juice
1/4 teaspoon rosewater

1 large mango, flesh diced
1 large red papaya, peeled, seeded and cut into wedges
12 fresh lychees, peeled, or 400 g (14 oz) tinned lychees, drained
shaved or shredded coconut, to serve

To make the rosewater syrup, put the sugar in a small saucepan with 125 ml (4 fl oz/1/2 cup) water and bring to the boil. Reduce the heat and simmer for 5 minutes, stirring occasionally to ensure that the sugar completely dissolves. Take the pan off the heat and allow to cool completely. Stir in the lime juice and rosewater, then pour the syrup into a small glass bowl and chill in the refrigerator until ready to use.

Divide the fruit among four bowls, scatter with coconut and drizzle with some of the syrup. Serves 4

pineapple and lime muffins

215 g (7 1/2 oz/1 3/4 cups) plain (all-purpose) flour
2 heaped teaspoons baking powder
165 g (5 3/4 oz/3/4 cup) sugar
1/4 teaspoon ground cardamom
a pinch of ground cloves
115 g (4 oz/1 1/4 cups) desiccated coconut
2 tablespoons unsalted butter, melted
125 ml (4 fl oz/1/2 cup) coconut milk
grated zest and juice of 2 limes
2 eggs
190 g (6 3/4 oz/1 cup) diced fresh pineapple

Preheat the oven to 180°C (350°F/Gas 4). Sift the flour, baking powder and a pinch of salt into a mixing bowl. Stir in the sugar, cardamom, cloves and coconut.

Make a well in the centre and add the melted butter, coconut milk, lime zest, lime juice and eggs. Mix until just combined, then fold the pineapple through.

Spoon the mixture into 10 holes of a greased standard muffin tin and bake for 25 minutes, or until a skewer inserted into the centre of a muffin comes out clean. Makes 10

pineapple salad

1 pineapple
8 mint leaves, finely sliced
2 tablespoons lime juice
1/2 teaspoon caster (superfine) sugar
1 teaspoon orange flower water
3 tablespoons passionfruit pulp

Slice the skin off the pineapple, cutting out any brown 'eyes'. Cut the pineapple into quarters lengthways and remove the woody core. Slice the trimmed quarters into bite-sized pieces and put them in a bowl with the mint.

In a small bowl, mix together the lime juice, sugar, orange flower water and passionfruit pulp. Pour the mixture over the pineapple and lightly toss to combine. Serves 4

seasonal ideas

- I can't think of a better way to greet the morning on a hot summer's day than with a selection of tropical fruit. Arranged on a platter they always look amazing in all their varied sunny hues — and with the addition of some fresh lime for the papaya, a big bowl of Greek-style yoghurt and a drizzle of sweet syrup you really are in heaven. Think pineapple, lychees, mangoes, melons, passionfruit, papaya and mangosteen. If you want to add some crunch, serve with muesli or a blend of sesame seeds, pepitas (pumpkin seeds) and toasted coconut.

- Another fresh idea is to make a tropical trifle. Drizzle rolled (porridge) oats and shredded coconut with a little maple syrup and toast until golden brown. Allow to cool, then layer with plain yoghurt and a mixture of diced mango and passionfruit.

- Finely chop a selection of tropical fruit and add some freshly squeezed orange juice. Serve in bowls topped with plain yoghurt and lightly toasted shredded coconut.

- Have some yummy fun with tropical pancakes. For a basic pancake batter follow the recipe on page 291. Spoon the batter into a hot buttered pan and top with some finely sliced banana or pineapple. When the surface begins to bubble, flip the pancakes over and cook for a further minute. Serve warm, with a drizzle of maple syrup.

- Serve chopped banana, pineapple and strawberries with crisp waffles and a drizzle of coconut cream.

opposite: tropical fruit with rosewater syrup
over: pineapple and lime muffins, and pineapple salad

A chilled pineapple salad on a hot summer day

4 summer jams

apricot and almond jam

1 kg (2 lb 4 oz) apricots, cut in half and stones removed
juice of 1 lemon
1 kg (2 lb 4 oz/4^1/$_2$ cups) sugar
100 g (3^1/$_2$ oz/heaped ^{3}/$_4$ cup) slivered almonds

Put a small saucer in the freezer. Put the apricots in a large saucepan with the lemon juice and 250 ml (9 fl oz/1 cup) water. Simmer, partially covered, over medium heat for 20 minutes. Add the sugar and almonds and simmer for a further 15 minutes, then turn the heat up to high and boil vigorously until the jam begins to thicken, stirring occasionally to prevent sticking and burning.

Test that the jam is done by dropping a small spoonful onto the cold saucer. When the jam forms a thick pool, it is ready. Remove from the heat and allow to stand for 10 minutes, then spoon into two 500 ml (17 fl oz/2 cup) sterilized jars. Seal with a lid and refrigerate until ready to use.

This jam will keep for several months in the refrigerator and is delicious with warm wholemeal (whole-wheat) toast, buttery brioche or fresh scones (Favourites). Makes about 4 cups

peach chutney

1.3 kg (3 lb/about 5) peaches, peeled and cut into large chunks
500 g (1 lb 2 oz/2^2/$_3$ cups) soft brown sugar
2 apples, peeled and finely diced
2 red onions, finely chopped
2 teaspoons chilli flakes
500 ml (19 fl oz/2 cups) cider vinegar
2 thumb-sized knobs of ginger, peeled and roughly chopped
12 black peppercorns
12 cloves

Put the peaches in a large saucepan with the sugar, apple, onion, chilli flakes and vinegar. Take a small square of muslin (cheesecloth) or cotton, then pile the ginger, peppercorns and cloves in the middle and tie the cloth up with string into a secure bundle. Add the spice bag to the pot.

Stir over high heat until the sugar has dissolved and the mixture begins to bubble. Reduce the heat and simmer for 1^1/$_2$ to 2^1/$_4$ hours, or until rich and thick. Remove from the heat and allow to stand for 15 minutes, then spoon into four 500 ml (17 fl oz/2 cup) sterilized jars. Seal with a lid and refrigerate until ready to use. This jam will keep for several months in the refrigerator and is delicious on ham and cheese sandwiches, cold roast meats or grilled sausages. Makes about 8 cups

summer jam

200 g (7 oz/1^1/$_3$ cups) strawberries, rinsed, hulled and cut in half
2 ripe peaches (300 g/10^1/$_2$ oz in total), skinned and chopped
400 g (14 oz/heaped 1^3/$_4$ cups) sugar

Put the strawberries and peaches in a bowl. Pour the sugar over the fruit and stir once or twice. Cover with plastic wrap and allow to macerate for 2 hours.

Put a small saucer in the freezer. Tip the fruit and sugar into a saucepan. Bring to the boil, then reduce the heat and simmer gently for 40 minutes, skimming off any froth that rises to the surface, and stirring occasionally to prevent sticking.

Test that the jam is done by dropping a small spoonful onto the cold saucer and returning to the freezer for 1 minute. When the jam begins to form a skin it is ready.

Pour the jam into a 300 ml (10^1/$_2$ fl oz) sterilized jar and allow to cool. Seal with a lid and refrigerate until ready to use. Serve on buttered toast, fresh scones (Favourites) or spooned over a sponge cake. This jam will keep for several weeks in the refrigerator. Makes about 1 cup

tomato and chilli jam

100 ml (3^1/$_2$ fl oz) olive oil
1 teaspoon cumin seeds
1 teaspoon mustard seeds
1 teaspoon ground turmeric
1 teaspoon finely grated fresh ginger
4 garlic cloves, finely chopped
5 large red chillies, seeded and sliced into long thin strips
1 kg (2 lb 4 oz) ripe tomatoes, roughly chopped
125 g (4^1/$_2$ oz/heaped ^{1}/$_2$ cup) sugar
100 ml (3^1/$_2$ fl oz) white wine vinegar
1 tablespoon fish sauce

Pour the oil into a heavy-based saucepan over medium heat and add the cumin seeds, mustard seeds, turmeric and ginger. When the mustard seeds begin to pop, add the garlic and chilli, stir a few times, then add the remaining ingredients. Bring to the boil, then reduce the heat and simmer, stirring occasionally, for 2 hours, or until the jam has thickened.

Pour the jam into a sterilized 500 ml (17 fl oz/2 cup) jar and allow to cool. Seal with a lid and refrigerate until ready to use. This jam will keep for several weeks in the refrigerator and is wonderful with fried eggs, roast beef, grilled pork or sausages. Makes about 2 cups

opposite: apricot and almond jam

prosciutto with papaya and basil

juice of 1 orange
1 teaspoon red wine vinegar
3 tablespoons olive oil
2 small red papayas
6 slices of prosciutto
15 small basil leaves

Put the orange juice, vinegar and olive oil in a small bowl and mix together to make a dressing.

Cut each papaya into quarters and remove the seeds and skin. Cut the flesh into wedges and arrange on a serving platter. Tear the prosciutto into bite-sized bits and toss them over the papaya. Scatter the basil leaves over the top.

Stir the dressing again, drizzle over the salad and sprinkle with freshly ground black pepper. Serves 4 as a starter

smoked salmon salad

2 tablespoons olive oil
1 tablespoon lemon juice
a handful of flat-leaf (Italian) parsley
1 tablespoon small salted capers, rinsed and drained
1 fennel bulb, trimmed and shaved
8–12 slices of smoked salmon
1 avocado, flesh finely sliced
8 grissini

Put the olive oil, lemon juice, parsley, capers and fennel in a bowl. Season lightly with sea salt and freshly ground black pepper and toss to combine. Arrange the smoked salmon on four serving plates. Top with the avocado, then the fennel salad, and serve with grissini. Serves 4 as a starter

chicken and peppered peach salad

$1^1/_2$ tablespoons white wine vinegar
125 ml (4 fl oz/$^1/_2$ cup) olive oil
$1^1/_2$ teaspoons freshly ground black pepper
4 ripe peaches
100 g ($3^1/_2$ oz/$2^1/_4$ cups) baby English spinach leaves
200 g (7 oz/2 cups) shredded roast chicken

In a large bowl, combine the vinegar, olive oil and pepper. Slice the peaches into the pepper dressing and lightly toss to coat.

Arrange the spinach leaves on a serving platter or in a bowl. Add the dressed peaches and chicken and season with a little sea salt. Serves 4 as a starter

seasonal ideas

- The savoury saltiness of prosciutto combines beautifully with ripe summer fruit. Scatter with a few rocket (arugula) or basil leaves for the perfect start to a summer meal.

- I've added a splash of citrus to the prosciutto salad opposite, but there are many possible variations. Wrap some prosciutto around wedges of rockmelon or other orange-fleshed melon for the classic approach. Or arrange several thin slices of prosciutto on a plate, top with sliced buffalo mozzarella cheese and a salsa of finely diced peach and papaya. Season with cracked black pepper and drizzle with olive oil and balsamic vinegar.

- Wrap prosciutto around little bundles of thin asparagus. Place on a baking tray, dab with butter and bake in a moderate oven until the asparagus is soft and the prosciutto is golden and crispy. Serve on a baby leaf salad with a dollop of crème fraîche.

- Pan-fry finely chopped prosciutto and leek in a pan, then add tinned chopped tomatoes. Spoon over warm pasta and sprinkle with some finely grated parmesan cheese.

- Top rounds of puff pastry with finely sliced red onion. Bake in a moderate oven until golden brown, then top with smoked salmon, capers and horseradish cream (Favourites).

- Toss finely diced red onion, finely sliced celery, capers, lemon zest, lemon juice and olive oil through warm spaghettini and top with fine slivers of smoked salmon.

- Finely slice witlof (chicory/Belgian endive) and toss with roughly chopped parsley, cucumber, celery and pear. Toss with a lemon vinaigrette (Favourites) and serve with slices of smoked salmon.

opposite: prosciutto with papaya and basil
over: smoked salmon salad, and
chicken and peppered peach salad

A sumptuous salad of sweet peppery peach

deep-fried whitebait

500 g (1 lb 2 oz) whitebait
125 g (4¹/₂ oz/1 cup) plain (all-purpose) flour
1 tablespoon sumac
¹/₂ teaspoon cayenne pepper
1 teaspoon sea salt
750 ml (26 fl oz/3 cups) vegetable oil

Rinse the whitebait under cold running water, then drain in a colander or large sieve. Put the flour, sumac, cayenne pepper and sea salt in a large bowl and mix well.

Heat the vegetable oil in a large deep saucepan until the surface begins to shimmer and a pinch of flour dropped into the oil fries immediately.

Pat the whitebait dry with paper towels. Toss them in the seasoned flour, ensuring all the fish are well coated. Lift them out of the bowl and shake off any excess flour, then deep-fry in batches for 3 minutes, or until crisp and golden. Serve with a sprinkle of sea salt. Serves 4–6 as a starter

a bowl of cold noodles

15 g (¹/₂ oz) instant dashi granules
125 ml (4 fl oz/¹/₂ cup) soy sauce
3 tablespoons mirin
1 teaspoon sugar
1 teaspoon wasabi paste
1 tablespoon finely grated fresh ginger
300 g (10¹/₂ oz) soba noodles
1 nori sheet
8 cm (3¹/₄ inch) piece of daikon, peeled and finely grated
2 spring onions (scallions), finely sliced

Put the dashi granules in a bowl and pour 375 ml (13 fl oz/1¹/₂ cups) boiling water over them. Stir until the granules have dissolved, then add the soy sauce, mirin, sugar, wasabi paste and ginger. Stir to make a dressing.

Bring a large pot of water to the boil and add the noodles. Allow the water to return to the boil, then add 125 ml (4 fl oz/¹/₂ cup) cold water to drop the temperature a little. Repeat this process three times, then drain the noodles. Rinse the noodles with cold water to remove the starch, then divide among four bowls.

Toast the nori sheet over a high flame or in a hot oven, then slice into thin strips. Pour the dressing over the noodles, toss lightly, then scatter with the daikon, spring onion and nori strips. Serves 4 as a starter

watermelon and feta salad

750 g (1 lb 10 oz) seedless watermelon
200 g (7 oz) Bulgarian feta cheese, cut into 2 cm (³/₄ inch) cubes
20 kalamata olives, pitted and sliced
12 mint leaves, finely sliced
2 celery stalks, finely diced
1 tablespoon red wine vinegar
2 tablespoons olive oil

Cut away the rind from the watermelon, then slice the flesh into bite-sized chunks. Roughly pile the feta and watermelon onto a serving platter, then scatter with the olives, mint and celery. Mix together the vinegar and olive oil and drizzle over the salad. Sprinkle with freshly ground black pepper. Serves 4 as a starter

seasonal ideas
- With its creamy, salty bite, feta is the perfect cheese for summer salads. There's the classic Greek salad of tomatoes, cucumbers, olives and feta, or crumble the cheese over blanched green beans and asparagus.

- Toss together some feta and mint, mix through green peas and serve with seared lamb cutlets.

- For a lighter take on the classic Sunday roast, serve the following salad with roast lamb. Arrange some thinly sliced feta cheese over a serving platter and top with finely diced cucumber and tomato. Scatter with parsley and mint leaves and drizzle with a little balsamic dressing.

opposite: deep-fried whitebait
over: a bowl of cold noodles, and watermelon and feta salad

summer salads

Summer is the time to enjoy the seasonal wonders of springy green salad leaves, ripe fruit and crisp vegetables, and what better way to enjoy them than all thrown together into a big bowl of wonderful flavours?

- Marinate farmhouse cheeses, balls of labneh or baby bocconcini (fresh baby mozzarella cheese) in olive oil and fresh herbs. Serve nestled in a pile of leafy greens, cherry tomatoes and small olives.

- Make a chunky salsa of sliced mango, diced cucumber and finely chopped red onion and red chilli. Serve with sliced leg ham and butter lettuce.

- Chickpeas and cannellini beans are a great addition to any salad with tuna or salami. Pep them up with a dressing flavoured with the warming earthiness of cumin, the hot smoky bite of paprika or the peppery lemon tang of sumac. Add roughly chopped parsley to lighten the flavours.

- Make a light summer salad of diced avocado, cucumber, spring onion (scallion), spinach leaves and finely chopped preserved lemon rind. Serve with chargrilled chicken.

- Blanch asparagus and snow peas (mangetout) and toss with baby rocket (arugula) leaves. Scatter with halved cherry tomatoes and shaved parmesan cheese.

- Make a salad of cucumber, avocado and finely sliced celery. Drizzle with chilli mint sauce (Favourites) and serve with poached chicken on a bed of mixed baby leaves.

- Chargrill asparagus on a barbecue or chargrill plate. Dress with a lemon vinaigrette (Favourites) and scatter with mint and parsley leaves. Serve with a thick slice of goat's cheese and strips of chargrilled red capsicum (pepper).

- Finely chop celery, tomato, radicchio and roasted red capsicum (pepper) (Favourites). Season well, then drizzle with olive oil and caramelized balsamic vinegar. Top with torn buffalo mozzarella cheese or sliced chicken breast.

- Make a salad of roasted red capsicums (peppers) (Favourites), green beans and chunky chopped tomato.

- Make a lunchtime salad of soft butter lettuce leaves, avocado, spring onion (scallion), capers and soft-boiled eggs. Top with a spoonful of mayonnaise and serve with seedy brown bread.

- Rinse and drain tinned kidney beans and put them in a bowl with black olives and parsley. Dress them in a simple vinaigrette flavoured with a few drops of Tabasco sauce. Spoon over rocket (arugula) leaves and top with crumbled feta or goat's cheese.

sashimi fish with soya beans and daikon salad

300 g (10¹/2 oz) piece of sashimi-grade ocean trout or salmon
100 g (3¹/2 oz/³/4 cup) frozen soya beans, or 100 g (3¹/2 oz/
   ²/3 cup) frozen broad (fava) beans
1 tablespoon finely grated fresh ginger
juice of 3 limes
1 tablespoon soy sauce
1 tablespoon sesame oil
200 g (7 oz/1¹/2 cups) peeled and finely julienned daikon
1 tablespoon sesame seeds, lightly toasted

Remove any small bones or skin from the fish, then wrap it in plastic wrap and freeze for 30 minutes.

Bring a pot of salted water to the boil and add the soya beans. Cook for 10 minutes, then drain and refresh under cold running water. Slip the beans from their pods and set aside.

Put the ginger, lime juice, soy sauce and sesame oil in a small bowl and stir to make a dressing.

Using a very sharp knife, cut the fish into paper-thin slices, then arrange on four serving plates. Toss the soya beans and daikon in the dressing and pile the mixture into the centre of each dish. Drizzle the fish with the remaining dressing and sprinkle with sesame seeds. Serves 4 as a starter

nutty rice

2 tablespoons olive oil
1 teaspoon cumin seeds
1 tablespoon sesame seeds
200 g (7 oz/1 cup) basmati rice
a handful of coriander (cilantro) leaves, roughly chopped

Heat the olive oil in a large saucepan over medium heat. Add the cumin and sesame seeds and fry for 1 minute, or until the sesame seeds turn golden brown.

Add the rice and stir for 1 minute. Pour in 500 ml (17 fl oz/ 2 cups) water and bring to the boil, stirring occasionally. Cover, reduce the heat to low and simmer for 15 minutes, or until the rice is fluffy and cooked through. Quickly stir in the coriander and serve with a vegetable curry, or chargrilled prawns (shrimp) or fish. Serves 4 as a side dish

steamed fish with watercress salad

4 x 150 g (5¹/2 oz) blue-eye cod fillets
1 telegraph (long) cucumber, peeled, seeded and finely julienned
2 large handfuls of watercress sprigs
2 tablespoons fish sauce
2 tablespoons lime juice
1¹/2 tablespoons white wine vinegar
1 tablespoon grated fresh ginger
1 teaspoon sugar
1 large red chilli, seeded and finely chopped
steamed white rice (Favourites), to serve

Fill a large, wide pot with 6 cm (2¹/2 inches) of water and bring to the boil.

Rest the base of a bamboo steamer in the boiling water. Line a second bamboo basket with a large square of baking paper, sit the fish fillets on the paper and sprinkle with a little sea salt. Cover the basket, then sit it on top of the bamboo steamer and steam the fish for 7–8 minutes, depending on the thickness of the fillets.

Meanwhile, toss the cucumber and watercress in a large bowl. In a small bowl mix together the fish sauce, lime juice, vinegar, ginger, sugar and chilli to make a dressing. Stir until the sugar has dissolved, then pour the dressing over the salad and lightly toss.

Arrange the fish on four plates. Top with the salad, drizzle with any remaining dressing and serve with steamed white rice. Serves 4

seasonal ideas

- Watercress has long been cast into the too-hard basket, which to my mind is an overly harsh judgment on a wonderful salad ingredient. With its peppery bite, it is the perfect accompaniment to chargrilled steak (especially when served with a flavoured butter), and rich seafoods such as salmon or swordfish.

- Buy watercress close to the day it is to be used and put it in a large bowl of water. Pick all the sprigs off the coarse stalks and place in an airtight container. Refrigerate until ready to use.

opposite: sashimi fish with soya beans and daikon salad
over: nutty rice, and steamed fish with watercress salad

carpaccio of three fish

150 g (5¹/2 oz) piece of sashimi-grade tuna
150 g (5¹/2 oz) piece of sashimi-grade ocean trout
150 g (5¹/2 oz) piece of sashimi-grade trevally or snapper
1 tablespoon lemon juice
a handful of baby rocket (arugula) leaves
2 tablespoons sesame oil
1/2 teaspoon sea salt
lightly toasted sesame seeds, to serve
lemon wedges, to serve

Remove any small bones or skin from all the fish, then wrap each portion in plastic wrap and freeze for 30 minutes.

Using a very sharp knife, cut the fish into paper-thin slices, then arrange on four serving plates. Put the rocket in a bowl and toss the lemon juice through. Pile the rocket into the centre of each dish. Drizzle with the sesame oil, sprinkle with the sea salt and sesame seeds and serve with lemon wedges. Serves 4 as a starter

crunchy noodle salad

1 tablespoon grated palm sugar (jaggery) or soft brown sugar
2 teaspoons balsamic vinegar
1 tablespoon kecap manis
1 large red chilli, seeded and finely chopped
2 garlic cloves, finely chopped
80 g (2³/4 oz/1/2 cup) peanuts, toasted and ground
125 ml (4 fl oz/1/2 cup) peanut oil
90 g (3¹/4 oz) dried Chinese egg vermicelli
2 witlof (chicory/Belgian endive), leaves separated
2 Lebanese (short) cucumbers, cut into long, thin strips
2 carrots, peeled and cut into long, thin strips
12 cherry tomatoes, cut in half
100 g (3¹/2 oz) deep-fried tofu, thinly sliced
4 boiled eggs, peeled and cut in half

Put the sugar in a bowl with 3 tablespoons of boiling water. Stir until the sugar has dissolved, then add the vinegar, kecap manis, chilli, garlic and ground peanuts. Stir well to make a peanut sauce.

Heat the peanut oil in a wok or small saucepan over high heat. When it begins to shimmer, add some of the vermicelli by crumbling the nest into broken strands. Fry for a minute or two, or until the threads begin to look golden brown rather than yellow, then remove with a slotted spoon and drain on paper towels — you'll probably need to fry the vermicelli in several batches.

Divide the witlof leaves among four serving plates and top with the vermicelli. Add the cucumber, carrot, cherry tomatoes and tofu. Top with the boiled egg halves and drizzle with the peanut sauce. Serves 4

grilled lemon prawns with five-spice salt

24 raw large prawns (shrimp)
juice of 2 lemons
1 tablespoon olive oil
1 teaspoon sea salt
1/4 teaspoon Chinese five-spice
1/4 teaspoon ground white pepper
lemon or lime cheeks, to serve

Peel and devein the prawns, leaving the tails intact. Put the lemon juice and olive oil in a non-metallic bowl, then add the prawns and toss to coat. Cover and set aside for 10 minutes.

In a small bowl mix together the sea salt, five-spice and white pepper.

Heat a non-stick frying pan over high heat. When the pan is hot, add the prawns and sear on both sides for a few minutes, until they turn pink and begin to curl up.

Arrange the prawns on a serving platter, drizzle with any pan juices and sprinkle with the five-spice salt. Serve with lemon or lime cheeks. Serves 4 as a starter

A delicate balance of seafood, sesame and salt

opposite: carpaccio of three fish
over: crunchy noodle salad, and
grilled lemon prawns with five-spice salt

4 nibbles

cherry bocconcini with a spice dip

2 roma (plum) tomatoes, cut into quarters
2 tablespoons sesame seeds, lightly toasted
1 tablespoon fresh thyme
1 teaspoon sumac
1 teaspoon sea salt
1/2 teaspoon ground cumin
1/4 teaspoon smoked paprika
300 g (10 1/2 oz) cherry bocconcini (fresh baby mozzarella cheese)

Preheat the oven to 180°C (350°F/Gas 4). Sit the tomatoes on a baking tray. Bake for 20 minutes, or until they are beginning to dry out and blacken.

Tip the tomatoes into a food processor and add the sesame seeds, thyme, sumac, sea salt, cumin and paprika. Process to a chunky paste, then spoon into a serving bowl. Serve with a pile of cherry bocconcini on the side. Serves 4–6 as a starter

oysters with a sherry dressing

1 tablespoon dry sherry
1 tablespoon lime juice
1/2 teaspoon fish sauce
1/4 teaspoon sesame oil
1 teaspoon soft brown sugar
1 spring onion (scallion)
24 small oysters, on the shell

Combine the sherry, lime juice, fish sauce, sesame oil and sugar in a small bowl. Stir to dissolve the sugar. Finely slice the green end of the spring onion on the diagonal and add to the dressing just before serving.

Serve the oysters with a drizzle of the dressing, or serve the dressing in a little bowl and allow your guests to help themselves. Serves 4 as a starter

chargrilled prawns with aïoli

1 large green chilli, seeded
1 garlic clove
1 teaspoon dried oregano
1/2 teaspoon ground cumin
grated zest and juice of 1 lime
juice of 1 orange
4 tablespoons olive oil
24 raw large prawns (shrimp), peeled and deveined, tails intact
aïoli (Favourites), to serve

Using a mortar and pestle or small blender, grind the chilli, garlic, oregano, cumin, lime zest, lime juice, orange juice and olive oil together to make a marinade. Season with sea salt and ground white pepper. Toss the prawns in the marinade, then cover and refrigerate for 1 hour. Meanwhile, soak 24 small bamboo skewers in cold water for 30 minutes.

Heat a barbecue flat plate, chargrill or grill (broiler) to high. Drain the skewers, thread a prawn onto each one and cook for 1 1/2 minutes, or until they just turn pink and start to curl. Turn and cook for a further 1 1/2 minutes, or until just opaque. Serve at once with a bowl of aïoli. Serves 4 as a starter

spiced nuts

1 teaspoon cumin seeds
1 teaspoon coriander seeds
1 teaspoon mustard seeds
1 teaspoon ground turmeric
1/4 teaspoon fennel seeds
1/2 cinnamon stick
1/2 teaspoon black peppercorns
2 tablespoons soft brown sugar
1 tablespoon finely grated orange zest
2 teaspoons sea salt
100 g (3 1/2 oz/1 cup) pecans
100 g (3 1/2 oz/2/3 cup) peanuts
100 g (3 1/2 oz/2/3 cup) cashew nuts
100 g (3 1/2 oz/2/3 cup) macadamia nuts
2 tablespoons olive oil

Preheat the oven to 170°C (325°F/Gas 3). Put all the spices in a spice grinder or small blender and grind to a fine powder.

Tip the mixture into a large bowl and add the sugar, orange zest, sea salt and nuts. Stir to combine, add the olive oil and mix well. Spread the nuts on a baking tray. Bake, stirring occasionally, for 10–15 minutes, or until they have coloured a little. Remove from the oven and allow to cool completely.

Store in an airtight container until ready to serve (keeps for up to 2 weeks). Makes 400 g (14 oz/3 cups)

A bowl of soft tofu with a nutty sweet dressing

tofu salad

600 g (1 lb 5 oz) silken tofu
1 tablespoon olive oil
6 French shallots, finely sliced
1 tablespoon tamarind paste
1 tablespoon bottled Thai sweet chilli sauce
2 tablespoons palm sugar (jaggery) or soft brown sugar
1 cucumber, finely diced
1 red capsicum (pepper), finely julienned
1 yellow capsicum (pepper), finely julienned
70 g (2¹/2 oz/scant ¹/2 cup) salted cashew nuts, roughly chopped

Remove the tofu from its packaging and allow to drain for several minutes on paper towels.

Heat a small saucepan over medium heat and add the olive oil and shallot. Sauté for several minutes, or until the shallot is golden brown, then add the tamarind paste, sweet chilli sauce, sugar and 125 ml (4 fl oz/¹/2 cup) water. Stir until the sugar has dissolved, then remove the dressing from the heat and allow to cool.

Pat the tofu dry and cut into bite-sized pieces. Arrange the tofu on a serving platter and scatter with the cucumber and capsicum. Spoon the cooled dressing over the top and scatter with the cashews. Serve as a salad or with steamed rice. Serves 4 as a starter or light meal

smoked salmon with vegetable salad

1 fennel bulb
2 zucchini (courgettes)
2 Lebanese (short) cucumbers
1 teaspoon finely chopped mint
1 teaspoon finely chopped dill
1 tablespoon olive oil
2 tablespoons lemon juice
1 teaspoon caster (superfine) sugar
¹/2 teaspoon sea salt
16 slices of smoked salmon

Trim the base of the fennel, slice the bulb as finely as possible and put it in a bowl. Slice the zucchini and cucumbers as finely as possible, cutting them on the diagonal, and add them

to the fennel. Add the mint, dill, olive oil, lemon juice, sugar and sea salt. Toss to combine, then set aside for 10 minutes.

Divide the smoked salmon slices among four plates. Toss the salad one more time before piling it on top of the salmon. Serves 4 as a starter

scallops with ginger and lemon grass

2 tablespoons finely chopped lemon grass, white part only
2 teaspoons grated fresh ginger
¹/2 red chilli, seeded and finely chopped
1 teaspoon sesame oil
2 tablespoons mirin
1 tablespoon fish sauce
1 tablespoon lime juice
10 scallops, on the shell
coriander (cilantro) leaves, to serve
lime wedges, to serve

Put the lemon grass, ginger, chilli, sesame oil, mirin, fish sauce and lime juice in a bowl. Mix well and allow the dressing to infuse for a few minutes.

To prepare the scallops, rinse away any sand from the shell. If the black stomach sac and extra membrane around the scallop are still present, remove them with a knife. Using a sharp knife, run the blade under the scallop meat, holding it close to the shell, and cut the scallop away, removing the connecting ligament. Return the scallop meat to the shell.

Heat the grill (broiler) to high. Sit the scallops on a baking tray and cook them under the grill for 2 minutes.

Arrange the scallops on a serving platter. Spoon the dressing over the scallops, garnish with coriander leaves and serve with lime wedges. Serves 4 as a starter

opposite: tofu salad
over: smoked salmon with vegetable salad,
and scallops with ginger and lemon grass   141

dill pancakes with smoked salmon

200 g (7 oz/heaped 1²/³ cups) plain (all-purpose) flour
¹/₂ teaspoon salt
2 teaspoons baking powder
2 eggs
250 ml (9 fl oz/1 cup) milk
grated zest of 1 lemon
1 tablespoon finely chopped dill
1 tablespoon butter
1 tablespoon lemon juice
100 g (3¹/₂ oz/heaped ¹/₃ cup) crème fraîche
12 slices of smoked salmon, cut in half
dill sprigs, to serve

To make the pancake batter, sift the flour and salt into a bowl. Stir in the baking powder, then make a well in the centre. In a separate bowl, beat the eggs and milk together. Pour the liquid ingredients into the dry ingredients and whisk together thoroughly. Stir in the lemon zest and dill. Allow the batter to rest at room temperature for 10 minutes.

Heat a non-stick frying pan over medium heat and grease the surface with a little of the butter. Using 1 tablespoon at a time, drop spoonfuls of batter into the hot pan and cook until the top of the pancake begins to bubble. Flip the pancakes over and cook for a further minute, then remove to a plate, stacking the pancakes to keep them warm. Repeat with the remaining batter — you should have about 24 small pancakes.

Fold the lemon juice through the crème fraîche and season with a little freshly ground black pepper.

Top the pancakes with smoked salmon, a dollop of the lemony crème fraîche, a sprinkle of freshly ground black pepper and a sprig of dill. Makes 24

beef salad with wasabi dressing

500 g (1 lb 2 oz) piece of beef sirloin
2 tablespoons lemon juice
1 tablespoon light olive oil
1 tablespoon soy sauce
1 tablespoon finely grated fresh ginger
1 teaspoon sesame oil
1 teaspoon wasabi paste
1 garlic clove, crushed
¹/₂ teaspoon wholegrain mustard
1 head of butter lettuce, leaves separated
4 radishes, trimmed and finely sliced
1 Lebanese (short) cucumber, diced
a handful of mint
a handful of coriander (cilantro) leaves

Trim the beef of all fat and sinew. Heat a frying pan or chargrill pan over high heat. When the pan is hot, add the beef and sear for 3 minutes on each side. Transfer to a plate, season with sea salt and cover loosely with foil.

Put the lemon juice, olive oil, soy sauce, ginger, sesame oil, wasabi paste, garlic and mustard in a large bowl and stir to make a dressing.

Arrange the lettuce, radish, cucumber, mint and coriander on a serving platter. Finely slice the beef and add it to the dressing, along with any meat juices. Toss the meat in the dressing, arrange over the salad and drizzle with any remaining dressing. Serves 4

lamb salad with walnut pesto

walnut pesto
a handful of basil
a handful of flat-leaf (Italian) parsley
50 g (1³/₄ oz/¹/₂ cup) grated parmesan cheese
1 garlic clove
100 g (3¹/₂ oz/1 cup) walnuts
170 ml (5¹/₂ fl oz/²/₃ cup) olive oil

250 g (9 oz) cherry tomatoes or truss tomatoes
2 x 300 g (10¹/₂ oz) lamb backstraps or loin fillets, trimmed
2 baby cos (romaine) lettuces, cut into quarters

Preheat the oven to 180°C (350°F/Gas 4). To make the walnut pesto, put the basil, parsley, parmesan, garlic and walnuts in a food processor with the olive oil and blend to a chunky paste. Transfer to a bowl and season to taste with sea salt and freshly ground black pepper.

Put the whole tomatoes on a baking tray and roast for 10 minutes, or until they start to split.

Heat a heavy-based frying pan over high heat and sear the lamb fillets for 2 minutes on each side. Put them on a baking tray and bake for 5 minutes, then transfer to a plate, season with sea salt, cover loosely with foil and leave to rest for 5 minutes.

Divide the lettuce quarters among four plates. Slice the lamb on the diagonal and arrange over the lettuce, then top with the roasted tomatoes and a large spoonful of the pesto. Serve drizzled with a little of the pesto oil. Serves 4

opposite: dill pancakes with smoked salmon
over: beef salad with wasabi dressing, and
lamb salad with walnut pesto

tomatoes

A bowl of ruby-red tomatoes ripening on the kitchen bench is a sign that summer is here and that I don't need to worry too much about tonight's dinner!

- Tomatoes are at their best at room temperature, and leaving them to ripen on a kitchen bench will ensure that they are richly red and very sweet when you come to use them. Adding salt draws the sweet juices out of the flesh and gives you a wonderfully flavoured salad. If time permits, always cut your tomatoes in advance of making a salad and salt them. Drizzle with a dressing and leave them to sit for half an hour. When you come to add the remaining ingredients you'll have a sweet tomato-flavoured dressing.

- Finely slice fennel and toss it in olive oil and lemon juice. Allow to sit for a few minutes and add some finely tossed mint and several large roughly chopped ripe tomatoes.

- Make a quick and easy salad of thick sliced tomato, rocket (arugula) leaves, shaved parmesan cheese, finely sliced salami, torn basil leaves and a scattering of rinsed and drained salted baby capers. Just add a drizzle of extra virgin olive oil and some sweet balsamic vinegar.

- Toss cherry tomatoes in a baking dish with some black olives and halved baby potatoes. Add a generous amount of olive oil, garlic, fresh rosemary and sea salt and bake in

a moderately hot oven until the potatoes are golden brown and the olives are nice and crinkly. Serve with roast meat, or cook in a covered baking dish on the barbecue and serve alongside chargrilled meats.

- Slow-bake cherry tomatoes with a drizzle of olive oil and sea salt until they are beginning to collapse. Arrange on a serving plate with baby bocconcini (fresh baby mozzarella cheese), thinly sliced prosciutto, wild rocket (arugula) leaves and garlicky bruschetta (Favourites).

- Slice ripe roma (plum) tomatoes in half, scatter with fresh thyme and sprinkle with sea salt and sugar. Bake in a

moderate oven for 40 minutes. Serve drizzled with extra virgin olive oil with grilled sausages.

- Roughly chop tomatoes and season generously with sea salt. Add some rinsed and drained tinned cannellini beans, a handful of flat-leaf (Italian) parsley, some extra virgin olive oil and a splash of balsamic vinegar. Add blanched green beans and freshly ground black pepper and toss to combine. Serve with chargrilled lamb or sausages.

poached tomato salad

4 large vine-ripened tomatoes
8 black peppercorns
2 teaspoons sea salt
1 tablespoon balsamic vinegar
1/2 red onion, finely sliced
70 g (2 1/2 oz/1/2 bunch) flat-leaf (Italian) parsley
a handful of wild rocket (arugula) leaves
8 basil leaves, roughly torn
150 g (5 1/2 oz/heaped 2/3 cup) drained and finely sliced
    marinated artichoke hearts
70 g (2 1/2 oz/3/4 cup) shaved pecorino cheese
2 tablespoons extra virgin olive oil
crusty bread, to serve

Preheat the oven to 180°C (350°F/Gas 4). Put the tomatoes in a small baking dish, then fill the dish with enough water to come halfway up the tomatoes. Add the peppercorns, sea salt, vinegar, onion and six parsley sprigs and bake for 40 minutes.

Lift the tomatoes out of the dish using a slotted spoon and sit them in the centre of four serving plates. Arrange the rocket, basil and a few parsley leaves around the tomatoes. Top with the artichoke slices, then scatter with the pecorino. Drizzle each salad with some of the tomato poaching liquid and a little olive oil. Serve with crusty bread. Serves 4 as a starter

fresh egg noodle salad

200 g (7 oz) fresh egg noodles
45 g (1 1/2 oz/1 cup) finely sliced Chinese cabbage
2 spring onions (scallions), finely sliced
100 g (3 1/2 oz/1 heaped cup) bean sprouts, trimmed
1 carrot, julienned
1 red capsicum (pepper), julienned
2 handfuls of coriander (cilantro) leaves
3 tablespoons hoisin sauce
1 1/2 tablespoons lime juice
1 teaspoon sesame oil
1 teaspoon sugar
2 tablespoons sesame seeds, toasted

Bring a large pot of salted water to the boil and add the egg noodles. Cook until *al dente*, then drain, rinse and set aside.

In a large bowl, toss together the cabbage, spring onion, bean sprouts, carrot, capsicum and coriander. In a small bowl, combine the hoisin sauce, lime juice, sesame oil and sugar, then pour over the vegetables.

Rinse and drain the noodles again, then toss them through the vegetables. Divide among four serving bowls and sprinkle with sesame seeds. Serves 4

somen noodle salad with seared prawns

soy and sesame dressing
3 tablespoons soy sauce
3 tablespoons sesame oil
1 1/2 tablespoons balsamic vinegar
2 tablespoons sugar
2 tablespoons lime juice
1 teaspoon finely grated fresh ginger
1 tablespoon finely chopped lemon grass, white part only

300 g (10 1/2 oz) somen noodles
2 handfuls of mint
2 handfuls of coriander (cilantro) leaves
12 cm (4 1/2 inch) piece of daikon, peeled and julienned
16 raw king prawns (shrimp), peeled and deveined
1 tablespoon olive oil
1 tablespoon lime juice

Put all the soy and sesame dressing ingredients in a large bowl and stir until the sugar has dissolved.

Bring a large pot of water to the boil and cook the noodles until *al dente*. Drain and rinse under cold running water, then toss the noodles in the dressing until well coated. Add the mint, coriander and daikon, toss together again, then pile into four serving bowls.

Put the prawns in a bowl with the olive oil and lime juice and toss until the prawns are well coated.

Heat a large non-stick frying pan over high heat. When the pan is hot, sear the prawns on both sides for a few minutes, until they turn pink and begin to curl up. Arrange over the noodles and serve immediately. Serves 4

opposite: poached tomato salad
over: fresh egg noodle salad, and
somen noodle salad with seared prawns

Comforting noodles with a touch of sesame and a crunch of vegetables

sweet and sour prawns

$1/2$ teaspoon cayenne pepper
1 teaspoon ground turmeric
1 tablespoon tamarind purée
20 raw king prawns (shrimp), peeled and deveined, tails intact
2 tablespoons vegetable oil
2 red onions, finely sliced
1 red capsicum (pepper), cut into 1 cm ($1/2$ inch) cubes
1 tablespoon grated palm sugar (jaggery) or soft brown sugar
1 tablespoon balsamic vinegar
steamed white rice (Favourites), to serve
100 ml ($3^1/2$ fl oz) coconut milk
a handful of coriander (cilantro) sprigs

Put the cayenne pepper, turmeric and tamarind purée in a non-metallic bowl and stir to combine. Add the prawns and toss until well coated. Cover and refrigerate until ready to use.

Put the vegetable oil in a large heavy-based frying pan over medium–low heat. Add the onion and cook for 20 minutes, stirring occasionally, until the onion is soft and beginning to caramelize. Add the capsicum, sugar and vinegar and cook for a further 2 minutes.

Add the prawns, laying them on their sides in a single layer over the onion mixture, and cook for $1^1/2$–2 minutes on each side, or until they are starting to curl up and turn pink — you may need to cook the prawns in two batches if your pan isn't quite large enough to fit them all at once.

Serve the prawns and sauce over steamed white rice, drizzled with the coconut milk and scattered with coriander. Serves 4

pan-fried bream with fennel, tomato and pancetta

1 large fennel bulb
2 tablespoons lemon juice
2 tablespoons extra virgin olive oil
10 mint leaves, finely sliced
2 tomatoes
60 g ($2^1/4$ oz) sliced pancetta
4 x 150 g ($5^1/2$ oz) bream fillets
2 tablespoons butter

Preheat the oven to 180°C (350°F/Gas 4).

Cut the fennel into paper-thin slices, reserving some of the feathery fronds as a garnish. Toss in a bowl with the lemon juice, olive oil and mint until well coated. Cut the tomatoes in half, scoop out the seeds with a teaspoon, then thinly slice the flesh. Add the tomato strips to the fennel and season with a little sea salt and freshly ground black pepper.

Heat a non-stick frying pan over high heat and fry the pancetta slices for 2–3 minutes, or until crisp and golden on both sides. Drain on paper towels and set aside.

Rinse the bream fillets under cold running water and pat dry with paper towels.

Heat the butter in the same frying pan and fry the bream over medium heat for 2 minutes on each side, or until lightly golden. Transfer the fish to a baking tray and bake for 5 minutes, or until cooked through. Top with pancetta and a fennel frond, and serve with the fennel and tomato. Serves 4

citrus couscous

185 g ($6^1/2$ oz/1 cup) instant couscous
grated zest and juice of 1 orange
grated zest and juice of 1 lemon
2 tablespoons olive oil
2 tablespoons finely chopped preserved lemon rind
2 Lebanese (short) cucumbers, peeled and finely diced
20 basil leaves

Put the couscous in a large bowl and pour 250 ml (9 fl oz/1 cup) boiling water over the top. Cover and allow to sit for 5 minutes, then fluff up the grains with a fork. Cover again and leave for a further 5 minutes. When the couscous has absorbed all the water, rub the grains with your fingertips to remove any lumps.

In a small bowl, mix together the citrus zest and citrus juice, olive oil and preserved lemon rind, then pour the mixture over the couscous. Add the cucumber and basil and toss to combine. Season with sea salt and freshly ground black pepper. Serve with smoked or roast chicken or chargrilled fish. Serves 4 as a side dish

opposite: sweet and sour prawns
over: pan-fried bream with fennel, tomato and pancetta, and citrus couscous

A shimmer of summer in the golden zest of oranges and lemons

4 salsas

herby harissa

1 roasted red capsicum (pepper) (Favourites)
2 garlic cloves, roughly chopped
4 red chillies, seeded and roughly chopped
1 teaspoon ground coriander
1 teaspoon ground cumin
90 g (3¹/₄ oz/1 bunch) coriander (cilantro), roughly chopped
3 tablespoons olive oil
1 tablespoon lemon juice

Remove any seeds, membrane and skin from the roasted capsicum. Roughly chop the flesh, put it in a food processor with the remaining ingredients and process to a thick sauce. Serve with roast chicken, chargrilled tuna or fried eggs.

The harissa will keep in an airtight container in the refrigerator for several weeks. Makes about 300 g (10¹/₂ oz/1 cup)

asian salsa

1 Lebanese (short) cucumber, finely diced
1 large red chilli, seeded and finely diced
¹/₂ yellow capsicum (pepper), finely diced
1 spring onion (scallion), finely sliced
1 tablespoon finely chopped coriander (cilantro)
1 teaspoon finely chopped lemon grass, white part only
1 teaspoon finely grated fresh ginger
2 tablespoons lime juice
1 tablespoon fish sauce
1 teaspoon sugar
1 teaspoon sesame oil

In a bowl, toss together the cucumber, chilli, capsicum, spring onion, coriander, lemon grass and ginger.

Put the remaining ingredients in another small bowl and stir until the sugar has dissolved. Gently toss the dressing through the salsa. Serve with seared fish or spooned over baked scallops. Makes about 300 g (10¹/₂ oz/¹/₂ cup)

chunky tomato, olive and basil salsa

12 cherry tomatoes, cut in half, or into quarters if large
10 basil leaves, torn
12 small black olives
1¹/₂ tablespoons balsamic vinegar
3 tablespoons extra virgin olive oil

Put all the ingredients in a bowl, season with sea salt and freshly ground black pepper and gently toss together. Spoon over grilled tuna, swordfish or marlin, drizzling any remaining dressing over the top. Makes about 200 g (7 oz/1¹/₂ cups)

lime and avocado salsa

1 ripe avocado, diced
1 Lebanese (short) cucumber, finely chopped
¹/₂ small red onion, finely diced
2 large red chillies, seeded and finely chopped
a large handful of coriander (cilantro) leaves
2 teaspoons fish sauce
2 tablespoons lime juice
4 tablespoons olive oil
1 lime

Put the avocado in a bowl with the cucumber, onion, chilli, coriander, fish sauce, lime juice and olive oil.

Using a sharp knife, cut the top and base off the lime. Sit the lime on a chopping board and run the knife down all sides, removing the skin and pith. Run the knife between the membranes to release the lime segments, then finely chop them and gently stir them into the salsa, being careful not to mash the avocado. Serve with grilled fish. Makes about 600 g (1 lb 5 oz/2 cups)

opposite: lime and avocado salsa

lamb skewers with herbed yoghurt

300 g (10¹/₂ oz/about 2¹/₄ cups) plain yoghurt
2 spring onions (scallions), finely sliced
1 teaspoon garam masala
1 teaspoon grated fresh ginger
1 garlic clove, crushed
¹/₂ teaspoon ground turmeric
¹/₂ teaspoon chilli powder
300 g (10¹/₂ oz) diced lamb, cut into 3 cm (1¹/₄ inch) cubes
15 mint leaves, finely chopped
25 g (1 oz/1 bunch) chives, finely snipped
baby leaf salad, to serve

Spoon 4 tablespoons of the yoghurt into a bowl and add the spring onion, garam masala, ginger, garlic, turmeric and chilli powder. Stir to combine, then add the lamb, mixing well to ensure all the cubes are well coated. Cover and refrigerate overnight.

One hour before cooking, soak eight wooden skewers in cold water to prevent scorching.

Mix the remaining yoghurt with the mint and chives, then spoon into four little serving dishes. Thread the lamb onto the soaked skewers and cook on a hot barbecue grill plate or chargrill pan for 4 minutes on each side, or until cooked to your liking. Remove from the heat and season with sea salt. Serve with the herbed yoghurt and a baby leaf salad. Serves 4

asian-style poached chicken

6 sichuan peppercorns
juice of 1 lemon
2 star anise
1 cinnamon stick
a thumb-sized knob of ginger, thinly sliced
3 tablespoons sweet mirin
3 tablespoons soy sauce
4 boneless, skinless chicken breasts
1 spring onion (scallion), finely sliced on the diagonal
2 large red chillies, seeded and finely chopped
100 g (3¹/₂ oz/²/₃ cup) unsalted toasted cashew nuts
10 mint leaves, torn
a handful of coriander (cilantro) leaves
steamed white rice (Favourites), to serve

Fill a saucepan with 1.5 litres (52 fl oz/6 cups) water and add the peppercorns, lemon juice, star anise, cinnamon stick, ginger, mirin and 2 tablespoons of the soy sauce. Bring to the boil, then reduce heat and simmer for 15 minutes.

Drop the chicken breasts into the simmering liquid. When the liquid returns to the boil, cover with a tightly fitting lid and remove from the heat. Allow to sit, covered, for 40 minutes — during this time the residual heat will gently poach the chicken.

Remove the chicken from the poaching liquid and shred it into a bowl. Add the spring onion, chilli, cashews, mint and coriander. Toss together, then pile into a serving bowl. Strain 500 ml (17 fl oz/2 cups) of the cooking stock into a jug and add the remaining soy sauce. Pour a generous amount of the warm liquid over the chicken and serve with steamed white rice. Serves 4

seared lamb with almond salad

almond salad
50 g (1³/₄ oz/heaped ¹/₂ cup) flaked almonds, toasted and finely chopped
1 garlic clove, crushed
a handful of flat-leaf (Italian) parsley, roughly chopped
10 basil leaves, roughly chopped
3 ripe roma (plum) tomatoes, finely chopped
¹/₄ red onion, finely diced
3 tablespoons extra virgin olive oil

2 x 300 g (10¹/₂ oz) lamb backstraps or loin fillets, trimmed
1 tablespoon olive oil

Put all the almond salad ingredients in a bowl. Season generously with sea salt and freshly ground black pepper, toss to combine and set aside.

Put the lamb fillets in a bowl with the olive oil and toss a few times to thoroughly coat the lamb. Heat a large heavy-based frying pan over high heat. Add the lamb and sear for 3 minutes on each side. Transfer to a warm plate, cover loosely with foil and allow to rest for 5 minutes.

Spoon the almond salad into the centre of four serving plates. Slice the lamb fillets on the diagonal, arrange the slices over the salad and pour any meat juices over the top. Serves 4

opposite: lamb skewers with herbed yoghurt
over: asian-style poached chicken, and
seared lamb with almond salad

A healthy, grainy twist on the classic niçoise salad

tuna and quinoa salad

150 g (5¹/2 oz/³/4 cup) quinoa
2 tablespoons lemon juice
2 tablespoons olive oil
1 tablespoon finely chopped preserved lemon rind
25 g (1 oz/1 bunch) chives, finely snipped
200 g (7 oz) green beans, blanched and cut into 3 cm (1¹/4 inch)
    lengths, on the diagonal
250 g (9 oz) cherry tomatoes, cut into quarters
200 g (7 oz) tinned tuna in oil, drained
a large handful of mizuna or baby salad leaves

Put the quinoa in a saucepan and cover with 500 ml
(17 fl oz/2 cups) water. Bring to the boil, then reduce
the heat and simmer for 5 minutes, or until the grains are
cooked through. Remove from the heat and drain.

Put the lemon juice, olive oil, preserved lemon rind and
chives in a bowl and add the quinoa. Toss together, then
add the beans, cherry tomatoes and tuna. Toss once more
and season to taste with sea salt and freshly ground black
pepper. Divide the salad leaves among four bowls and
spoon the tuna and quinoa salad over the top. Serves 4

chicken and preserved lemon salad

1 tablespoon sea salt
juice of 2 lemons
2 boneless, skinless chicken breasts
3 tablespoons olive oil
1 teaspoon ground cumin
1 tablespoon finely chopped preserved lemon rind
90 g (3¹/4 oz/1 cup) flaked almonds, toasted
a handful of coriander (cilantro), roughly chopped
a handful of mint, roughly chopped
1 Lebanese (short) cucumber, diced
50 g (1³/4 oz/¹/3 cup) currants
steamed couscous (Favourites), to serve

Bring a saucepan of water to the boil. Add the sea salt, half
the lemon juice and the chicken breasts. When the liquid
returns to the boil, cover with a tightly fitting lid and remove
from the heat. Allow to sit, covered, for 40 minutes — during
this time the residual heat will gently poach the chicken.

Remove the chicken from the poaching liquid and roughly
shred it into a large bowl. Add the remaining lemon juice, olive
oil, cumin, preserved lemon rind and flaked almonds. Toss
together briefly, then add the remaining salad ingredients and
toss again. Serve with steamed couscous. Serves 4

barbecue butterflied chicken with a chilli tomato sauce

chilli tomato sauce
1 tablespoon light olive oil
1 onion, finely chopped
2 garlic cloves, finely chopped
1 tablespoon finely grated lemon zest
1 tablespoon soft brown sugar
2 tablespoons lemon juice
1 cup tomato passata (puréed tomatoes)
1 tablespoon finely chopped tinned chipotle chilli
2 tablespoons red wine vinegar
2 tablespoons soy sauce

1 large organic chicken, butterflied (ask your butcher to do this)
crusty bread, to serve
baby leaf salad, to serve

To make the chilli tomato sauce, heat the olive oil in a
saucepan over medium heat and add the onion and garlic.
Sauté for 5 minutes, or until the onion is transparent. Add the
remaining sauce ingredients and stir in 125 ml (4 fl oz/¹/2 cup)
water. Stir until well combined, then simmer for 5 minutes.
Allow the sauce to cool, then pour over the chicken and rub
into the flesh. Leave to marinate for 30 minutes.

Preheat a barbecue grill plate to medium. Place the chicken
on the barbecue, skin side down. Cook for 10 minutes, then
turn the chicken over and cover with a barbecue lid or a baking
tray. Cook for a further 20–30 minutes, depending on the size
of the chicken.

If you like your chicken slightly less charred, cook the chicken
on a shallow baking tray sitting on the grill plate. This method
will also retain most of the spicy juices.

If you prefer, you can also cook the chicken in the oven. Line
a shallow baking dish with baking paper and sit the chicken in
the dish, skin side up. Spoon the sauce over the chicken and
bake in a preheated 200°C (400°F/Gas 6) oven for 40 minutes.
Turn the chicken over, then cook for a further 20 minutes.

Carve the chicken into pieces, pour the cooking juices over
and serve with crusty bread and a baby leaf salad. Serves 4–6

opposite: tuna and quinoa salad
over: chicken and preserved lemon salad, and
barbecue butterflied chicken with a chilli tomato sauce

tangy shellfish broth

8 raw king prawns (shrimp)
3 lemon grass stems
100 g (3¹/₂ oz) oyster mushrooms, cut in half
100 g (3¹/₂ oz) enoki mushrooms
6 makrut (kaffir lime) leaves
3 roma (plum) tomatoes, finely chopped
2 spring onions (scallions), finely sliced
juice of 3 limes
1 large red chilli, seeded and finely chopped
2–4 tablespoons fish sauce, or to taste
50 g (1³/₄ oz/¹/₂ cup) fresh crabmeat
a handful of coriander (cilantro), roughly chopped
a handful of mint

Peel and devein the prawns, reserving the shells. Slice off and reserve the white ends of the lemon grass stems, then cut the long green stalks into 2 cm (³/₄ inch) longths and flatten them with a cleaver or the ond of a heavy-handled knife.

Heat 1 litre (35 fl oz/4 cups) water in a saucepan. Add the prawn shells and the white ends of the lemon grass and bring to the boil. Take the pan off the heat and strain the prawn stock into a large bowl to remove the solids.

Pour the prawn stock back into the saucepan, then add the crushed green lemon grass stalks, mushrooms, lime leaves and tomato. Return to the boil, then reduce the heat and simmer for 3–4 minutes. Add the prawns, and when they start to turn pink, add the spring onion, lime juice, chilli, fish sauce and crabmeat. Stir well, then season to taste. Ladle into bowls and serve with a scattering of coriander and mint. Serves 4 as a starter, or 2 as a main meal

whiting with jewelled butter

1 tablespoon finely diced red onion
1 tablespoon finely diced red capsicum (pepper)
1 tablespoon finely diced green capsicum (pepper)
1 small ripe tomato
70 g (2¹/₂ oz) butter, softened
8 small whiting fillets
2 tablespoons cornflour (cornstarch)
2 tablespoons light olive oil
mixed leaf salad, to serve
lemon wedges, to serve

Put the onion and capsicum in a bowl. Cut the tomato into quarters and scoop out the seeds using a teaspoon. Finely dice the flesh and add it to the diced vegetables. Add the melted butter, mix well and set aside.

Rinse the whiting fillets and pat dry with paper towels. Put the cornflour on a plate and use it to lightly dust the fish fillets. Set aside.

Heat a non-stick frying pan over high heat and add the olive oil. Fry the whiting for 1–2 minutes on each side, or until crisp and golden. Divide among four serving plates, then spoon the vegetable butter over the fish. Serve with a mixed leaf salad and lemon wedges. Serves 4

red snapper with tomato salsa

tomato salsa
250 g (9 oz) cherry tomatoes, cut into quarters
1 teaspoon finely grated fresh ginger
2 tablespoons finely diced red onion
6 basil leaves, finely sliced
1¹/₂ tablespoons lime juice
1¹/₂ tablespoons coconut cream

2 tablespoons vegetable oil
4 x 200 g (7 oz) red snapper fillets, skin on
lime wedges, to serve

Preheat the oven to 200°C (400°F/Gas 0). Put all the tomato salsa ingredients in a small bowl. Mix together and set aside.

Put the vegetable oil in a large heavy-based frying pan over high heat. Rinse the snapper fillets and pat dry with paper towels. Coacon generously with sea salt and sit the fillets, skin side down, in the hot pan. Sear for 1–2 minutes, or until the skin is crisp and golden, then turn the fillets over.

Lift the fish, skin side up, onto a baking tray lined with foil. Bake for 8–10 minutes, or until cooked through. Lift the fillets onto serving plates, then spoon the tomato salsa over the top and serve with lime wedges. Serves 4

seasonal ideas

Flavoured butters are a great way to add zing to steamed or grilled fish, baked scallops or barbecued prawns (shrimp). Simply blend some softened butter with your chosen flavouring and refrigerate until needed. Try these:

- grated lemon zest and finely chopped parsley or dill
- finely chopped coriander (cilantro), chilli and lime zest
- curry powder or a little Thai curry paste
- chopped capers, parsley and anchovies
- finely chopped sun-dried tomato, black olives and basil.

opposite: tangy shellfish broth
over: whiting with jewelled butter, and
red snapper with tomato salsa

passionfruit jelly with lychees

400 g (14 oz) tin lychees
1 teaspoon lime juice
3 tablespoons caster (superfine) sugar
6 gelatine leaves or 2 teaspoons powdered gelatine*
160 ml (5^{1}/$_{4}$ fl oz) strained passionfruit pulp (about 8 passionfruit)
juice of 2 oranges

Drain the lychees, reserving the juice. Put the lychees in a bowl, cover with water and add the lime juice. Chill in the refrigerator until ready to serve.

Pour the reserved lychee juice into a saucepan with the sugar and heat over low heat, stirring until the sugar has dissolved.

If using gelatine leaves, soak them in a bowl of cold water for 5 minutes, or until dissolved to a jellied consistency. Squeeze out the excess water, then stir the leaves into the warm lychee syrup. If using powdered gelatine, stir the powdered gelatine into 3 tablespoons of boiling water until the crystals have completely dissolved, then pour into the warm lychee syrup.

Pour the warm syrup into a measuring container, then add the passionfruit juice and enough orange juice to make 600 ml (21 fl oz) liquid. Stir well, pour into four 200 ml (7 fl oz) glasses and refrigerate for 3 hours or overnight, until set.

Drain the lychees and serve with the passionfruit jelly. Serves 4

* When using powdered gelatine, always check the manufacturer's instructions.

macerated plums with coconut sorbet

145 g (5 oz/^{2}/$_{3}$ cup) caster (superfine) sugar
1 vanilla bean
250 ml (9 fl oz/1 cup) milk
400 ml (14 fl oz) tin coconut milk
1 tablespoon golden rum
10 blood plums (about 800 g/1 lb 12 oz in total)
2 tablespoons dark brown sugar
juice of 1 orange

Put the caster sugar, vanilla bean and 150 ml (5 fl oz) water in a saucepan over medium heat. Stir well to dissolve the sugar. When the syrup comes to the boil, let it bubble for 10 minutes. Discard the vanilla bean and pour the syrup into a bowl.

To make the coconut sorbet, pour the milk and coconut milk into the saucepan and let it warm through. Take the pan off the heat, stir in the vanilla syrup and rum, then allow to cool. Churn the mixture in an ice cream machine, or pour it into a shallow container, place it in the freezer, then stir every hour until the sorbet freezes.

Cut the plums into thick slices, removing the stones as you go. Put the plums in a bowl, add the brown sugar and orange juice and toss until well coated. Cover and refrigerate for 1 hour. Divide the chilled plums among six bowls and serve with scoops of the coconut sorbet. Serves 6

peach and fig semifreddo

4 egg yolks
150 g (5^{1}/$_{2}$ oz/scant ^{1}/$_{2}$ cup) honey
300 ml (10^{1}/$_{2}$ fl oz) pouring (whipping) cream
2 peaches, flesh diced
5 dried figs, finely chopped
fresh berries, to serve

Line a 10 x 20 cm (4 x 8 inch) loaf (bar) tin with plastic wrap. Beat the egg yolks with the honey until light and frothy. Whip the cream until it forms soft peaks, then fold it into the honey mixture. Stir in the peach and fig. Pour into the prepared tin, cover with plastic wrap and freeze overnight.

When ready to serve, turn the semifreddo out onto a serving plate and cut into thick slices. Scatter with berries. Serves 6

seasonal ideas

- Blend white peaches, raspberries and orange juice with a handful of crushed ice for the perfect summer afternoon drink.

- Poach plums in orange juice with cinnamon or vanilla and serve chilled with whipped cream and some plain chocolate biscuits (cookies).

- Slice peaches in half, sprinkle with sugar and bake in a moderate oven until soft and golden. Top with a tumble of fresh raspberries and thick (double/heavy) cream.

- Slice a banana in half lengthways, top with a large scoop of vanilla ice cream and drizzle with passionfruit syrup (Favourites).

opposite: passionfruit jelly with lychees
over: peach and fig semifreddo, and
macerated plums with coconut sorbet

A warm sunset and the taste of icy sweet coconut

4 granitas

lemon grass granita

2 lemon grass stems
145 g (5¼ oz/⅔ cup) caster (superfine) sugar
250 ml (9 fl oz/1 cup) pineapple juice
juice of 2 limes
100 ml (3½ fl oz) vodka
½ small ripe pineapple

Trim away the root end of the lemon grass stems, then cut the stems into thirds and bruise them with the end of a heavy-handled knife. Put them in a saucepan with the sugar and 500 ml (17 fl oz/2 cups) water. Bring to the boil, reduce the heat and simmer for 5 minutes. Take the syrup off the heat and allow to cool. Stir in the pineapple juice, lime juice and vodka, then strain into a wide, shallow container and freeze for 1 hour.

Using a fork, scrape the ice from the side of the container back into the mixture. Return to the freezer and repeat another three times, until the granita looks like crushed ice.

Cut the pineapple into quarters, then into thin wedges. Serve the granita spooned into chilled glasses, with the pineapple wedges on the side. Serves 4–6

coffee granita

1 litre (35 fl oz/4 cups) strong plunger or filter coffee
220 g (7¾ oz/1 cup) sugar
6 thick strips of lemon zest
4 tablespoons Frangelico or other hazelnut liqueur
almond bread, to serve

Put the coffee and sugar in a saucepan with the lemon zest strips and bring to the boil. Reduce the heat and allow to simmer for a few minutes, stirring to dissolve the sugar. Remove from the heat and allow to cool.

Stir in the liqueur, then pour into a 20 cm (8 inch) square plastic container. Place in the freezer and leave for an hour or two. As crystals start to form, use a large fork to scrape them away from the side of the container back into the mixture. Repeat every hour for 3–4 hours until the granita is frozen into large shards of ice. Return to the freezer until ready to serve.

To serve, scrape the ice with a fork before spooning into four tall chilled glasses. Serve with almond bread. Serves 4

blood orange and campari granita

200 g (7 oz/1 scant cup) sugar
600 ml (21 fl oz) fresh blood orange juice
3 tablespoons Campari

Put the sugar and 400 ml (14 fl oz) water in a saucepan and bring to the boil. Reduce the heat to low and simmer for 10 minutes, stirring to dissolve the sugar. Remove from the heat and allow to cool.

Pour 400 ml (14 fl oz) of the sugar syrup into a measuring container. Stir in the blood orange juice and Campari, then pour into a 20 cm (8 inch) square plastic container. Place in the freezer and leave for an hour or two. As crystals start to form, use a large fork to scrape them away from the side of the container back into the mixture. Repeat every hour for 3–4 hours until the granita is frozen into large shards of ice. Return to the freezer until ready to serve.

To serve, scrape the ice with a fork before spooning into four tall chilled glasses. Serves 4

rum and pineapple ice

55 g (2 oz/¼ cup) caster (superfine) sugar
500 ml (17 fl oz/2 cups) pineapple juice
1 teaspoon natural vanilla extract
100 ml (3½ fl oz) golden rum
170 ml (5½ fl oz/⅔ cup) coconut milk

Put the sugar and pineapple juice in a saucepan over medium heat. Stir until the sugar has dissolved, then remove from the heat and stir in the vanilla and rum.

Pour the liquid into a wide shallow container and freeze for 4–5 hours, or until frozen. Remove from the freezer and allow to soften, then break the mixture up using a fork until it looks like crushed ice. Return to the freezer until ready to serve.

Spoon into four chilled glasses and drizzle with the coconut milk. Serves 4

passionfruit tart

23 cm (9 inch) pre-baked sweet shortcrust tart case (Favourites)
125 ml (4 fl oz/^{1}/$_2$ cup) strained passionfruit pulp
2 tablespoons lime juice
100 g (3^1/$_2$ oz/^{1}/$_2$ cup) sugar
300 ml (10^1/$_2$ fl oz) pouring (whipping) cream
6 egg yolks
icing (confectioners') sugar, to serve
whipped cream, to serve

passionfruit sauce
pulp of 3 passionfruit
3 tablespoons caster (superfine) sugar

Preheat the oven to 180°C (350°F/Gas 4). Put the tart case on a baking tray.

Put the passionfruit pulp, lime juice and sugar in a small saucepan and stir over low heat until the sugar has dissolved. Whisk together the cream and egg yolks, then whisk the warm passionfruit mixture into the cream.

Pour the passionfruit cream into the tart case and carefully place in the oven. Bake for 30–35 minutes, or until the tart is lightly golden on top and the filling is slightly wobbly in the centre. Remove from the oven and allow to cool.

To make the passionfruit sauce, put the passionfruit pulp and sugar in a saucepan, then stir and simmer over low heat for a few minutes. Remove from the heat and allow to cool.

Remove the tart from the baking tray, drizzle with the passionfruit sauce and sprinkle with icing sugar. Serve with whipped cream. Serves 8–10

apricot tart

fruit tart base
2^1/$_2$ tablespoons unsalted butter
3 tablespoons sour cream
125 g (4^1/$_2$ oz/1 cup) plain (all-purpose) flour
1 heaped teaspoon caster (superfine) sugar

100 g (3^1/$_2$ oz/heaped 1 cup) flaked almonds
1 tablespoon butter
1 egg
3 tablespoons honey
8 small ripe apricots, cut in half and stones removed
icing (confectioners') sugar, to serve
vanilla ice cream, to serve

Preheat the oven to 160°C (315°F/Gas 2–3). Line a baking tray with baking paper.

Put all the ingredients for the fruit tart base in a food processor and chop until the pastry begins to come together. Remove from the processor, cover with plastic wrap and refrigerate for 10 minutes.

Wipe the processor bowl clean and add the flaked almonds, butter, egg and honey. Process to a thick, uneven paste.

Roll out the chilled pastry between two sheets of baking paper to form a 30 cm (12 inch) square. Lay the pastry on the baking tray and create an edge for the finished tart by rolling over 1 cm (^{1}/$_2$ inch) of pastry all the way round.

Spread the almond mixture over the pastry, then arrange the apricot halves over the top, cut side up. Cover with foil and bake for 30 minutes, then remove the foil and bake for a further 15 minutes. Dust with icing sugar and serve sliced with vanilla ice cream. Serves 6

drunken peaches with raspberry sorbet

170 g (6 oz/^{3}/$_4$ cup) caster (superfine) sugar
300 g (10^1/$_2$ oz/about 2^1/$_2$ cups) frozen raspberries
6 ripe peaches
750 ml (26 fl oz/3 cups) Prosecco or sparkling wine

Put the sugar in a small saucepan with 185 ml (6 fl oz/^{3}/$_4$ cup) water and stir to dissolve sugar. Bring to the boil, then reduce the heat and simmer for a few minutes. Remove from the heat and allow the sugar syrup to cool.

To make the raspberry sorbet, put the raspberries and 250 ml (4 fl oz/1 cup) of the sugar syrup in a blender or food processor. Blend to a smooth purée, then strain the liquid through a fine sieve into a bowl. Cover with plastic wrap and freeze for several hours, or overnight.

Remove the skin from the peaches and slice them into six glass coupe bowls or parfait glasses. Pour the Prosecco over, add a scoop of raspberry sorbet and serve immediately. Serves 6

opposite: passionfruit tart
over: apricot tart, and drunken peaches with raspberry sorbet

fragrant peach tart

6–7 small ripe peaches
25 cm (10 inch) pre-baked sweet shortcrust tart case (Favourites),
    with 3 cm (1¹/4 inch) deep sides
2 eggs
115 g (4 oz/¹/2 cup) caster (superfine) sugar
4 tablespoons plain (all-purpose) flour
¹/2 teaspoon rosewater
110 g (3³/4 oz) unsalted butter
thick (double/heavy) cream, to serve

Preheat the oven to 180°C (350°F/Gas 4). Cut the peaches in half and remove the stones. Slice the flesh into thick wedges and arrange around the base of the tart case, skin side down.

Crack the eggs into a mixing bowl, add the sugar and beat using electric beaters until pale and fluffy. Fold in the flour and rosewater.

Heat the butter in a saucepan over high heat. When it begins to froth and turn pale golden brown, pour it into the egg mixture and beat for 1 minute.

Pour the filling over the peaches and bake for 35 minutes. Cover the tart with foil and bake for a further 15 minutes, or until the filling has set. Remove from the oven and allow to cool, then cut into slices and serve with cream. Serves 8

passionfruit sponge

2 eggs, separated
115 g (4 oz/¹/2 cup) caster (superfine) sugar
70 g (2¹/2 oz/heaped ¹/2 cup) plain (all-purpose) flour
¹/2 teaspoon baking powder
150 ml (5 fl oz) pouring (whipping) cream, whipped
125 ml (4¹/2 oz/¹/2 cup) passionfruit pulp (about 6–7 passionfruit)
icing (confectioners') sugar, to serve

Preheat the oven to 190°C (375°F/Gas 5). Line the base of a 20 cm (8 inch) round cake tin, then grease it and lightly flour the side and base.

In a bowl, beat the egg yolks with the sugar for a few minutes using electric beaters, then add 2 tablespoons of warm water. Continue to beat for a further 8 minutes, or until the mixture is very pale and fluffy.

Sift the flour and baking powder onto a plate. Lightly fold the flour into the egg yolk mixture, a few spoonfuls at a time. In a separate bowl, beat the egg whites until soft peaks form, then fold the egg whites through the flour mixture. Pour the batter into the prepared cake tin and bake for 20–25 minutes, or until the sponge springs back when tapped.

Turn out onto a wire rack to cool. When cool, slice in half horizontally. Cover the bottom layer with whipped cream, then spoon the passionfruit pulp over. Place the remaining sponge half on top, then dust generously with icing sugar. Serves 6

rosy plum crumbles

10 blood plums (about 800 g/1 lb 12 oz in total)
80 g (2³/4 oz/¹/3 cup) caster (superfine) sugar
1 teaspoon rosewater
115 g (4 oz/¹/2 cup) dark brown sugar
60 g (2¹/4 oz/¹/2 cup) plain (all purpose) flour
45 g (1¹/2 oz/¹/2 cup) desiccated coconut
75 g (2¹/2 oz) unsalted butter
whipped cream, thick (double/heavy) cream or ice cream, to serve

Preheat the oven to 180°C (350°F/Gas 4). Slice the plums, removing the stones, and put them in a bowl. Add the caster sugar and rosewater and toss until the plums are well coated in sugar. Set aside for 10 minutes.

Toss the brown sugar, flour and coconut together in a bowl. Rub the butter in with your fingertips until the mixture resembles breadcrumbs. Set aside.

Stir the plums again to ensure they are well coated, then divide among six 150 ml (5 fl oz) ovenproof bowls, piling the plums above the top of the bowls as they will cook down quite a bit.

Top the plums with the coconut mixture, then set the bowls on a baking tray and bake for 30 minutes, or until the crumbles are golden and the juices are bubbling over the sides of the bowls. Serve warm with cream, or at room temperature with ice cream. Serves 6

opposite: fragrant peach tart
over: passionfruit sponge, and rosy plum crumbles

Syrupy plums and crisp sweet crumbs

summer fruit

Who can resist summer's glorious array of succulent fruit? Their wonderful flavours and colours need very little embellishment — just add a drizzle of flavourful sauce or a scoop of ice cream and sorbet.

- Serve a fresh fruit salad of sliced banana, peach, passionfruit and orange juice with vanilla ice cream or mango sorbet.

- Serve wedges of chilled ripe pineapple with lime sorbet.

- Slice fresh mango onto a plate, drizzle with a little coconut cream and top with a crumble of palm sugar (jaggery) and toasted shredded coconut.

- Finely slice mango and drizzle with raspberry coulis (Favourites), or make a sweet mango salsa with diced mango, pineapple, lime juice and mint. Serve spooned over squares of vanilla ice cream.

- Drizzle lychees with rosewater syrup (page 115). Add a wedge of fresh lime and vanilla ice cream, or spoon the syrup over a salad of fresh strawberries and raspberries and serve with thick (double/heavy) cream and biscotti.

- Drizzle ripe strawberries with aromatic honey and a few drops of caramelized balsamic vinegar. Serve with mascarpone cheese and biscotti.

- Mix orange juice with soft brown sugar and finely grated fresh ginger and drizzle over sliced nectarines and banana.

- Stew apricots with a little sugar and $1/2$ teaspoon orange flower water. Serve with yoghurt or ice cream, sprinkled with toasted flaked almonds or crushed pecans.

- Put 8 sliced blood plums in a small baking dish with 150 g (5$1/2$ oz) blackberries. Sprinkle generously with caster (superfine) sugar, dab with butter and drizzle with dessert wine. Cover and bake in a moderate oven until soft. Serve warm with a dollop of mascarpone cheese and almond bread.

- Sit some halved plums, skin side down, on a baking tray lined with baking paper. Place a thin slice of quince paste in each and bake in a moderately hot oven until soft. Serve with vanilla ice cream.

- Stew plums to a soft velvety richness and serve with caramel ice cream or thick (double/heavy) cream.

- Roughly chop poached peaches and layer in trifle glasses with whipped cream, broken savoiardi (lady fingers/sponge finger biscuits) and strawberry coulis (Favourites).

chocolate plum cake

165 g (5³/4 oz/³/4 cup firmly packed) dark brown sugar
280 g (10 oz/2¹/4 cups) plain (all-purpose) flour
185 g (6¹/2 oz) cold unsalted butter
2 teaspoons baking powder
3 tablespoons dark cocoa powder
¹/4 teaspoon salt
230 g (8 oz/1 cup) caster (superfine) sugar
3 eggs, lightly beaten
185 ml (6 fl oz/³/4 cup) milk
16 small plums (550 g/1 lb 4 oz), stones removed, cut in half
ice cream or thick (double/heavy) cream, to serve

Preheat the oven to 180°C (350°F/Gas 4). Grease a 25 cm (10 inch) spring-form cake tin.

Put the brown sugar in a bowl with 30 g (1 oz/¹/4 cup) of the flour and mix together. Add 3 tablespoons of the cold butter (leave the rest at room temperature to soften) and rub the butter in with your fingertips until the mixture resembles coarse breadcrumbs.

Sift the remaining flour into a mixing bowl along with the baking powder, cocoa and salt. Put the caster sugar and softened butter in a separate bowl and cream together using electric beaters, then add the eggs and mix well. Add half the flour mixture, then half the milk, mixing well after each addition. Mix in the remaining flour mixture, then the remaining milk.

Pour the batter into the prepared cake tin and arrange the plum halves on top, cut side down. Sprinkle with the brown sugar mixture and bake for 50–60 minutes, or until a skewer inserted into the centre of the cake comes out clean.

Remove the cake from the oven and allow to cool before turning out of the tin. Serve with ice cream or cream. Serves 10

peach cake

4 eggs, separated
150 g (5¹/2 oz/1¹/4 cups) plain (all-purpose) flour
1 teaspoon baking powder
150 g (5¹/2 oz/²/3 cup) caster (superfine) sugar
120 g (4¹/4 oz) unsalted butter, melted
1 tablespoon grated lemon zest
500 g (1 lb 2 oz/about 3) ripe peaches, peeled and cut into
    thick wedges
icing (confectioners') sugar, to serve

Preheat the oven to 180°C (350°F/Gas 4). Grease and line a 23 cm (9 inch) spring-form cake tin.

In a bowl, beat the egg whites using electric beaters until soft peaks form. Sift the flour and baking powder into another bowl, then add the sugar. Stir to combine, then make a well in the centre.

In another bowl, whisk together the melted butter, egg yolks and lemon zest. Stir the liquid ingredients and one-third of the egg whites into the dry ingredients to form a smooth batter, then fold the remaining egg whites through.

Pour the batter into the prepared cake tin. Arrange the peach slices in a single layer over the top and bake for 30–40 minutes, or until the cake is golden brown and a skewer inserted into the centre comes out clean. Allow to cool, then turn the cake out of the tin and dust with icing sugar. Serves 8

mango jellies with summer fruit salad

mango jellies
1 large ripe mango, flesh diced
juice of 2 limes
115 g (4 oz/¹/2 cup) caster (superfine) sugar
375 ml (13 fl oz/1¹/2 cups) orange juice
3 teaspoons powdered gelatine*

200 g (7 oz/1 cup) finely diced pineapple
1 ripe peach, cut into wedges
pulp of 2 passionfruit
juice of 1 orange
sansho pepper, optional (available from Japanese speciality stores)

To make the mango jellies, purée the mango in a blender with the lime juice, then pour the mixture into a measuring container — you will need 250 ml (9 fl oz/1 cup) liquid. If you don't have quite enough, top up with water or orange juice. Set aside.

Put the sugar and orange juice in a small saucepan over medium heat. Stir until the sugar has dissolved, then pour the liquid into a bowl. Sprinkle the gelatine over the warm liquid and stir for a minute or two to ensure that it is evenly dissolved. Stir in the mango purée, then ladle into four 150 ml (5 fl oz) jelly moulds or ramekins. Cover with plastic wrap and refrigerate overnight.

Just before serving, put the pineapple, peach, passionfruit pulp and orange juice in a bowl and gently mix together.

Dip the moulds in hot water, then turn the jellies out onto four dessert plates. Spoon the fruit salad around them and sprinkle with a little sansho pepper if desired. Serves 4

* When using powdered gelatine, always check the manufacturer's instructions.

opposite: chocolate plum cake
over: peach cake, and mango jellies with summer fruit salad

The sudden appearance of chilly mornings and falling leaves announces the arrival of autumn. And it's not just the trees that are turning golden brown. In the kitchen the luscious colours of summer are slowly giving way to soft browns, creams and russet reds. However, this is not a time to mourn the end of all things tropical, as autumn has its own treats in store. This is the season when all the deeply delicious root vegetables are harvested and food has a distinctly woodland feel. Explore the wonderfully earthy flavours of mushrooms, eggplant (aubergine) and beetroot (beet) and the fruity richness of quinces and figs. Embrace the earthy rush of all things autumnal by pulling out the baking tins, roasting pans and cake tins and making the most of these great flavours. Start thinking of creamy, flavourful cheeses scattered with pomegranate seeds, freshly sliced pears tossed with walnuts and pecans, warm greens sweetened with nutty oils, and roasted pumpkin (winter squash) and the spicy sweetness of cinnamon.

pumpkins baked breads

beetroot witlof

warm breakfasts

mushrooms cheesy tarts

celeriac hearty salads

fennel spooning sauces

olives spinach

daikon leeks

grilled meats

filling grains onions

sweet potatoes

pomegranates

pears

whisking and whirring

poached fruits nuts

figs oranges

baking trays

quinces biscuit stacks

wholemeal muffins with raspberry jam

250 g (9 oz/1²/₃ cups) wholemeal (whole-wheat) self-raising flour
1 teaspoon ground cinnamon
60 g (2¹/₄ oz/¹/₃ cup) soft brown sugar
1 egg
120 g (4¹/₄ oz) butter, melted
125 ml (4 fl oz/¹/₂ cup) milk
1/2 teaspoon finely grated lemon zest
160 g (5¹/₂ oz/¹/₂ cup) raspberry jam
extra soft brown sugar, for sprinkling

Preheat the oven to 180°C (350°F/Gas 4). Lightly grease a six-hole muffin tin and line with baking paper or paper cases.

Sift the flour and cinnamon into a bowl, tipping the wheatgerm from the sieve back into the bowl. Stir in the sugar and a pinch of salt, then make a well in the centre.

In a separate bowl, whisk together the egg, melted butter, milk and lemon zest. Pour the liquid ingredients into the dry ingredients and stir to combine.

Spoon the batter into the muffin holes to about one-third full, then spoon a tablespoon of jam onto each muffin. Top with the remaining batter, sprinkle with a little extra sugar and bake for 20–25 minutes, or until the muffins are golden brown and cooked through. Makes 6

pan-baked eggs with chilli salsa

chilli salsa
1 small Lebanese (short) cucumber, finely diced
1 red chilli, seeded and finely diced
a handful of coriander (cilantro) leaves

2 tablespoons olive oil
1/2 red onion, finely sliced
1/2 red capsicum (pepper), roughly diced
185 g (6¹/₂ oz/³/₄ cup) tinned chopped tomatoes
2 eggs
40 g (1¹/₂ oz) goat's cheese
buttered toast, to serve

Preheat the oven to 180°C (350°F/Gas 4). Put all the chilli salsa ingredients in a bowl. Toss together and set aside.

Heat the olive oil in a small ovenproof frying pan. Add the onion and sauté over medium heat for 5 minutes, or until the onion is soft and transparent. Add the capsicum, tomato and 125 ml (4 fl oz/¹/₂ cup) water and cook for 5 minutes, or until the capsicum is beginning to soften. Season to taste with sea salt.

Make two small wells in the tomato mixture and break the eggs into them. Bake for 10 minutes, or until the whites of the eggs are cooked through.

Crumble the goat's cheese over the top and serve with the chilli salsa and buttered toast. Serves 2

orange soda bread with mixed seeds

450 g (1 lb/heaped 3²/₃ cups) plain (all-purpose) flour
1 heaped teaspoon bicarbonate of soda (baking soda)
1 heaped teaspoon cream of tartar
2 tablespoons soft brown sugar
1 tablespoon finely grated orange zest
2 tablespoons sunflower seeds
2 tablespoons poppy seeds
1 tablespoon sesame seeds
1 teaspoon salt
500 ml (17 fl oz/2 cups) buttermilk
2 tablespoons butter, melted
butter, extra, to serve

Preheat the oven to 200°C (400°F/Gas 6). Sift the flour into a large bowl, add the rest of the dry ingredients and stir to combine. Make a well in the centre and gradually pour in the buttermilk, mixing to form a soft dough.

Brush a 10 x 21 cm (4 x 8¹/₄ inch) loaf (bar) tin with the melted butter. Scoop the dough into the greased tin and pour any remaining butter over. Bake for 30 minutes, then reduce the oven temperature to 150°C (300°F/Gas 2) and bake for a further 30 minutes, or until a skewer inserted into the centre of the loaf comes out clean.

Turn the bread out onto a wire rack to cool. Serve warm, spread with butter. Also delicious spread with honey, or topped with sliced banana. Makes 1 loaf

A golden muffin with a jammy surprise

opposite: wholemeal muffins with raspberry jam
over: pan-baked eggs with chilli salsa, and
orange soda bread with mixed seeds

baked eggs with bacon and mushrooms

2 tablespoons butter
2 slices of bacon, finely chopped
100 g (3^1/$_2$ oz/1 cup) finely sliced button mushrooms
1 ripe tomato, diced
4 eggs
3 tablespoons grated cheddar cheese
buttered toast, to serve

Preheat the oven to 180°C (350°F/Gas 4). Use some of the butter to generously grease two 8 cm (3^1/$_2$ inch) ramekins and sit them in a roasting tin half filled with water.

Put the remaining butter in a non-stick frying pan and sauté the bacon and mushrooms over medium heat until golden brown. Add the diced tomato and cook for a further minute. Divide the mixture between the two ramekins.

Crack the eggs into a bowl, add a little sea salt and freshly ground black pepper and whisk together. Pour the mixture into the ramekins and sprinkle with the cheese. Bake for 15 minutes, or until the egg is cooked through. Serve with fingers of buttered toast. Serves 2

date and banana loaf

160 g (5^1/$_2$ oz/1 cup) chopped dates
2 bananas, mashed
2 tablespoons unsalted butter
^{1}/$_2$ teaspoon bicarbonate of soda (baking soda)
170 g (6 oz/^{3}/$_4$ cup) castor (superfine) sugar
1 egg
250 g (9 oz/2 cups) self-raising flour, sifted
1 teaspoon baking powder
butter, to serve

Preheat the oven to 180°C (350°F/Gas 4). Grease and line a 10 x 20 cm (4 x 8 inch) loaf (bar) tin with baking paper.

Put the dates, banana, butter, bicarbonate of soda and sugar in a bowl. Pour in 250 ml (9 fl oz/1 cup) boiling water, stir to dissolve the sugar, then leave to soak for a few minutes. Stir the egg through, then fold the flour and baking powder through.

Pour the batter into the prepared tin and bake for 45 minutes, or until a skewer inserted into the centre of the loaf comes out clean. Cut into thick slices and serve toasted with butter. Makes 1 loaf

sweet couscous

1 orange
1 teaspoon butter
2–4 teaspoons honey, to taste
100 g (3^1/$_2$ oz/^{1}/$_2$ cup) couscous
^{1}/$_2$ teaspoon ground cinnamon
50 g (1^3/$_4$ oz/^{1}/$_3$ cup) currants
50 g (1^3/$_4$ oz/^{1}/$_2$ cup) pecans, roughly chopped
plain yoghurt, to serve

Grate the orange to give 1 teaspoon of zest, then juice the orange. Pour the juice into a saucepan and add the butter, honey and 100 ml (3^1/$_2$ fl oz) water.

Bring to the boil, then pour in the couscous. Stir once or twice, then remove the pan from the heat and cover with a lid. Leave to sit for 10 minutes, then fluff up the grains with a fork. Keep covered until the couscous has cooled completely, then rub the grains with your fingertips to remove any lumps.

Add the cinnamon, currants, pecans and grated orange zest. Stir well, divide among four bowls and serve with yoghurt. Serves 4

seasonal ideas

When it comes to baked eggs you are really only limited by your imagination in terms of what you can flavour or serve them with. Experiment with the following combinations:

- sautéed spinach and pancetta
- roast tomato and basil
- goat's cheese and finely chopped olives
- thinly sliced and fried salami with parmesan cheese
- smoked river trout and finely chopped parsley
- pan-fried wild mushrooms with gruyère cheese.

Serve the eggs with grilled flat bread, oven-warmed baguette, wholemeal (whole-wheat) toast, seedy grissini, toasted fingers of pide (Turkish/flat) bread or oven-dried crispbread.

opposite: baked eggs with bacon and mushrooms
over: date and banana loaf, and sweet couscous

breakfast

Well, yes you can have the usual spreads such as jam or honey, but here are a few toppings to rekindle your interest in the humble piece of toast.

- Sour cream, chives and smoked salmon.
- Grilled bacon, avocado and sliced tomato.
- Mashed boiled egg with butter and seasoning.
- Bolognese sauce with a dash of Tabasco sauce.
- Fresh ricotta cheese, aromatic honey and a cinnamon sprinkle.
- Fried egg and sweet chilli sauce (Favourites).
- Peppery butter-fried mushrooms.
- Baked beans with crispy pancetta.
- Tapenade, roast tomatoes and goat's cheese.

- Squished sardines, black pepper and lemon juice.
- Leg ham and thinly sliced cheese.
- Butter and cinnamon sugar.

- Serve dried fruit compote (Favourites) with Greek-style yoghurt, or spoon over a bowl of muesli, sweet couscous (page 205) or warm porridge.

- Spoon stewed rhubarb or apple (Favourites) over yoghurt and muesli.

- To make bircher muesli, soak rolled (porridge) oats in apple juice for an hour or overnight. Stir in some grated apple, plain yoghurt and a pinch of cinnamon.

Pancakes are a good excuse to enjoy some of the really yummy things in life like maple syrup, honey and sweetly flavoured butters. Try sliced banana, mango and mixed berries, butter flavoured with crushed honeycomb or fresh berries, good-quality fruit jams, and the all-time classic of butter, lemon juice and a sprinkle of sugar.

Everyone has their favourite side dishes for scrambled eggs (Favourites), but here are a few other suggestions.
- Mushrooms slow-baked in an oven with butter, garlic and a scatter of thyme leaves.
- Crisp bacon and grilled breakfast sausages.
- Thinly sliced smoked salmon scattered with sprigs of fresh dill.

- Chunks of hot-smoked salmon with coriander (cilantro) sprigs and sweet chilli sauce (Favourites).

The most basic omelette is simply a few eggs whisked together with a dash of water and poured into a hot pan with a little butter. Cook for a few minutes and then either finish in a hot oven or under a grill (broiler) until the egg is puffy and golden.

To this simple recipe can be added a feast of other ingredients such as fresh herbs, grated cheddar or parmesan cheese, crumbled goat's cheese, sautéed spinach or semi-dried (sun-blushed) tomatoes.

salt and pepper crab cakes

4 thick slices of sourdough bread
300 g (10¹/2 oz/about 2 cups) fresh crabmeat
¹/2 teaspoon fresh oregano
a handful of flat-leaf (Italian) parsley, roughly chopped
2 spring onions (scallions), finely sliced
¹/2 teaspoon white pepper
3 eggs, beaten
vegetable oil, for pan-frying
lemon cheeks, to serve
lemon mayonnaise (Favourites), to serve

Tear the bread into small bits and place in a food processor
or blender. Process to form rough breadcrumbs. Tip them
into a large bowl and add the crabmeat, oregano, parsley,
spring onion and white pepper. Season generously with sea
salt, then toss until well combined. Stir in the beaten eggs.
Form the mixture into 12 round cakes and set them on a tray.

Pour enough vegetable oil into a frying pan to fill it to about
5 mm (¹/4 inch). Place over medium heat. When the surface
of the oil begins to shimmer, cook the crab cakes a few at
a time for 2–3 minutes, or until deep golden on both sides.
Remove and drain on paper towels, then place on a baking
tray and keep in a warm oven while cooking the remaining
crab cakes.

Serve the warm crab cakes with lemon cheeks and a bowl
of lemon mayonnaise. Makes 12

steamed prawn wontons

juice of 2 limes
3 tablespoons mirin
1 red chilli, seeded and finely chopped
2 egg whites
300 g (10¹/2 oz/1¹/2 cups) minced (ground) prawn meat
¹/4 teaspoon Chinese five-spice
2 spring onions (scallions), finely sliced
1 teaspoon finely grated fresh ginger
¹/2 teaspoon sea salt
24 square (8.5 cm/3¹/2 inch) wonton wrappers

Put the lime juice, mirin and chilli in a small bowl and stir to
make a dipping sauce. Set aside.

Lightly whisk the egg whites in a bowl. Add the prawn meat,
five-spice, spring onion, ginger and sea salt and stir together.

Lay a wonton wrapper on a clean surface and moisten the
edges with a little water. Put a heaped teaspoon of the prawn
mixture in the centre of the wrapper, then bring the four corners
together, sealing the sides. Repeat with the remaining mixture
to make 24 wontons.

Sit the wontons in a bamboo steamer basket lined with oiled
baking paper. Set the basket over a large saucepan of boiling
water and steam the wontons for 10–12 minutes, or until the
pastry turns opaque. Serve immediately with the dipping
sauce. Makes 24

lobster salad with brown butter and capers

350 g (12 oz/2 bunches) asparagus, trimmed
2 handfuls of baby English spinach leaves
2 cooked lobster tails, shells removed and flesh sliced
1 large red chilli, seeded and finely chopped
1 tablespoon small salted capers, rinsed and drained
2 tablespoons lemon juice
80 g (2³/4 oz) butter

Blanch the asparagus spears in a pot of boiling water for
2 minutes, or until they turn emerald green. Drain and rinse
under cold running water.

Divide the spinach leaves, asparagus and lobster slices
among four serving plates.

Combine the chilli, capers and lemon juice in a small bowl.
Put the butter in a small saucepan over high heat. When it
begins to froth and turn brown, add the caper mixture and stir
once. Remove from the heat and spoon the caper butter over
the salad. Serves 4 as a starter or light meal

opposite: salt and pepper crab cakes
over: steamed prawn wontons, and
lobster salad with brown butter and capers

fig and goat's cheese salad

1 teaspoon wildflower honey
1 teaspoon balsamic vinegar
1 teaspoon wholegrain mustard
3 teaspoons extra virgin olive oil
6 slices of prosciutto
6 large figs
100 g (3^1/$_2$ oz/3 cups) wild rocket (arugula) leaves
100 g (3^1/$_2$ oz) goat's cheese, cut into 4 rounds

Combine the honey, vinegar, mustard and olive oil in a large bowl and stir to combine.

Heat a non-stick frying pan over medium heat and fry the prosciutto until crisp and golden. Remove from the pan and drain on paper towels.

Finely slice the figs and arrange on four serving plates. Stir the dressing one more time, then add the rocket and toss lightly. Crumble the prosciutto over the rocket and toss again before piling the salad onto the sliced figs. Top each salad with a slice of goat's cheese. Serves 4 as a starter

goat's cheese tartlets

1 sheet of frozen puff pastry
100 g (3^1/$_2$ oz) goat's cheese, thinly sliced
2 tablespoons extra virgin olive oil
1 teaspoon red wine vinegar
a handful of baby rocket (arugula) leaves
40 g (1^1/$_2$ oz/^{1}/$_4$ cup) finely sliced semi-dried (sun-blushed) tomatoes
16 small olives

Preheat the oven to 230°C (450°F/Gas 8). Line a baking tray with baking paper.

Cut the puff pastry into four rounds, each about 10 cm (4 inches) in diameter. Place them on the baking tray and cover with the goat's cheese slices. Bake for 10 minutes, or until the pastry is puffed and golden.

Meanwhile, put the remaining ingredients in a bowl and toss to combine. Remove the hot tartlets from the oven and place on warmed serving plates. Arrange the salad over the top. Serves 4 as a starter

pumpkin and hazelnut salad

1 kg (2 lb 4 oz) jap or kent pumpkin
1 tablespoon vegetable oil
100 g (3^1/$_2$ oz/^{3}/$_4$ cup) hazelnuts
3 tablespoons tahini
125 g (4^1/$_2$ oz/^{1}/$_2$ cup) plain yoghurt
1 teaspoon ground cumin
^{1}/$_2$ teaspoon finely chopped garlic
1 tablespoon lemon juice
200 g (7 oz/2 small bunches) rocket (arugula), stalks removed
1 tablespoon olive oil
1 teaspoon red wine vinegar

Preheat the oven to 180°C (350°F/Gas 4). Peel the pumpkin, remove any seeds and cut the flesh into bite-sized chunks. Toss in a bowl with the vegetable oil and season with sea salt and freshly ground black pepper. Spread the pumpkin on a baking tray and roast for 20 minutes, or until golden brown. Meanwhile, roast the hazelnuts on another baking tray for 5 minutes, or until the skins start splitting. Remove from the oven and allow to cool.

In a small bowl, mix the tahini, yoghurt, cumin, garlic and lemon juice to a smooth paste, then season to taste.

Rub the skins off the cooled hazelnuts. Roughly chop the nuts and put them in a bowl with the rocket. Add the olive oil and vinegar, toss together, then divide among four shallow bowls. Top with the pumpkin chunks and dollop with the tahini mixture. Serves 4 as a starter or side dish

seasonal ideas

Goat's cheese is one of the predominant flavours of autumn.

- Crumble some over a warming tomato, pumpkin or mushroom soup to add a filling richness.

- Make a salad of leafy greens and sliced pear or apple. Add a scattering of pecans or walnuts and top with some creamy goat's cheese.

- Combine goat's cheese and pouring (whipping) cream until the cheese has a smooth texture, then serve a spoonful on top of a salad of roast tomatoes, prosciutto and basil, or spoon it on top of a sweet onion tart.

opposite: fig and goat's cheese salad
over: goat's cheese tartlets, and
pumpkin and hazelnut salad

4 autumn salads

tofu, broccolini and almonds

300 g (10^1/$_2$ oz) silken tofu
235 g (8^1/$_2$ oz/1 bunch) broccolini
2 tablespoons olive oil
2 teaspoons finely grated fresh ginger
2 garlic cloves, crushed
2 tablespoons soy sauce
2 tablespoons mirin
3 large red chillies, seeded and cut into fine, long strips
1 tablespoon butter
50 g (1^3/$_4$ oz/heaped ^{1}/$_2$ cup) flaked almonds

Slice the tofu into 2 cm (^{3}/$_4$ inch) cubes and put them in a large serving bowl. Cut the broccolini in half, then slice the thicker pieces in half along the stalk.

Heat the olive oil in a wok over high heat. Add the ginger and garlic. As soon as they start to sizzle, add the soy sauce and mirin. When the sauce begins to bubble, add the broccolini and stir-fry for 2 minutes. Add the chilli and stir-fry for 1 minute, then scoop the vegetables over the tofu, leaving the sauce in the wok.

Add the butter to the wok, then the flaked almonds. Stir for 30 seconds, or until the sauce thickly coats the almonds, then spoon the almonds over the vegetables. Serves 4 as a side dish

rocket and pear salad

200 g (7 oz/2 small bunches) rocket (arugula)
2 beurre bosc pears, thinly sliced
100 g (3^1/$_2$ oz/1^1/$_2$ cups) shaved parmesan cheese
1 teaspoon white wine vinegar
1 teaspoon dijon mustard
^{1}/$_2$ teaspoon honey
2 tablespoons olive oil

Trim the stalks from the rocket and put the leaves in a salad bowl with the pear and parmesan.

In a small bowl, mix together the vinegar, mustard and honey. Slowly whisk in the olive oil, season with sea salt and freshly ground black pepper and drizzle over the salad. Serves 4 as a side dish

baby beets with a walnut dressing

625 g (1 lb 6 oz/1 bunch) small beetroot (beets), scrubbed
2 tablespoons walnut oil
1 tablespoon balsamic vinegar
1 teaspoon honey
a handful of rocket (arugula) leaves
50 g (1^3/$_4$ oz/^{1}/$_3$ cup) roasted cashew nuts

Preheat the oven to 180°C (350°F/Gas 4). Cut the leafy tops from the beetroot and rinse and reserve any small tender leaves. Place the bulbs in a roasting tin and add 250 ml (9 fl oz/ 1 cup) water. Cover with foil and bake for 1 hour, or until tender when pierced with a skewer. Allow to cool. Wearing rubber gloves to stop your hands staining, peel the skins from the beetroot — they should slip free quite easily. Slice the larger bulbs in half and place in a bowl.

In a smaller bowl combine the walnut oil, vinegar and honey. Stir until the honey has dissolved, then pour the dressing over the beetroot. Season, then toss well.

Arrange the rocket leaves on a serving platter, then add the beetroot and scatter with the cashews and any reserved small beetroot leaves. Serves 4 as a side dish

roast pumpkin and tofu salad

700 g (1 lb 9 oz) jap or kent pumpkin
2 tablespoons olive oil
grated zest and juice of 1 lime
1 tablespoon fish sauce
1 tablespoon soy sauce
100 ml (3^1/$_2$ fl oz) mirin
2 bunches broccolini (about 400 g/14 oz in total), trimmed
200 g (7 oz) firm tofu, cut into 2 cm (^{3}/$_4$ inch) cubes
1 tablespoon sesame seeds, toasted

Preheat the oven to 180°C (350°F/Gas 4). Peel the pumpkin, remove any seeds, cut the flesh into bite-sized chunks and place in a large bowl. Add the olive oil and season with sea salt and freshly ground black pepper. Toss until the pumpkin is well coated, then spread on a baking tray and roast for 20 minutes, or until golden brown and tender.

Put the lime zest, lime juice, fish sauce, soy sauce and mirin in a large non-metallic bowl and stir to make a dressing.

Bring a pot of water to the boil. Add the broccolini and blanch for 2 minutes, or until just tender. Drain, then add to the dressing along with the pumpkin, tofu and sesame seeds. Gently toss to mix the dressing through. Serves 4–6 as a starter

lentil and pumpkin salad

1 kg (2 lb 4 oz) jap or kent pumpkin
1 large red onion
2 tablespoons olive oil
120 g (4^1/$_4$ oz/^{2}/$_3$ cup) puy lentils or tiny blue-green lentils
^{1}/$_2$ teaspoon sea salt
1 teaspoon wholegrain mustard
1 tablespoon balsamic vinegar
2 tablespoons extra virgin olive oil
a handful of flat-leaf (Italian) parsley, roughly chopped
50 g (1^3/$_4$ oz/1^1/$_2$ cups) wild rocket (arugula) leaves
100 g (3^1/$_2$ oz) goat's cheese

Preheat the oven to 180°C (350°F/Gas 4). Peel the pumpkin, remove any seeds, cut the flesh into bite-sized chunks and spread on a baking tray. Peel the onion and cut it in half, then slice into small half-moons. Scatter the onion over the pumpkin. Drizzle with the olive oil and season with a little sea salt and freshly ground black pepper. Bake for 25 minutes, or until the pumpkin is cooked through and the onion is starting to blacken a little on the ends.

Meanwhile, put the lentils in a small saucepan with the sea salt and 500 ml (17 fl oz/2 cups) water. Bring to the boil, then reduce the heat and simmer for 30 minutes, or until tender. Drain the lentils of any excess water, then stir in the mustard, vinegar, extra virgin olive oil and parsley.

Arrange the rocket leaves on a serving plate, top with the baked pumpkin and onion, then spoon the lentils over. Crumble the goat's cheese over the top. Serves 4 as a side dish or starter

baked ricotta with a tomato herb salsa

600 g (1 lb 5 oz/heaped 2^1/$_3$ cups) fresh ricotta cheese
1 teaspoon fresh thyme leaves
10 kalamata olives, pitted and roughly chopped
2 tablespoons grated parmesan cheese
1 egg
2 ripe tomatoes
^{1}/$_2$ red onion, finely diced
6 large basil leaves, finely sliced
a handful of flat-leaf (Italian) parsley, roughly chopped
1 teaspoon balsamic vinegar
2 tablespoons extra virgin olive oil
bruschetta (Favourites), to serve

Preheat the oven to 180°C (350°F/Gas 4). Line a baking tray with baking paper.

Put the ricotta in a large bowl with the thyme, olives, parmesan and egg. Stir to combine. Sit a 20 cm (8 inch) spring-form cake tin on a baking tray and spoon the ricotta mixture into the tin. Bake for 35–40 minutes, or until firm and lightly golden. Remove and allow to cool to room temperature.

To make the salsa, slice the tomatoes in half and scoop out the seeds using a teaspoon. Finely chop the flesh and place in a bowl with the onion, basil and parsley. Add the vinegar and olive oil and stir together until well combined.

Transfer the baked ricotta to a serving plate and spoon the salsa over the top. Season with a little sea salt and a good grind of black pepper. Serve with bruschetta. Serves 6

parmesan-crusted eggplant with a cherry tomato salad

75 g (2^1/$_2$ oz/^{3}/$_4$ cup) finely grated parmesan cheese
^{1}/$_4$ teaspoon paprika
60 g (2^1/$_4$ oz/^{3}/$_4$ cup) fresh breadcrumbs
4 tablespoons plain (all-purpose) flour
2 eggs
2 eggplants (aubergines), cut into 1 cm (^{1}/$_2$ inch) rounds
vegetable oil, for pan-frying
500 g (1 lb 2 oz) cherry tomatoes, cut in half
a handful of basil
a handful of flat-leaf (Italian) parsley
2 tablespoons olive oil
1 tablespoon balsamic vinegar

Mix the parmesan, paprika and breadcrumbs together in a bowl. Put the flour in another bowl and lightly season with sea salt and freshly ground black pepper. In a third bowl, whisk the eggs.

Dip an eggplant round in the flour, then dip it into the egg so that it is completely covered. Now turn the eggplant in the breadcrumbs, ensuring it is well coated on both sides. Set on a tray and repeat with the remaining eggplant slices.

Pour enough vegetable oil into a frying pan to fill it to about 5 mm (^{1}/$_4$ inch) and place over medium heat. When the surface of the oil begins to shimmer, add several eggplant rounds. Fry for 2–3 minutes, or until golden brown underneath, then flip and cook for a further 2–3 minutes. Remove and drain on paper towels. Cook the remaining eggplant in the same way, adding more vegetable oil as you need it.

Toss the tomatoes, herbs, olive oil and vinegar together in a small bowl. Stack the eggplant rounds on four warmed plates and spoon the salad over the top. Serves 4

opposite: lentil and pumpkin salad
over: baked ricotta with a tomato herb salsa, and
parmesan-crusted eggplant with a cherry tomato salad

seared prawns with tomato parsley broth

16 raw large prawns (shrimp)
1 tablespoon butter
a pinch of saffron threads
1 teaspoon sea salt
6 black peppercorns
4 parsley stalks
2 spring onions (scallions)
1 teaspoon fish sauce
2 tablespoons lemon juice
2 vine-ripened tomatoes, seeds removed and flesh diced
buttered crusty bread, to serve

Peel and devein the prawns, reserving the shells and heads. Put the prawns in a bowl, cover and refrigerate until ready to use.

Put the butter and saffron in a saucepan over medium heat. When the butter has melted, add the prawn shells and heads and cook for several minutes, stirring occasionally, until all the heads have turned orange. Add 1 litre (35 fl oz/4 cups) water, the sea salt and peppercorns. Remove the leaves from the parsley stalks and reserve for later use. Roughly chop a spring onion and add it to the broth with the parsley stalks. Bring to the boil, then reduce the heat and simmer for 30 minutes.

Remove the stock from the heat and strain into a bowl. Rinse the saucepan, then pour in the strained stock and continue to simmer over low heat. Add the fish sauce, lemon juice and tomato. Roughly chop the reserved parsley leaves, finely chop the remaining spring onion, and add them to the broth.

Heat a non-stick frying pan over high heat. When the pan is hot, sear the prawns on both sides until they turn pink and begin to curl up.

Ladle the stock into four warmed pasta bowls and pile the prawns in the centre. Serve with buttered crusty bread. Serves 4 as a starter

prosciutto with braised fennel and zucchini

2 fennel bulbs
3 tablespoons olive oil
juice of 1 lemon
2 zucchini (courgettes)
6 thin slices of prosciutto
10 mint leaves, torn

Preheat the oven to 200°C (400°F/Gas 6). Line a baking tray with baking paper. Trim the fennel, reserving any feathery green fronds, and cut each bulb into eight wedges. Place them on the baking tray and drizzle with the olive oil and 1 tablespoon of the lemon juice. Season with sea salt and freshly ground black pepper, cover with foil and bake for 30 minutes. Remove from the oven and allow the fennel to cool a little.

Slice the zucchini into long thin ribbons using a vegetable peeler. Tear the prosciutto into strips. Arrange the fennel, zucchini and prosciutto on a serving platter and scatter with the mint and reserved fennel fronds. Pour the cooking juices from the fennel over the salad and drizzle with the remaining lemon juice. Serves 4 as a side dish

minute steak with mushroom salad

1 red onion, finely sliced
1 tablespoon sea salt
1 tablespoon fresh rosemary
2 garlic cloves, roughly chopped
2 tablespoons olive oil
650 g (1 lb 7 oz) piece of sirloin, or 3 x 200 g (7 oz) sirloin steaks, cut into 12 fine slices
250 g (9 oz/2⅔ cups) finely sliced button mushrooms
3 tablespoons extra virgin olive oil
1 tablespoon red wine vinegar
250 g (9 oz) cherry tomatoes, cut in half
a large handful of baby rocket (arugula) leaves

Put the onion in a bowl with the sea salt. Toss to ensure the onion is well coated, then cover and set aside for 20 minutes.

Meanwhile, put the rosemary, garlic, olive oil and steak slices in a separate bowl and toss until the beef is well coated in the marinade. Toss the mushrooms in another bowl with the extra virgin olive oil and vinegar.

Put the onion in a sieve and lightly rinse under cold running water. Squeeze off any excess water, then add the onion to the mushrooms, along with the cherry tomatoes.

Heat a non-stick frying pan over high heat and cook the steak slices in batches for 1 minute on each side. As you finish cooking each piece of steak allow it to rest on a warm plate until all the meat is cooked. Stack the steak slices on four warmed plates, alternating each slice with some mushroom salad and a few rocket leaves. Drizzle with any remaining dressing or meat juices. Serves 4

opposite: seared prawns with tomato parsley broth
over: prosciutto with braised fennel and zucchini, and minute steak with mushroom salad

warming vegetables

- Roast parsnips in a moderate oven until they are golden brown and sweetly caramelized.

- Slow-roast halved red onions with sprigs of rosemary, a light sprinkle of sugar and a drizzle of olive oil. Serve with seared steak or lamb fillets.

- Put some roughly chopped leeks (white part only) in a baking dish. Cover with chicken stock (Favourites), a few dabs of butter and some saffron threads. Bake in a moderate oven for 40 minutes. Sprinkle with finely chopped parsley and serve as a side dish to chicken or seafood, with some creamy mashed potato (Favourites).

- Wrap a whole head of garlic in foil and roast in a moderate oven for an hour. Squeeze the garlic cloves from their skins and mix with a little butter. Spread over seared beef or fold through creamy mashed potato (Favourites).

- Toss steamed carrots in a little honey and orange juice or bake with a sprinkle of ground cumin.

- Peel 1 kg (2 lb 4 oz) pumpkin (winter squash) and remove the seeds. Cut into 2 cm (3/4 inch) cubes and place in a large bowl with 4 tablespoons olive oil, 3 finely chopped garlic cloves and 1/2 teaspoon finely chopped rosemary. Season with sea salt and ground white pepper and toss

228

well to coat. Tip into a baking dish and bake in a moderate oven for 40 minutes. Serve sprinkled with parsley.

- Pour béchamel sauce (Favourites) over blanched cauliflower and top with grated parmesan cheese. Bake in a moderate oven until golden and bubbling. Or stir-fry cauliflower florets, Indian style, with some oil, sliced onion, mustard seeds, green chillies, desiccated coconut, finely grated fresh ginger and a sprinkle of ground turmeric.

- Peel beetroot (beets) and cut them in half. Place in a baking dish and scatter with fresh thyme. Season and drizzle with a little oil. Add a few tablespoons water and

cover with foil. Bake in a moderate oven for 40 minutes, or until tender. Serve sprinkled with some finely chopped parsley or mint and a light drizzle of balsamic vinegar or pomegranate molasses.

- When horseradish is in season, savour its bite with fresh horseradish cream (Favourites). Serve with smoked salmon, roast beef or a roast vegetable salad.

- With a jar of onion jam (Favourites) in the fridge you can always pep up a quick meal of seared beef or grilled sausages. It's also great with crumbly aged cheddar cheese and some crusty bread.

spiced salmon

4 tablespoons olive oil
1 tablespoon ground cumin
1 teaspoon smoked paprika
1 teaspoon chilli flakes
juice of 2 limes
1 tablespoon small salted capers, rinsed and drained
1 tablespoon finely chopped preserved lemon rind
2 tablespoons finely chopped coriander (cilantro)
4 x 150 g (5¹/2 oz) salmon steaks
steamed couscous (Favourites), to serve
small mint leaves, to serve

Put the olive oil, cumin, paprika, chilli flakes, lime juice, capers, preserved lemon rind and coriander in a bowl. Stir to combine.

Line a baking tray with foil and lay the salmon steaks on top. Spoon the spice mixture over the salmon, then cover with plastic wrap and refrigerate for 1 hour.

Preheat the oven to 180°C (350°F/Gas 4). Bake the salmon for 10 minutes, or until cooked to your liking. Serve with steamed couscous and a scattering of mint. Serves 4

chestnut and mushroom soup

1¹/2 tablespoons butter
1 onion, finely chopped
1 garlic clove, finely chopped
400 g (14 oz) Swiss brown mushrooms, roughly chopped
300 g (10¹/2 oz/1¹/2 cups) tinned chestnuts, drained
1 litre (35 fl oz/4 cups) chicken stock (Favourites)
2 tablespoons crème fraîche or light sour cream

Heat the butter in a saucepan over medium heat and add the onion and garlic. Sauté for 5 minutes, or until the onion is soft and transparent, then add the mushrooms. Cover and cook for 5 minutes, or until the mushrooms have reduced by half. Add the chestnuts and stock and simmer for 15 minutes. Remove from the heat, season to taste with sea salt and allow to cool.

Transfer the soup to a food processor or blender and purée in batches until smooth. Return to the saucepan and gently reheat. Ladle the hot soup into four warmed bowls and top with a dollop of crème fraîche and some coarsely ground black pepper. Serves 4 as a starter

simmered vegetables and tofu

1 garlic clove, finely sliced
2 tablespoons soy sauce
2 teaspoons sesame oil
125 ml (4 fl oz/¹/2 cup) shaoxing rice wine
125 ml (4 fl oz/¹/2 cup) mirin
2 star anise
1 tablespoon finely sliced fresh ginger
12 fresh shiitake mushrooms, cut in half if large
1 red capsicum (pepper), cut into 1 cm (¹/2 inch) cubes
1 yellow capsicum (pepper), cut into 1 cm (¹/2 inch) cubes
300 g (10¹/2 oz) silken tofu
2 spring onions (scallions), finely sliced on the diagonal
steamed white rice (Favourites), nutty rice (page 131) or
    brown rice, to serve

Put the garlic, soy sauce, sesame oil, rice wine, mirin, star anise, ginger, mushrooms and all the capsicum in a large saucepan. Add 125 ml (4 fl oz/¹/2 cup) water and bring to the boil over high heat. Reduce the heat to low and allow the broth to simmer for 10 minutes.

Cut the tofu into 1.5 cm (⁵/8 inch) cubes and divide among four warmed bowls. Spoon the vegetables and broth over the top. Garnish with spring onion and serve with rice. Serves 4

seasonal ideas

- Sauté some sliced Swiss brown and wild mushrooms. When they are softly cooked spoon them into small pre-baked savoury shortcrust tartlet cases (Favourites) and top with creamed goat's cheese or goat's curd.

- Line a baking dish with vine leaves and top with field mushrooms. Add some roughly chopped garlic cloves, a few fresh thyme sprigs and a drizzle of extra virgin olive oil. Cover with another layer of vine leaves and bake in a moderately slow oven for an hour. Serve with a spoonful of goat's curd.

- Sauté a selection of small wild mushrooms in garlicky butter and serve alongside pan-seared beef fillets.

opposite: spiced salmon
over: chestnut and mushroom soup, and
simmered vegetables and tofu

4 quick pastas

lemon and parmesan spaghettini

grated zest and juice of 2 lemons
400 g (14 oz) spaghettini
3 tablespoons olive oil
2 garlic cloves, finely chopped
2 leeks, white part only, rinsed and sliced
2 tablespoons small salted capers, rinsed and drained
a handful of flat-leaf (Italian) parsley, roughly chopped
25 g (1 oz/1 bunch) chives, finely snipped
75 g (2¹/2 oz/³/4 cup) grated parmesan cheese

Bring a large pot of salted water to the boil. Add the juice
of one lemon and the spaghettini and cook until *al dente*.
Drain and return to the warm pot.

Meanwhile, heat the olive oil in a large frying pan over
medium heat. Add the garlic and leek and sauté for
5 minutes, or until the leek is soft and transparent.
Season with a little freshly ground black pepper.

Tip the mixture into the pasta, then add the lemon zest,
remaining lemon juice, capers, parsley and chives, stirring
them through the pasta. Divide among four warmed pasta
bowls and sprinkle with the parmesan. Serves 4

chilli bacon penne

400 g (14 oz) penne
3 tablespoons butter
1 red onion, diced
2 garlic cloves, finely chopped
2 red chillies, seeded and finely chopped
3 slices of bacon, chopped
4 roma (plum) tomatoes, roughly chopped
75 g (2¹/2 oz/³/4 cup) grated parmesan cheese
8 basil leaves, roughly torn

Bring a large pot of salted water to the boil, add the penne
and cook until *al dente*. Drain and return to the warm pot.

Meanwhile, melt the butter in a large frying pan over medium
heat. Add the onion, garlic and chilli and sauté for 5 minutes,
or until the onion is soft and transparent. Add the bacon and
cook for 2 minutes.

Add the tomato, then cover and allow to simmer over low
heat for 10 minutes. Using a spoon, roughly break up the
tomato chunks, then season with sea salt and freshly ground
black pepper.

Stir the tomato mixture through the pasta over low heat until it
coats all the pasta. Divide among four warmed pasta bowls
and sprinkle with the parmesan and basil. Serves 4

pesto and goat's cheese linguine

400 g (14 oz) linguine
150 g (5¹/2 oz) crumbled goat's cheese
4 heaped tablespoons pesto (Favourites)
50 g (1³/4 oz/1¹/2 cups) wild rocket (arugula) leaves
extra virgin olive oil, to serve

Bring a large pot of salted water to the boil, add the linguine
and cook until *al dente*. Drain and return to the warm pot.

Crumble the goat's cheese over the pasta, add the pesto
and rocket and stir them through the pasta. Divide among
four warmed pasta bowls, drizzle with a little olive oil and
season to taste with sea salt and freshly ground black
pepper. Serves 4

fresh tomato pasta

4 very ripe large tomatoes
1 teaspoon sea salt
2 tablespoons small salted capers, rinsed and drained
15 basil leaves, finely chopped
a handful of flat-leaf (Italian) parsley, roughly chopped
500 g (1 lb 2 oz) casareccia or penne
75 g (2¹/2 oz/³/4 cup) finely grated parmesan cheese
3 tablespoons olive oil
20 niçoise olives
finely grated parmesan cheese, extra, to serve

Chop the tomatoes and put them in a bowl with the sea salt,
capers, basil and parsley. Stir gently to coat all the tomato,
then set aside.

Bring a large pot of salted water to the boil, add the pasta
and cook until *al dente*. Drain and return to the warm pot.

Add the parmesan and olive oil, stir a few times, then add
the tomato mixture. Season with freshly ground black pepper,
toss together well and divide among four warmed pasta
bowls. Scatter with the olives and sprinkle with some extra
parmesan. Serves 4

smoked trout salad

1 red onion
1 tablespoon sea salt
1 teaspoon sugar
3 tablespoons lemon juice
1 egg yolk
4 tablespoons olive oil
1 telegraph (long) cucumber
1 teaspoon poppy seeds
2 x 200 g (7 oz) smoked river trout
2 large handfuls of picked watercress sprigs

Peel the onion, cut it in half, then finely slice into half-moons. Put the onion in a bowl and add the sea salt. Toss several times to ensure the onion is well coated, then cover and set aside for 30 minutes.

Drain the onion, then rinse under cold running water and squeeze out any excess liquid. Put the onion in a clean bowl and add the sugar and 2 tablespoons of the lemon juice. Stir to combine, then set aside for a further 30 minutes.

Put the egg yolk in a small bowl with the remaining lemon juice. Whisk until creamy, then slowly add the olive oil, whisking continually until a thin mayonnaise forms. Season to taste with sea salt and freshly ground black pepper.

Peel the cucumber and slice it in half lengthways. Remove the seeds using a teaspoon, then finely slice the flesh. Gently toss the cucumber in a bowl with the poppy seeds.

Remove the skin from the trout, then gently pull away the flesh, ensuring that you remove all the bones. Slice or tear the flesh into generous portions.

Arrange the watercress sprigs on four serving plates. Top with the cucumber and pile the trout in the middle. Drizzle with the mayonnaise and top with a mound of pink onions. Serves 4 as a starter

eggplant and mozzarella salad

2 eggplants (aubergines)
2 roasted red capsicums (peppers) (Favourites)
vegetable oil, for pan-frying
1 buffalo mozzarella or 4 bocconcini (fresh baby mozzarella cheese), torn into chunks
2 tablespoons pine nuts, toasted
10 large basil leaves
2 tablespoons extra virgin olive oil
1 tablespoon balsamic vinegar

Slice the eggplants into 5 mm (1/4 inch) thick rounds and place in a colander. Sprinkle generously with sea salt and leave for 1 hour.

Slice the roasted capsicum flesh into thick strips. Rinse the eggplant and drain well on paper towels.

Pour enough vegetable oil into a frying pan to fill it to about 5 mm (1/4 inch) and place over medium–high heat. When the surface of the oil begins to shimmer, add several eggplant rounds. Fry until golden brown on both sides, then remove and drain on paper towels. Cook the remaining eggplant in the same way, adding more vegetable oil as you need it.

Arrange the eggplant slices on a platter and top with the capsicum, mozzarella chunks, pine nuts and basil. Season lightly with sea salt and freshly ground black pepper. In a small bowl combine the olive oil and vinegar and stir to blend. Spoon over the salad. Serves 4–6 as a starter or side dish

blue-eye cod with chermoula

chermoula paste
1 roasted red capsicum (pepper) (Favourites), flesh chopped
1 tablespoon chopped preserved lemon rind
a handful of coriander (cilantro) leaves
a handful of flat-leaf (Italian) parsley
2 garlic cloves
1 teaspoon cumin
1/2 teaspoon paprika
1/4 teaspoon chilli powder
1 tablespoon lemon juice
2 tablespoons olive oil

4 x 200 g (7 oz) blue-eye cod fillets
grilled zucchini (courgette), to serve
steamed couscous (Favourites), to serve

Preheat the oven to 200°C (400°F/Gas 2–3). Line a baking tray with baking paper.

Put all the chermoula paste ingredients in a food processor and blend to form a thick paste, or use a mortar and pestle to grind them to a chunky paste.

Rinse the cod fillets under cold running water, then pat dry with paper towels. Rub the chermoula paste over the fillets, then sit them on the baking tray and bake for 15 minutes, or until cooked through. Serve with grilled zucchini and steamed couscous. Serves 4

opposite: smoked trout salad
over: eggplant and mozzarella salad, and
blue-eye cod with chermoula

wild rice, chickpea and goat's cheese salad

95 g (3¹/₄ oz/¹/₂ cup) wild rice blend
2 vine-ripened tomatoes
1 tablespoon balsamic vinegar
2 tablespoons olive oil
400 g (14 oz) tin chickpeas, drained
a handful of baby rocket (arugula) leaves
a handful of flat-leaf (Italian) parsley
70 g (2¹/₃ oz) goat's cheese
extra virgin olive oil, to serve

Bring a pot of salted water to the boil and add the rice. Cook for 30 minutes, or until tender, then drain and rinse under cold running water.

Dice the tomatoes and put them in a bowl. Season well with sea salt and freshly ground black pepper, then add the vinegar and olive oil. Toss several times to ensure the tomatoes are well coated in the vinaigrette. Add the rice and chickpeas and toss once more.

Arrange the rocket and parsley on a serving platter. Spoon the rice salad over, crumble the goat's cheese over the top and drizzle with a little extra virgin olive oil. Serves 4 as a side dish or light meal

lamb cutlets with smoky eggplant

1 large roasted eggplant (aubergine) (Favourites)
3 tablespoons plain creamy yoghurt
¹/₂ teaspoon ground cumin
¹/₂ garlic clove
250 g (9 oz) cherry tomatoes, cut into quarters
6 bottled artichoke hearts, drained and cut into wedges
a handful of flat-leaf (Italian) parsley
12 frenched lamb cutlets (French trimmed rib chops)

Peel away the charred skin from the eggplant. Put the eggplant in a colander over a bowl. Using a pair of kitchen scissors, roughly cut the flesh into small pieces. Using your hands, press down on the eggplant to remove any excess liquid.

Put the eggplant flesh in a food processor or blender and purée with the yoghurt, cumin and garlic. Season to taste with sea salt and freshly ground black pepper.

Toss the cherry tomatoes in a bowl with the artichoke and parsley and set aside.

Heat a large non-stick frying pan or chargrill pan over high heat. Add the lamb cutlets and sear for 2–3 minutes on each side. Transfer to a warm plate, cover loosely with foil and allow to rest for 5 minutes.

Spoon the eggplant purée onto four plates and cross the lamb cutlets over the top. Add any lamb juices to the tomato salad, toss once, then pile beside the cutlets. Serves 4

duck salad

2 tablespoons tamarind concentrate
1 teaspoon soy sauce
2 teaspoons finely grated fresh ginger
1 tablespoon grated palm sugar (jaggery) or soft brown sugar
¹/₂ teaspoon ground cumin
1 large red chilli, seeded and finely chopped
1 Chinese roasted duck
2 ripe mangoes
500 g (1 lb 2 oz/1 large bunch) watercress, leaves picked
200 g (7 oz/³/₄ cup) tinned water chestnuts, drained and sliced

Put the tamarind concentrate in a large bowl and add 125 ml (4 fl oz/¹/₂ cup) water. Stir together, then add the soy sauce, ginger, sugar, cumin and chilli. Stir to make a dressing.

Pull the skin off the duck and cut it into thin strips, scraping off any fat. Put the skin strips on a baking tray and briefly cook under a hot grill (broiler) until crisp. Remove and place on paper towels to drain off any fat.

Pull the meat from the duck and tear it into strips, then add it to the dressing. Remove the skin from the mangoes, cut the flesh into thin strips and add it to the salad, along with the watercress, water chestnuts and crispy strips of duck skin. Gently toss together. Serves 4–6

seasonal ideas
- Tinned chickpeas are a great store-cupboard ingredient. Drained and lightly rinsed they can be added to simple autumn salads, steamed couscous (Favourites) or warming vegetable soups. They work well with roast vegetables, cumin or paprika-spiced dressings, salami, eggplant (aubergine), rocket (arugula), roasted capsicums (peppers) (Favourites) and fresh herbs such as parsley and coriander (cilantro).

- Toss tinned chickpeas with finely chopped preserved lemon rind, tomato chunks and fresh basil and serve with seared lamb, or purée the chickpeas with a touch of garlic and ground cumin and serve with grilled sausages.

opposite: wild rice, chickpea and goat's cheese salad
over: lamb cutlets with smoky eggplant, and duck salad

seared lamb fillets with chipotle chilli couscous

16 truss tomatoes
185 g (6¹/2 oz/1 cup) instant couscous
1 tablespoon butter
1 tablespoon finely chopped tinned chipotle chilli
1 Lebanese (short) cucumber, diced
a handful of coriander (cilantro) leaves
600 g (1 lb 5 oz) lamb loin fillets

Preheat the oven to 180°C (350°F/Gas 4). Cut the tomatoes in half and place on a baking tray. Season with a little sea salt and freshly ground black pepper and bake for 30 minutes.

Meanwhile, put the couscous, butter and chilli in a large bowl and pour 250 ml (9 fl oz/1 cup) boiling water over the top. Cover and allow to sit for 5 minutes, then fluff up the grains with a fork. Cover again and leave for a further 5 minutes. When the couscous has absorbed all the water, rub the grains with your fingertips to remove any lumps. When the couscous has cooled, add the cucumber and coriander.

Heat a large non-stick frying pan over high heat. Add the lamb fillets and sear for 2 minutes. Turn them over, reduce the heat to low and cook for a further 3–4 minutes. Transfer to a warm plate, cover with foil and allow to rest for 5 minutes.

Divide the couscous among four plates. Slice the lamb fillets diagonally and arrange over the couscous. Top with the baked tomatoes and drizzle with any meat juices. Serves 4

sumac buttered chicken with coriander pesto

80 g (2³/4 oz) butter, softened
1 tablespoon sumac
1 teaspoon ground cumin
1 kg (2 lb 4 oz) whole organic chicken
1 lemon, quartered
rocket (arugula) leaves, to serve

coriander pesto
25 g (1 oz/¹/4 cup) flaked almonds
45 g (1¹/2 oz/¹/2 bunch) coriander (cilantro)
2 teaspoons lemon juice
4 tablespoons olive oil

Preheat the oven to 200°C (400°F/Gas 6). In a small bowl, mix together the butter, sumac and cumin.

Rinse the chicken under cold running water and pat dry with paper towels. Sit the chicken in a roasting dish, breast side up, and put the lemon quarters inside the cavity. Run your finger under the skin of the breast, then put some sumac butter in the space between the skin and the breast meat. Rub the remaining butter over the skin of the chicken. Season generously with sea salt, then bake for 1 hour 20 minutes. To check that the chicken is cooked, pull a leg away from the body — the juices that run out should be clear. Remove from the oven, cover with foil and leave to rest for 10 minutes before carving.

While the chicken is resting, make the coriander pesto. Spread the flaked almonds on a baking tray and toast in the hot oven until golden brown. Remove from the oven and allow to cool. Tip the almonds into a food processor or blender, add the coriander, lemon juice and olive oil and blend to a thick paste.

Carve the chicken and arrange on a platter. Serve with rocket leaves and a bowl of the coriander pesto. Serves 4

roast pork with soy-roasted pumpkin

1.5 kg (3 lb 5 oz) piece of pork shoulder, skin scored
    (ask your butcher to do this)
4 fresh sage sprigs
1 kg (2 lb 4 oz) jap or kent pumpkin
3 tablespoons olive oil
1 tablespoon soy sauce
1 red chilli, seeded and finely chopped
¹/2 teaspoon Chinese five-spice
steamed green beans, to serve

Preheat the oven to 220°C (425°F/Gas 7). Pat the pork dry with paper towels and rub the scored skin with a generous amount of sea salt. Season with freshly ground black pepper. Scatter the sage sprigs into a roasting tin, then sit the pork on top, skin side up. Roast for 25 minutes, then turn the oven temperature down to 180°C (350°F/Gas 4) and cook for a further 1 hour.

Meanwhile, peel the pumpkin, remove any seeds and cut the flesh into bite-sized chunks. Place in a large bowl and add the olive oil, soy sauce, chilli and five-spice. Toss well, then spread on a baking tray. Add to the oven 30 minutes before the pork is due to be completely cooked.

Remove the pork from the oven and reduce the heat to low to keep the pumpkin warm. To test if the meat is done insert a sharp knife or skewer into the centre — the juices should run clear. Transfer the pork to a warm serving platter, then cover loosely with foil and leave to rest for 15 minutes. If the skin isn't quite crunchy and needs further cooking, slice it off using a sharp knife, put it back in the roasting tin and roast on the top shelf of the oven for a few minutes. Carve the pork and serve drizzled with any roasting juices, alongside the roast pumpkin and steamed green beans. Serves 6

opposite: seared lamb fillets with chipotle chilli couscous
over: sumac buttered chicken with coriander pesto, and
roast pork with soy-roasted pumpkin

seared beef and noodle salad

zest and juice of 2 limes
zest and juice of 1 orange
2 tablespoons fish sauce
1 teaspoon sesame oil
1 tablespoon grated palm sugar (jaggery) or soft brown sugar
1 garlic clove, crushed
2 tablespoons finely chopped lemon grass, white part only
1 tablespoon julienned fresh ginger
1 large red chilli, seeded and finely sliced
2 tablespoons olive oil
250 g (9 oz) piece of beef sirloin
200 g (7 oz) somen noodles
a handful of coriander (cilantro) leaves
a handful of Thai basil

In a small bowl, mix together the citrus zest, citrus juice, fish sauce, sesame oil, sugar, garlic, lemon grass, ginger and chilli. Stir until the sugar has dissolved, then cover the dressing and set aside until ready to use.

Heat the olive oil in a frying pan over high heat. Add the beef sirloin and sear on each side for 2–3 minutes. Transfer the meat to a bowl, cover loosely with foil and leave to rest.

Bring a large pot of salted water to the boil. Add the noodles and cook for 2 minutes, then drain and rinse under running water. Place in a large bowl, pour half the dressing over, toss well to coat, then divide among four warmed bowls.

Finely slice the beef and arrange over the noodles. Scatter with the coriander and basil and spoon the remaining dressing over the top. Serves 4

tomato and prosciutto risotto

1 litre (35 fl oz/4 cups) chicken or vegetable stock (Favourites)
4 large slices of prosciutto, cut in half crossways
2 tablespoons butter
2 garlic cloves, finely chopped
2 leeks, white part only, rinsed and finely sliced
325 g (11½ oz/1½ cups) risotto rice
3 ripe roma (plum) tomatoes, diced
2 tablespoons dry sherry
4 tablespoons grated parmesan cheese
extra virgin olive oil, to serve
rocket (arugula) or basil, to serve

Bring the stock to the boil in a saucepan, then reduce the heat and keep at a low simmer.

Heat a large saucepan over medium heat. Add the prosciutto and cook on both sides until golden and crisp, then remove and drain on paper towels. Add the butter, garlic and leek to the pan and sauté for 4–5 minutes, or until the leek is soft

and transparent. Add the rice and stir for 1 minute, or until the rice is well coated and the grains are glossy.

Ladle 250 ml (9 fl oz/1 cup) of the hot stock into the pan and simmer, stirring occasionally, until it has been completely absorbed. Add another 250 ml (9 fl oz/1 cup) stock and the tomato. Cook, stirring, for a further few minutes until the stock has been completely absorbed, then add another 250 ml (9 fl oz/1 cup) stock. Cook, stirring occasionally, until all the liquid has been absorbed, then test the rice to see if it is al dente. If it needs more cooking, add the remaining stock. Splash in the sherry, then lightly fold half the parmesan through.

Spoon into four warmed pasta bowls and sprinkle with the remaining parmesan. Crumble the prosciutto into smaller pieces and scatter over the risotto. Drizzle with a little olive oil and garnish with rocket or basil. Serves 4

figgy duck breast with lemon couscous

4 boneless duck breasts, skin on
¼ teaspoon Chinese five spice
2 tablespoons soft brown sugar
1 tablespoon sea salt
100 ml (3½ fl oz) brandy
185 g (6½ oz/1 cup) instant couscous
1 tablespoon butter
finely grated zest and juice of 1 lemon
8 ripe black figs, sliced in half
1 spring onion (scallion), finely sliced on the diagonal
1 tablespoon balsamic vinegar

Preheat the oven to 200°C (400°F/Gas 6).

Score the duck skin in a crisscross pattern. Combine the five-spice, sugar and sea salt in a small bowl, then rub the mixture into the duck skin. Put the brandy in a dish and add the duck breasts, skin side up. Cover and marinate in the refrigerator for at least 1 hour, or preferably overnight.

Put the couscous and butter in a bowl and pour 250 ml (9 fl oz/1 cup) boiling water over the top. Cover and leave the couscous to absorb the liquid for 10 minutes. Fluff up the grains with a fork, then stir in the lemon zest and lemon juice.

Heat a frying pan over high heat. Add the duck breasts, skin side down, and sear for 3 minutes, or until lightly browned underneath. Put the figs in a baking tray and drizzle with any remaining marinade. Sit the duck breasts on a rack, skin side up, and set the rack over the baking tray. Roast for 15 minutes. If the duck skin hasn't completely crisped up in your oven, blast the duck under a hot grill (broiler) for 1 minute. Remove from the heat and cover loosely with foil.

Toss the spring onion through the couscous and divide among four warmed plates. Add the duck breasts, top with the figs and drizzle with a little vinegar. Serves 4

opposite: seared beef and noodle salad
over: tomato and prosciutto risotto, and
figgy duck breast with lemon couscous

255

4 marinades

lamb

125 ml (4 fl oz/1/2 cup) white wine
4 tablespoons olive oil
juice of 1 lemon
1 tablespoon fresh oregano
1 garlic clove, finely sliced
4 lamb backstraps, 8 lamb loin fillets or 1 boned leg of lamb

Put the wine, olive oil, lemon juice, oregano and garlic in a large non-metallic bowl and mix together well.

Add your chosen cut of lamb to the marinade. Toss to ensure all the meat is thoroughly coated, then cover and marinate in the refrigerator for 2–3 hours.

Remove the lamb from the marinade and cook until it is still a little pink in the centre. Remove from the heat and season with sea salt and freshly ground black pepper. Cover loosely with foil and allow to rest for 5 minutes before serving. Serves 4

chicken

3 tablespoons lemon juice
3 tablespoons olive oil
1 tablespoon dijon mustard
1 teaspoon finely chopped garlic
1 teaspoon fresh thyme
1/2 teaspoon ground white pepper
4–6 chicken drumsticks, chicken leg quarters or boneless, skinless chicken breasts

Put the lemon juice, olive oil, mustard, garlic, thyme and white pepper in a large non-metallic bowl and mix together well.

Add the chicken pieces to the marinade. Toss to ensure all the chicken is thoroughly coated, then cover and marinate in the refrigerator for 2–3 hours.

Remove the chicken from the marinade, then barbecue or roast until cooked. Season with sea salt. Serves 4

seafood

1 teaspoon finely grated fresh ginger
2 tablespoons coriander (cilantro) leaves
2 tablespoons lime juice
3 tablespoons olive oil
4 x 200 g (7 oz) fish fillets

Put the ginger, coriander, lime juice and olive oil in a large non-metallic bowl and mix together well.

Add the fish fillets, gently turn them about to ensure all the fish is thoroughly coated, then cover and marinate in the refrigerator for 30 minutes.

Remove the fish fillets from the marinade, then grill, bake or pan-fry. Serves 4

beef

250 ml (9 fl oz/1 cup) red wine
2 garlic cloves, finely chopped
1/2 teaspoon finely chopped fresh rosemary
125 ml (4 fl oz/1/2 cup) olive oil
4 sirloin or fillet steaks

Put the wine, garlic, rosemary and olive oil in a large non-metallic bowl and mix together well.

Add the steaks to the marinade. Turn them about to ensure all the meat is thoroughly coated, then cover and marinate in the refrigerator for 2–3 hours.

Remove the steaks from the marinade and season well with freshly ground black pepper. Cook on the barbecue or in a frying pan until cooked to your liking. Remove from the heat and season with sea salt, then cover loosely with foil and allow to rest for 5 minutes before serving. Serves 4

seared swordfish with a roast almond sauce

1 slice of white sourdough bread, crusts removed
100 g (3¹/₂ oz/heaped 1 cup) flaked almonds, lightly toasted
¹/₂ garlic clove
2 tablespoons lemon juice
1 teaspoon ground cumin
¹/₂ teaspoon paprika
250 g (9 oz) cherry tomatoes, cut in half
1 telegraph (long) cucumber, diced
10 fresh oregano leaves, torn
a handful of flat-leaf (Italian) parsley
1 tablespoon olive oil
4 x 175 g (6 oz) swordfish steaks

Soak the bread in 125 ml (4 fl oz/¹/₂ cup) cold water. Put the soaked bread and the water in a food processor or blender and add the almonds, garlic, lemon juice, cumin and paprika. Blend to a smooth mayonnaise consistency — if the mixture is quite thick, add a little extra water. Season to taste with sea salt and freshly ground black pepper.

Put the cherry tomatoes in a bowl with the cucumber and herbs. Sprinkle generously with sea salt and freshly ground black pepper and toss to combine. Set aside.

Heat the olive oil in a large frying pan over high heat. Add the swordfish steaks and sear for 2 minutes, or until golden brown underneath. Turn them over, reduce the heat and cook the other side for 2–3 minutes, or until the steaks are cooked through — they should feel firm when you press them.

Lift the swordfish steaks onto four warmed plates, spoon the tomato salad over and serve with the almond sauce. Serves 4

crushed eggplant and tomato salad

4 roma (plum) tomatoes
1 teaspoon sugar
1 teaspoon ground cumin
1 large roasted eggplant (aubergine) (Favourites)
1 tablespoon balsamic vinegar
2 tablespoons extra virgin olive oil
a handful of chopped flat-leaf (Italian) parsley
10 mint leaves, finely chopped
2 spring onions (scallions), thinly sliced

Dice the tomatoes and put them in a large bowl. Sprinkle with the sugar and cumin and season generously with sea salt and freshly ground black pepper. Set aside.

Peel away the charred skin from the eggplant. Put the eggplant in a colander over a bowl, then cut or tear into long strips. Using your hands, press down on the eggplant to remove any excess liquid, then add the eggplant to the tomatoes, along with the vinegar, olive oil, parsley, mint and spring onion. Season to taste with sea salt and freshly ground black pepper and gently mix together.

Delicious served with seared tuna steaks or grilled sausages. Serves 4 as a side dish

chorizo and white bean salad

2 tablespoons extra virgin olive oil
1 tablespoon red wine vinegar
1 teaspoon dijon mustard
400 g (14 oz) tin cannellini beans, rinsed and drained
250 g (9 oz) cherry tomatoes, cut in half
¹/₂ red onion, finely sliced
2 celery stalks, finely sliced
a handful of flat-leaf (Italian) parsley, roughly chopped
250 g (9 oz) chorizo sausages
150 g (5¹/₂ oz/1 bunch) rocket (arugula), stalks trimmed

Put the olive oil, vinegar and mustard in a large bowl and whisk together. Add the beans, cherry tomatoes, onion, celery and parsley and toss lightly to combine.

Heat a non-stick frying pan over medium heat. Thinly slice the chorizo, then lightly sauté for several minutes, or until golden on both sides. Toss the warm chorizo through the salad.

Divide the rocket leaves among four serving plates, then spoon the chorizo salad over the top. Serves 4 as a starter or light meal

seasonal ideas

- Fry thinly sliced rounds of eggplant (aubergine) in oil until crisp and golden. Drain on paper towels, then toss with roughly chopped tomato, coriander (cilantro) leaves, a pinch of paprika and a little balsamic vinegar. Serve with seared swordfish or tuna.

- For a rich pasta sauce, lightly fry some eggplant (aubergine) chunks with garlic, roasted red capsicum (pepper) (Favourites) and a late addition of tinned tomatoes. Add fresh basil to finish.

- Finely slice a large eggplant (aubergine) and lightly fry it. Roll each slice around a spoonful of ricotta cheese that has been flavoured with parsley, basil and a little grated parmesan cheese. Bake in a moderately hot oven for half an hour, then drizzle with a rich tomato sauce and serve with a green salad.

opposite: seared swordfish with a roast almond sauce
over: crushed eggplant and tomato salad, and
chorizo and white bean salad

The hot spice of chorizo is softened with
white beans and rocket

marsala-baked figs

8 figs
4 tablespoons soft brown sugar
1 1/2 tablespoons unsalted butter
125 ml (4 fl oz/1/2 cup) marsala
grated zest and juice of 1 lemon
4 tablespoons flaked or slivered almonds
mascarpone cheese, to serve

Preheat the oven to 180°C (350°F/Gas 4). Slit a cross in the top of each fig and slice halfway down the figs, keeping them attached at the base. Sit them in a baking dish and slightly open the figs at the top. Spoon a heaped teaspoon of sugar and some of the butter into the centre of each fig. Pour the marsala into the baking dish, then add the lemon zest, lemon juice and the remaining butter and sugar. Bake for 10 minutes.

Spread the almonds on a baking tray and toast in the oven for 2–3 minutes, or until golden brown.

Serve the figs with a dollop of mascarpone, some toasted almonds and a drizzle of the fig baking liquid. Serves 4

rustic apple and blueberry pie

3 green apples (500 g/1 lb 2 oz in total)
220 g (7 3/4 oz/1 cup) sugar
grated zest and juice of 1 lemon
250 g (9 oz/2 cups) plain (all-purpose) flour
125 g (4 1/2 oz) unsalted butter, cut into cubes and chilled
3 tablespoons sugar, extra
2–0 tablespoons chilled water
150 g (5 1/2 oz/1 cup) blueberries
whipped cream or custard (page 91), to serve

Peel and core the apples, then cut them into eighths. Place in a saucepan with the sugar, lemon zest, 1 tablespoon of the lemon juice and 750 ml (26 fl oz/3 cups) water. Bring to the boil, then reduce the heat and simmer for 15–20 minutes, or until the apple is tender. Remove with a slotted spoon, draining away as much liquid as possible, and allow to cool completely. Meanwhile, continue simmering the syrup until it has reduced to one-third of its original volume, then remove the pan from the heat.

While the syrup is simmering, put the flour in a food processor with the butter and 1 tablespoon of the extra sugar. Process until the mixture begins to resemble breadcrumbs, then add the chilled water. Process briefly until the dough comes together, then remove, cover with plastic wrap and chill in the refrigerator for 10 minutes.

Preheat the oven to 200°C (400°F/Gas 6). Roll the dough out between two large pieces of baking paper into a large circle about 30 cm (12 inches) in diameter, and about 5 mm (1/4 inch) thick. Remove the top sheet of paper, then lift the lower sheet of baking paper and dough onto a baking tray.

Pile the cooled apple into the centre of the pastry, leaving a margin around the edge, then add the blueberries. Pull the dough up around the sides, scrunching it in over the fruit. Sprinkle with the remaining sugar, then bake for 40 minutes, or until the pastry is golden brown. Remove from the oven and allow to cool. Brush some of the apple syrup over the pie before serving with whipped cream or custard. Serves 6

maple panna cotta

8 teaspoons maple syrup
250 ml (9 fl oz/1 cup) pouring (whipping) cream
250 ml (9 fl oz/1 cup) milk
2 tablespoons sugar
1 vanilla bean
2 teaspoons gelatine powder*
4 ripe figs, cut in half

Spoon the maple syrup into four 150 ml (5 fl oz) ramekins, allowing 2 teaspoons per ramekin. Place in the freezer.

Put the cream, milk and sugar in a small saucepan. Rub the vanilla bean between your fingers to soften it. Using the tip of a sharp knife, split the vanilla bean in half along its length and add it to the cream. Cook over low heat for 10 minutes, then remove from the heat and discard the vanilla bean. Sprinkle the gelatine powder over the warm cream and stir for 2 minutes to ensure that it has dissolved thoroughly into the mixture.

When the cream has cooled, remove the ramekins from the freezer. Gently pour the cream over the maple syrup. Cover with plastic wrap, then refrigerate for several hours.

Just before serving, run a sharp knife around the inside of the ramekins and turn out onto serving plates. Serve with the fig halves. Serves 4

* When using powdered gelatine, always check the manufacturer's instructions.

opposite: marsala-baked figs
over: rustic apple and blueberry pie, and maple panna cotta

autumn fruit

Autumn fruits love to be baked and then drizzled with rich cream.

- Slice pears in half and remove the core. Press softened butter into the hollow, then place skin side up in a baking dish. Cover with 250 ml (9 fl oz/1 cup) dessert wine and add a split vanilla bean. Cover with foil and bake in a moderate oven for an hour. Serve with a drizzle of the syrup and thick (double/heavy) cream.

- Cut 4 quinces into quarters and remove the cores. Peel and then cut the quarters in half lengthways. Arrange in a large baking dish and add 3 tablespoons unsalted

butter, cut into cubes, 4 tablespoons honey and 125 ml (4 fl oz/1/2 cup) water. Cover with foil and bake for 4 hours in a 150°C (300°F/Gas 2) oven. Serve with a drizzle of the syrup and vanilla or caramel ice cream.

- Slice 8 fresh figs into quarters lengthways, from the top downwards, being careful to only slice halfway down. In a small bowl combine 2 tablespoons soft brown sugar with 1 tablespoon softened butter and 1 teaspoon finely chopped crystallized ginger. Stir to combine, then spoon some of the mixture into the centre of each fig. Arrange in a small baking dish and bake in a moderate oven for 10 minutes. Serve with thick (double/heavy) cream.

- Replace the apricots in the apricot tart recipe (page 181) with thin slices of baked quince. Bake as per recipe and serve with vanilla ice cream.

- Put 400 g (14 oz/scant 1²/₃ cups) ricotta cheese in a food processor or blender with 2 tablespoons sugar and ¹/₂ teaspoon grated orange zest. Blend to a smooth paste and divide among four serving bowls. Scatter with pomegranate seeds and dried barberries. Serves 4

- Sometimes it's easy to forget that a simple dessert of stewed apple or rhubarb (Favourites) topped with a rich home-made custard (page 91) is really a grand thing!

- Slice fresh figs crossways into thin rounds and arrange on a serving platter. Top with thinly sliced orange, sprinkle with cinnamon and drizzle with aromatic honey. Serve with Greek-style yoghurt.

- Serve ripe pears with thin slices of pecorino cheese and fresh walnuts.

- Serve a ripe goat's cheese or brie with fresh figs and muscatel grapes.

Sweet red wine and cinnamon flavour this pretty pear

red wine pears

225 g (8 oz/1 cup) caster (superfine) sugar
350 ml (12 fl oz) red wine
2 strips of lemon zest
1 cinnamon stick
6 cooking pears
sweet mascarpone (Favourites), to serve

Put the sugar, wine, lemon zest strips, cinnamon stick and 750 ml (26 fl oz/3 cups) water in a saucepan large enough to comfortably fit six pears standing upright.

Bring the syrup to the boil over high heat, stirring until the sugar has dissolved. Remove from the heat and discard the cinnamon stick. Peel the pears, leaving the stems on. Insert the tip of a small sharp knife into the base of the pears and remove the cores in one circular movement. Stand the pears upright in the syrup and cover with a sheet of baking paper. Weigh the paper down with a saucepan lid or saucer, then gently simmer for 1 1/2 hours.

To test if the pears are cooked, insert a skewer into the fattest section — they should feel tender. Remove from the heat and allow the pears to cool in the syrup. Serve with sweet mascarpone. Serves 6

cherry and cinnamon tartlets

670 g (1 lb 7 oz) bottle of sour cherries
1/4 teaspoon ground cinnamon
1 tablespoon unsalted butter
3 tablespoons soft brown sugar
2 sheets of frozen butter puff pastry, thawed
thick (double/heavy) cream, to serve
icing (confectioners') sugar, to serve

Preheat the oven to 180°C (350°F/Gas 4).

Strain the cherries, reserving the liquid. Pour 125 ml (4 fl oz/ 1/2 cup) of the cherry liquid into a small saucepan and add the cinnamon, butter and sugar. Cook over medium heat for 8–10 minutes, or until the liquid has reduced to a thick syrup. Remove from the heat and allow to cool.

Cut four 10 cm (4 inch) rounds from the puff pastry. Generously butter four egg rings and place them on a non-stick baking tray. Press the pastry into the egg rings, in a fairly free-form shape. Spoon the strained cherries into the tart cases and bake for 25 minutes, or until the pastry is golden brown and crisp.

Remove the egg rings by gently pulling away the tartlets and place on four serving plates. Spoon the cherry syrup over the cherries, top with a dollop of cream and dust with icing sugar. Serve warm. Makes 8

pomegranate syrup cake

125 g (4 1/2 oz) butter
230 g (8 oz/1 cup) caster (superfine) sugar
3 eggs
125 g (4 1/2 oz/1 cup) plain (all-purpose) flour
60 g (2 1/4 oz/1/2 cup) semolina
55 g (2 oz/1/2 cup) ground almonds
2 teaspoons baking powder
2 teaspoons rosewater

pomegranate syrup
3 pomegranates
55 g (2 oz/1/4 cup) sugar
whipped cream, to serve

Preheat the oven to 160°C (315°F/Gas 2–3). Generously grease a 27 cm (10 3/4 inch) bundt or ring tin.

Cream the butter and sugar using electric beaters, then add the eggs. Fold in the flour, semolina, ground almonds, baking powder and rosewater. Spoon the batter into the prepared cake tin and bake for 45 minutes, or until a skewer inserted into the centre of the cake comes out clean. Remove from the oven and allow to cool.

Meanwhile, make the pomegranate syrup. Cut the pomegranates in half. Squeeze the seeds and juice out of two of them and strain the juice into a saucepan. Add the sugar and simmer over low heat for 10 minutes, stirring to dissolve the sugar.

Invert the cooled cake onto a serving plate. Prick the cake all over with a skewer, then spoon the warm pomegranate syrup over. Decorate with the seeds of the remaining pomegranate and serve with whipped cream. Serves 10

opposite: red wine pears
over: cherry and cinnamon tartlets, and
pomegranate syrup cake

spiced filo with fig and pomegranate salad

cardamom syrup
115 g (4 oz/^{1}/2 cup) caster (superfine) sugar
1 teaspoon lemon juice
5 cardamom pods, lightly crushed
^{1}/2 teaspoon rosewater

75 g (2^1/2 oz/^{1}/2 cup) shelled pistachio nuts
2 tablespoons honey
2 teaspoons lemon zest
2 teaspoons lemon juice
1 teaspoon cinnamon
2 sheets of filo pastry
2 tablespoons butter, melted
4 figs
2 pomegranates
thick (double/heavy) cream, to serve

Preheat the oven to 160°C (315°F/Gas 2–3). Line a baking tray with baking paper.

To make the cardamom syrup, put the sugar, lemon juice and cardamom pods in a small saucepan with 250 ml (9 fl oz/1 cup) water. Bring slowly to the boil, stirring to ensure that the sugar dissolves completely, then reduce the heat and simmer for 5 minutes. Remove from the heat and stir in the rosewater. Allow to cool and set aside.

Finely chop the pistachios in a food processor or blender and put them in a bowl with the honey, lemon zest, lemon juice and cinnamon. Stir to combine.

Lay a sheet of filo pastry on a clean work surface and brush with melted butter. Fold one-third of the sheet over, then fold the remaining third over the top, to make a rectangle measuring about 15 x 28 cm (6 x 11^1/4 inches). Put the pastry on the baking tray, brush with more butter and spread all the pistachio mixture over the top. Repeat the folding and buttering process with the remaining sheet of filo, then lay it over the pistachio mixture and firmly press to form a sandwich. Brush the top with any remaining butter.

Using kitchen scissors, cut the finished pastry rectangle in half widthways. Cut each of those pieces in half, then in half again. You should have eight pastry strips, each measuring 3 x 15 cm (1^1/4 x 6 inches). Bake for 10 minutes, or until golden brown, then remove from the oven and cool on a wire rack.

Finely slice the figs and arrange in the centre of four dessert plates. Remove the seeds and juice from the pomegranates and spoon them over the figs. Dollop some cream in the centre and cross two pastry strips over each plate. Drizzle with the cardamom syrup. Serves 4

caramelized apple tartlets

3 small green apples
2^1/2 tablespoons unsalted butter
1 vanilla bean
4 tablespoons caster (superfine) sugar
2 tablespoons brandy
1 sheet of puff pastry
whipped cream, to serve

Preheat the oven to 200°C (400°F/Gas 6). Line a baking tray with baking paper.

Cut the apples into quarters and remove the cores. Cut each quarter into wedges.

Melt the butter in a frying pan. Rub the vanilla bean between your fingertips to soften it. Using the tip of a sharp knife, split the vanilla bean in half along its length and scrape the seeds into the melted butter. When the butter begins to bubble, add the apple wedges and cook for 2 minutes on each side. Add the sugar and brandy and cook until the apple starts to caramelize. Remove from the heat.

Cut the puff pastry into four squares and place them on the baking tray. Arrange the apple over the pastry, reserving the syrup in the pan. Bake for 20 minutes, or until golden brown. Spoon the remaining syrup over the top and serve with a dollop of whipped cream. Serves 4

rhubarb fool

500 g (1 lb 2 oz/about 30 stalks) rhubarb, trimmed
115 g (4 oz/^{1}/2 cup) caster (superfine) sugar
juice of 1 orange
^{1}/2 teaspoon ground cinnamon
300 ml (10^1/2 fl oz) pouring (whipping) cream, whipped
almond bread or pistachio biscotti (page 278), to serve

Cut the rhubarb into 5 cm (2 inch) lengths and place in a saucepan with the sugar, orange juice and cinnamon. Cover and cook over low heat for 10 minutes, or until the rhubarb has dissolved. Remove from the heat and set aside for an hour or so to cool completely.

Gently fold the rhubarb through the whipped cream until they are almost combined, yet still slightly distinct. Spoon into dessert bowls and serve with almond bread or pistachio biscotti. Serves 6

opposite: spiced filo with fig and pomegranate salad
over: caramelized apple tartlets, and rhubarb fool

4 biscuits

strawberry swirls

250 g (9 oz/2 cups) plain (all-purpose) flour
1/2 teaspoon baking powder
115 g (4 oz/1/2 cup) caster (superfine) sugar
125 g (41/2 oz) unsalted butter, chopped
2 eggs, lightly beaten
100 g (31/2 oz/1/3 cup) strawberry jam
2 teaspoons ground cinnamon
icing (confectioners') sugar, to serve

Sift the flour and baking powder into a large bowl, then add the sugar. Using your fingertips, rub in the butter until the mixture resembles coarse breadcrumbs. Slowly work in the eggs to make a stiff dough.

Roll the dough out on a sheet of baking paper into a 20 x 30 cm (8 x 12 inch) rectangle. Spread the jam evenly over the top and sprinkle with the cinnamon. Roll the dough up, Swiss-roll (jelly-roll) style, from the widest edge, peeling off the paper as you go. Wrap in plastic wrap and refrigerate for 30 minutes.

Preheat the oven to 180°C (350°F/Gas 4). Line a baking tray with baking paper. Cut the roll into 1 cm (1/2 inch) slices, sit the rounds on the baking tray and bake for 15 minutes. Remove from the oven and cool on wire racks, then dust with icing sugar. Makes about 20

peanut butter cookies

90 g (31/4 oz) unsalted butter, softened
4 heaped tablespoons crunchy peanut butter
150 g (51/2 oz/2/3 cup firmly packed) soft brown sugar
1 egg
125 g (41/2 oz/1 cup) plain (all-purpose) flour
1/2 teaspoon bicarbonate of soda (baking soda)
1/4 teaspoon ground cinnamon

Preheat the oven to 180°C (350°F/Gas 4). Line a baking tray with baking paper.

Cream the butter, peanut butter and sugar using electric beaters until pale, then add the egg and stir thoroughly. Sift in the flour, bicarbonate of soda and cinnamon and mix well.

Drop teaspoonfuls of the mixture onto the baking tray, leaving room for the cookies to spread. Bake for 12 minutes, then remove from the oven. Allow the cookies to cool a little on the baking tray before lifting onto a wire rack to cool completely. Makes about 35

pistachio biscotti

125 g (41/2 oz/1 cup) plain (all-purpose) flour
115 g (4 oz/1/2 cup) caster (superfine) sugar
1 teaspoon baking powder
150 g (51/2 oz/1 cup) shelled pistachio nuts
2 teaspoons grated orange zest
2 eggs, beaten

Preheat the oven to 180°C (350°F/Gas 4). Line two baking trays with baking paper.

Mix the flour, sugar, baking powder, pistachios and orange zest together in a large bowl. Make a well in the centre and fold in the eggs to make a sticky dough.

Turn the dough out onto a clean, floured surface. Divide into two portions, then roll each one into a log about 4 cm (11/2 inches) long. Sit them on one of the baking trays, leaving some space in between for spreading. Bake for 30 minutes, then remove from the oven and allow to cool.

Reduce the oven temperature to 140°C (275°F/Gas 1). Using a very sharp bread knife, cut each loaf into thin slices about 5 mm (1/4 inch) thick. Spread the biscuits on the baking trays and bake for 20 minutes, turning once during baking. Remove from the oven and cool on wire racks. Makes 30 to 40

chocolate and hazelnut cookies

150 g (51/2 oz) good-quality dark chocolate
80 g (23/4 oz) unsalted butter
200 g (7 oz/1 heaped cup, lightly packed) dark brown sugar
100 g (31/2 oz/heaped 3/4 cup) plain (all-purpose) flour
1 teaspoon natural vanilla extract
55 g (2 oz/1/2 cup) ground hazelnuts
1 egg

Melt the chocolate and butter in a small saucepan over low heat. Add the sugar and stir for 1 minute, or until the sugar has dissolved. Sift in the flour, then stir in the vanilla and ground hazelnuts. Add the egg and stir to form a thick dough. Remove, cover with plastic wrap and refrigerate for 1 hour.

Preheat the oven to 180°C (350°F/Gas 4). Line two baking trays with baking paper. Shape the dough into small walnut-sized balls and sit them on the baking trays, leaving some space in between for spreading. Bake for 15–20 minutes, or until they look dry. Remove from the oven and cool on the baking trays. For a decadent treat, serve the cookies with a blob of cream and some fresh figs marinated in soft brown sugar and Grand Marnier. Makes about 30

ginger parfait with a mulled wine syrup

1 vanilla bean
125 g (4^1/2 oz/heaped ^{1}/2 cup) caster (superfine) sugar
4 cm (1^1/2 inch) knob of fresh ginger, peeled and chopped
5 egg yolks
500 g (1 lb 2 oz/2 cups) crème fraîche or sour cream

mulled wine syrup
250 ml (9 fl oz/1 cup) red wine
110 g (3^3/4 oz/^{1}/2 cup) sugar
1 cinnamon stick
2 cloves
2 cardamom pods, crushed

Rub the vanilla bean between your fingertips to soften it. Using the tip of a sharp knife, split the vanilla bean in half along its length and scrape the seeds into a small heavy-based saucepan. Add the vanilla bean, sugar, ginger and 125 ml (4 fl oz/^{1}/2 cup) water. Place the pan over medium heat, stir to dissolve the sugar and simmer for 5 minutes, or until a syrup forms. Strain the syrup into a bowl.

Whisk the egg yolks in a large bowl until light and fluffy, then add the warm sugar syrup. Whisk for a minute, then add the crème fraîche and whisk again to combine. Pour into an 8 x 22 cm (3^1/4 x 8^1/2 inch) loaf (bar) tin lined with baking paper. Freeze overnight.

To make the mulled wine syrup, pour the wine into a small saucepan and add the sugar and spices. Bring to the boil, then reduce the heat and simmer for 10 minutes. Strain into a bowl and allow the syrup to cool completely.

Cut the parfait into thick slices. Serve on chilled plates, drizzled with the mulled wine syrup. Serves 6

creamed rice with pomegranate molasses

1 tablespoon pomegranate molasses
2 tablespoons soft brown sugar
110 g (3^3/4 oz/^{1}/2 cup) short-grain white rice
1 vanilla bean
500 ml (17 fl oz/2 cups) milk
4 tablespoons caster (superfine) sugar
125 ml (4 fl oz/^{1}/2 cup) pouring (whipping) cream, whipped
fresh pomegranate seeds or strawberries, to serve

Put the pomegranate molasses in a small bowl with the brown sugar and 1 tablespoon of boiling water. Stir until the sugar has dissolved, then set aside.

Rinse the rice in cold water, then drain. Rub the vanilla bean between your fingertips to soften it. Using the tip of a sharp knife, split the vanilla bean in half along its length and scrape the seeds into a small heavy-based saucepan. Add the vanilla bean, milk and caster sugar and bring almost to the boil. Stir in the rice, reduce the heat and simmer gently for 30 minutes, stirring occasionally.

When the rice is tender, remove the pan from the heat and discard the vanilla bean. Transfer the rice to a bowl and allow to cool completely.

Fold the whipped cream through the rice and divide among six dessert bowls. Drizzle with some of the pomegranate molasses syrup and serve with fresh pomegranate seeds or strawberries. Serves 6

hazelnut affogato

375 ml (13 fl oz/1^1/2 cups) milk
250 ml (9 fl oz/1 cup) pouring (whipping) cream
2 tablespoons finely ground toasted hazelnuts
4 egg yolks
125 g (4^1/2 oz/heaped ^{1}/2 cup) caster (superfine) sugar
4 teaspoons hazelnut or coffee liqueur
4 shots of freshly brewed espresso coffee

To make the ice cream, pour the milk and cream into a heavy-based saucepan and add the ground hazelnuts. Place the saucepan over medium heat and bring the mixture just to simmering point. Remove from the heat.

In a large bowl, whisk the egg yolks with the sugar until light and creamy. Whisk in a little of the warm milk mixture, then add the remaining liquid and whisk to combine.

Rinse and dry the saucepan, then pour the mixture back into the pan. Cook over medium heat, stirring constantly with a wooden spoon, until the mixture thickens and coats the back of the spoon. Quickly remove from the heat, strain into a chilled bowl and allow to cool completely.

Churn in an ice-cream machine according to the manufacturer's instructions, then spoon into a container and freeze for at least 1 hour before serving. If you don't have an ice-cream machine, pour the mixture into a metal bowl, cover with plastic wrap and freeze. Every hour, stir the ice cream with a fork, scraping the frozen bits from the side of the bowl and folding it back through the ice cream. Repeat until the ice cream is quite stiff, then freeze overnight.

To serve, scoop two small balls of ice cream into four small heatproof glasses or cups and pour a teaspoon of liqueur over each. Serve the espresso coffee on the side for guests to pour over their ice cream. Serves 4 (makes enough ice cream for 10 serves)

opposite: ginger parfait with a mulled wine syrup
over: creamed rice with pomegranate molasses, and
hazelnut affogato

Hazelnut ice cream, liqueur and coffee …
one of my favourite treats

winter

I love winter. It's an easy statement to make when you come from a relatively mild climate, but I do get excited when it's time to unpack the winter woollies. The prospect of winter food gives me the same cosy feeling. Suddenly there is no excuse not to enjoy thick and hearty soups, crackly roast meats, creamy mashed potato and rich gooey desserts. Winter food is shared around a communal table, where the warmth of the oven fills the room with the rich aromas of baking and roasting. It is the time of slow food and big pots. The cupboards fill with potatoes, the fridge chills the cream, butter and stocks, and the crisper stores carrots and parsnips. Meanwhile, the shared table fills with large casseroles brimming with rich sauces and hot platters of juicy meat. But don't panic, this can be the kind of food that takes some time but little effort to prepare — so set the oven timer and add some winter drama to the table.

warming breakfasts

potatoes brussels sprouts

turnips

shallots shiny pots parsnips

kale horseradish hearty soups

garlic cabbages

spooning ladles

carrots broccoli

chestnuts

brown onions

rich cakes

stirring

apples lemons

rhubarb

pears creamy desserts

grapefruit hot porridge

omelette

3 eggs, separated
1 tablespoon butter
1 teaspoon finely snipped chives
50 g (1³/4 oz) goat's cheese, crumbled
buttered toast, to serve

Whisk the egg whites into soft peaks. In a separate bowl, lightly whisk the egg yolks, then gently fold them into the egg whites.

Heat a 25 cm (10 inch) non-stick frying pan over high heat and add the butter. When the butter has melted and begins to sizzle, pour in the egg mixture. Using a spatula, fold the edges of the egg into the centre as it cooks. When the egg is nearly cooked, sprinkle with the chives and crumbled goat's cheese. Flip one half of the omelette over the other and take the pan off the heat.

Divide the omelette between two plates and serve with buttered toast. Serves 2

espresso french toast with banana

2 x 100 g (3¹/2 oz) panettone
4 large egg yolks
125 ml (4 fl oz/¹/2 cup) strong freshly brewed espresso coffee
2 tablespoons unsalted butter
2 bananas
4 tablespoons maple syrup

Trim the top and bottom off each panettone, then cut each cake widthways into four round discs approximately 2 cm (³/4 inch) wide. Whisk the egg yolks and coffee together until well combined. Dip the panettone slices, one at a time, into the egg mixture, ensuring they are well coated.

Heat the butter in a non-stick frying pan over medium heat. When it starts to sizzle, add the panettone slices and fry for a minute or two on each side, until crisp and golden. Place on serving plates. Slice each banana on the diagonal and pile them over the panettone, then drizzle with the maple syrup. Serves 4

pancakes with chocolate butter

chocolate butter
150 g (5¹/2 oz) unsalted butter, softened
50 g (1³/4 oz) dark eating chocolate
¹/4 teaspoon ground cinnamon
4 tablespoons maple syrup

90 g (3¹/4 oz/³/4 cup) plain (all-purpose) flour
1 heaped teaspoon baking powder
1 tablespoon caster (superfine) sugar
1 egg, lightly beaten
250 ml (9 fl oz/1 cup) milk
1 teaspoon natural vanilla extract
butter, for greasing
maple syrup, extra, to serve
bottled morello cherries, drained, or fresh berries, to serve

Put all the chocolate butter ingredients in a food processor and blend to form a smooth butter. Spoon onto a length of plastic wrap and roll up to form a log. Refrigerate until needed.

To make the pancake batter, sift the flour into a bowl, add the baking powder, sugar and a pinch of salt, then make a well in the centre. In a separate bowl, whisk together the egg, milk and vanilla. Pour the liquid into the dry ingredients and whisk to form a smooth batter. Cover and refrigerate for 30 minutes.

Remove the chocolate butter and the batter from the refrigerator. Grease a small non-stick frying pan with butter and place over medium heat. As the butter begins to sizzle, spoon the batter into the pan to form two or three 8 cm (3¹/4 inch) rounds. Cook for 1 minute, or until bubbles appear on the surface, then flip the pancakes over and cook for a further minute. Stack the pancakes on a warm plate while cooking the remaining batter.

Divide the pancakes among four serving plates and top with slices of the chocolate butter and a drizzle of maple syrup. Serve with morello cherries or fresh berries. Serves 4

Golden eggs, creamy cheese and the crisp
crunch of buttered toast

opposite: omelette
over: espresso french toast with banana, and
pancakes with chocolate butter

Wake up to warm pancakes with bittersweet chocolate butter

mixed berry muffins

250 g (9 oz/1 cup) plain yoghurt
100 ml (3¹/₂ fl oz) vegetable oil
2 eggs
2 teaspoons natural vanilla extract
280 g (10 oz/2¹/₄ cups) plain (all-purpose) flour
2 heaped teaspoons baking powder
140 g (5 oz/³/₄ cup) soft brown sugar
250 g (9 oz/1³/₄ cups) frozen mixed berries
raw (demerara) sugar, for sprinkling

Preheat the oven to 180°C (350°F/Gas 4). Grease 12 holes of a standard muffin tin or line with paper cases.

Put the yoghurt, vegetable oil, eggs and vanilla in a bowl and whisk to combine. Sift the flour and baking powder into a large bowl and add the brown sugar and frozen berries (reserve 12 large berries for decorating the muffins). Stir lightly to mix the berries through the flour, then add the yoghurt mixture and lightly fold together.

Spoon into the prepared muffin holes, then top each muffin with a reserved frozen berry and about 1 heaped teaspoon of raw sugar. Bake for 25 minutes, or until the tops are golden and a skewer inserted into the centre of a muffin comes out clean. Makes 12

mushroom ragout on brioche

10 g (¹/₄ oz) dried porcini mushrooms
500 g (1 lb 2 oz) mixed mushrooms, such as Swiss brown, shiitake, morel and field
2 tablespoons olive oil
1 onion (preferably brown), diced
2 garlic cloves, finely chopped
2 slices of bacon, finely chopped
250 ml (9 fl oz/1 cup) red wine
2 tablespoons tomato paste (concentrated purée)
4 thick slices of brioche
1 tablespoon cornflour (cornstarch)
2 handfuls of flat-leaf (Italian) parsley, roughly chopped
50 g (1³/₄ oz/¹/₂ cup) shaved pecorino cheese

Put the dried porcini in a small bowl and cover with 250 ml (9 fl oz/1 cup) boiling water. Allow to soak for 15 minutes.

Wipe any grit off the fresh mushrooms and cut away the stems. Thickly slice all the mushrooms.

Heat the oil in a saucepan over medium heat. Add the onion, garlic and bacon and cook for 5 minutes, or until the onion is soft and transparent. Add the fresh mushrooms. Strain the liquid from the porcini mushrooms into the pan and stir. Finely chop the soaked porcini and add to the pan with the wine and tomato paste. Season with sea salt and freshly ground black pepper, then cover and simmer for 40 minutes.

Toast the brioche. Meanwhile, put the cornflour in a small bowl with 3 tablespoons of water and stir until the cornflour has dissolved. Add the cornflour paste to the mushrooms and stir until thickened, then remove the pan from the heat. Sprinkle with the parsley.

Place the toasted brioche on four serving plates, spoon the mushroom ragout over and top with the shaved pecorino. Serves 4

potato and spinach frittata

400 g (14 oz) boiling potatoes, such as long white, pink eye or kipfler (fingerling), peeled
250 ml (9 fl oz/1 cup) vegetable stock (Favourites)
3 tablespoons olive oil
1 red onion, diced
2 celery stalks, finely sliced
100 g (3¹/₂ oz/2¹/₄ cups) baby English spinach leaves
6 eggs, lightly beaten
70 g (2¹/₂ oz/³/₄ cup) grated parmesan cheese

Cut the potatoes into 2 cm (³/₄ inch) chunks. Put them in a deep heavy-based frying pan and pour in the stock. Heat over high heat until most of the stock has evaporated, then reduce the heat to medium and add the oil, onion and celery. Season with sea salt and freshly ground black pepper, then toss to lightly coat the vegetables in the oil. Allow to cook for a few minutes, or until the vegetables are slightly softened.

Add the spinach leaves, stir for a few minutes until the leaves have wilted, then pour the beaten eggs over the top. Sprinkle with the parmesan and cook for 10 minutes, or until the egg is almost set.

Briefly cook under a hot grill (broiler) until the cheese is golden and the frittata begins to puff up. Serve warm, cut into thick wedges. Serves 4–6

opposite: mixed berry muffins
over: mushroom ragout on brioche, and
potato and spinach frittata

295

4 dips

hummus

400 g (14 oz) tin chickpeas, rinsed and drained
2 teaspoons ground cumin
juice of 1 lemon
3 tablespoons tahini
3 tablespoons extra virgin olive oil
ground cumin, extra, to serve
extra virgin olive oil, extra, to serve
lightly toasted bread, to serve

Put the chickpeas, cumin, lemon juice, tahini and olive oil in a food processor and blend to a chunky purée, adding several tablespoons of warm water to give a smooth consistency.

Spoon into a serving bowl. Sprinkle with a little extra cumin and some freshly ground black pepper, then drizzle with a little more olive oil. Serve with lightly toasted bread. Serves 4

italian white bean and tuna dip

400 g (14 oz) tin cannellini beans, rinsed and drained
3 tablespoons extra virgin olive oil
1 tablespoon lemon juice
95 g (3¼ oz) tin tuna in oil, drained
a handful of flat-leaf (Italian) parsley, chopped
8 kalamata olives, pitted and finely chopped
extra virgin olive oil, extra, to serve
toasted pide (Turkish/flat bread), to serve

Put the cannellini beans, olive oil, lemon juice and tuna in a food processor or blender and pulse several times so that the beans are broken up but not mashed.

Scoop into a bowl and fold the parsley and olives through. Drizzle with a little more olive oil and serve with fingers of toasted pide. Serves 4–6

eggplant dip

2 roasted eggplants (aubergines) (Favourites)
1 small garlic clove, finely chopped
100 g (3½ oz) plain yoghurt
juice of 1 lemon
2 tablespoons tahini
a handful of flat-leaf (Italian) parsley, roughly chopped
½ teaspoon ground cumin
2 tablespoons pine nuts, toasted
lightly toasted ciabatta bread, to serve

Peel away the charred skin from the eggplants. Put the eggplants in a colander over a bowl. Using kitchen scissors, roughly cut the flesh into small pieces. Using your hands, press down on the eggplants to remove any excess liquid.

Mix the garlic with the yoghurt, then add the eggplant pulp, lemon juice, tahini and parsley. Stir the mixture thoroughly, breaking up the eggplant as you go. Season with the cumin, a little sea salt and a pinch of ground white pepper. Spoon into a serving bowl, sprinkle with the pine nuts and serve with lightly toasted slices of ciabatta bread. Serves 4

beetroot dip

4 beetroot (beets) (about 150 g/5½ oz each), scrubbed
4 fresh thyme sprigs
250 g (9 oz/1 cup) plain yoghurt
1 teaspoon pomegranate molasses
crispbread or crudités, to serve

Preheat the oven to 200°C (400°F/Gas 8). Put the beetroot in a roasting tin with the thyme sprigs and 250 ml (9 fl oz/1 cup) water. Cover with foil and bake for 1 hour, or until a knife passes easily through the beetroot. Remove the beetroot from the roasting tin and leave to cool.

Wearing rubber gloves to stop your hands staining, peel the skins from the beetroot — they should slip free quite easily. Roughly chop the flesh, then place in a food processor and blend to a smooth paste.

Transfer to a bowl and stir in the yoghurt and pomegranate molasses. Season to taste with sea salt and a generous grind of black pepper. Serve with crispbread or a plate of crudités. Serves 4–6

bread salad with fried sardines

3 ripe tomatoes, diced
1 Lebanese (short) cucumber, diced
1 garlic clove, finely chopped
1 red chilli, seeded and finely chopped
a handful of flat-leaf (Italian) parsley, roughly chopped
4 basil leaves, finely sliced
2 tablespoons red wine vinegar
4 slices of sourdough, lightly toasted
1 tablespoon butter
8–16 fresh sardine fillets, depending on their size

In a large bowl, combine the tomato, cucumber, garlic, chilli, parsley and basil. Pour the vinegar over. Tear the bread into small chunks and add them to the salad. Season with sea salt and freshly ground black pepper and toss to combine. Spoon the salad onto a large serving platter or divide among four plates.

Melt the butter in a large non-stick frying pan over high heat. Fry the sardine fillets for 1–2 minutes on each side, or until they are opaque and slightly browned, then arrange them over the salad. Serves 4 as a starter or light meal

trout salad

8 small boiling potatoes, such as long white, pink eye or
    kiptler (fingerling)
1/2 teaspoon fennel seeds
1 teaspoon mustard seeds
1 egg yolk
1 tablespoon lemon juice
4 tablespoons light olive oil
1/2 teaspoon caster (superfine) sugar
1 tablespoon finely chopped dill
1 butter lettuce
400 g (14 oz) hot-smoked trout fillet

Put the potatoes in a saucepan of cold water and bring to the boil. Reduce the heat and simmer for 15 minutes, or until the potatoes are cooked through.

Meanwhile, grind the fennel and mustard seeds using a mortar and pestle or spice grinder, then tip the spices into a bowl. Add the egg yolk and lemon juice and whisk until pale and creamy. Slowly drizzle in the olive oil and whisk until a thin mayonnaise forms. Stir in the sugar and dill and season to taste with sea salt and freshly ground black pepper.

Arrange the lettuce leaves on a platter or individual serving plates. Drain the warm potatoes and cut them into halves or quarters. Toss them in the dill mayonnaise, then arrange over the lettuce. Roughly break the trout into bite-sized pieces and scatter them over the salad. Serves 4

prosciutto and beetroot salad

2 ripe roma (plum) tomatoes, diced
1/2 red onion, diced
1 Lebanese (short) cucumber, diced
1 tablespoon salted capers, rinsed and drained
1 teaspoon red wine vinegar
8 slices of prosciutto, cut in half
1 large beetroot (beet), peeled and grated
2 hard-boiled eggs, grated
2 tablespoons finely chopped parsley
3 tablespoons extra virgin olive oil
sourdough or crispbread, to serve

Put the tomato, onion, cucumber, capers and vinegar in a bowl and toss together.

Arrange the prosciutto over a round serving platter and pile the grated beetroot in the middle. Spoon the tomato salad over the beetroot, then top with the grated egg. Sprinkle with the parsley, season with freshly ground black pepper and drizzle with the olive oil. Serve with thin slices of sourdough or crispbread. Serves 4 as a starter

seasonal ideas

- Make a salad of roasted beetroot (beets) and pumpkin (winter squash). Scatter with rocket (arugula) leaves and drizzle with a walnut oil dressing (Favourites).

- Toss warm green lentils and diced roasted beetroot (beets) together with some thinly sliced red onion and parsley. Serve with grilled sausages.

- Combine roughly chopped roasted beetroot (beets) with watercress sprigs and horseradish cream (Favourites). Serve with pan-fried beef.

- Finely chop roasted beetroot (beets) and scatter over a bed of rocket (arugula) leaves. Top with finely chopped fresh walnuts and a spoonful of creamed goat's cheese.

opposite: bread salad with fried sardines
over: trout salad, and prosciutto and beetroot salad

A platter of great flavours to gather around
and share with friends

lentil and beetroot salad

4 beetroot (beets) (about 150 g/5¹/₂ oz each), scrubbed
100 g (3¹/₂ oz/¹/₂ cup) puy lentils or tiny blue-green lentils
¹/₂ teaspoon sea salt
1 teaspoon balsamic vinegar
1 tablespoon extra virgin olive oil
juice of 1 orange
100 g (3¹/₂ oz/2¹/₃ cups) baby rocket (arugula) leaves
100 g (3¹/₂ oz) marinated goat's cheese

Preheat the oven to 200°C (400°F/Gas 6). Put the beetroot in a roasting tin and pour in 250 ml (9 fl oz/1 cup) water. Cover with foil and bake for 1 hour, or until a knife passes easily through the beetroot. Remove the beetroot from the roasting tin and leave to cool.

Meanwhile, put the lentils in a saucepan with 500 ml (17 fl oz/ 2 cups) water. Add the sea salt and bring to the boil, then reduce the heat and simmer for 20–30 minutes, or until the lentils are tender. Drain off any excess water, tip the lentils into a bowl and stir in the vinegar and olive oil.

Wearing rubber gloves to stop your hands staining, peel the skins from the beetroot — they should slip free quite easily. Cut the bulbs into wedges, put them in a bowl and pour the orange juice over the top.

Scatter the rocket on a serving platter and sit the beetroot wedges on top. Spoon the lentils over the salad, season with sea salt and freshly ground black pepper and drizzle with any remaining orange and beetroot juice. Crumble the goat's cheese over the top. Serves 4 as a starter or side dish

beetroot and buffalo mozzarella salad

750 g (1 lb 10 oz/about 16) baby beetroot (beets)
500 ml (17 fl oz/2 cups) vegetable stock (Favourites)
1 fresh thyme sprig
2 buffalo mozzarella cheeses
a handful of baby rocket (arugula) leaves
60 g (2¹/₄ oz/¹/₂ cup) sliced semi-dried (sun-blushed) tomatoes
1 tablespoon finely chopped parsley
extra virgin olive oil, to serve

Wearing rubber gloves to prevent your hands staining, peel the beetroot and place them in a saucepan. Pour in the stock and add the thyme sprig. Bring to the boil over high heat, then reduce the heat and simmer for 30 minutes. Remove from the heat and leave to cool slightly.

Thickly slice the mozzarella and divide among four plates. Top with a layer of rocket leaves. Cut half the warm beetroot into halves or quarters, then arrange all the beetroot over the rocket and scatter with the semi-dried tomato. Sprinkle with parsley, spoon a little of the beetroot poaching liquid over the top and drizzle with extra virgin olive oil. Serves 4 as a starter

minestrone

150 g (5¹/₂ oz/³/₄ cup) dried cannellini beans
2 tablespoons butter
100 g (3¹/₂ oz) pancetta, finely chopped
2 red onions, finely chopped
2 carrots, peeled and grated
2 celery stalks, finely sliced
3 large ripe tomatoes, roughly chopped
1 litre (35 fl oz/4 cups) chicken or vegetable stock (Favourites)
1 bay leaf
1 rosemary sprig
2 zucchini (courgettes), diced
100 g (3¹/₂ oz) green beans, trimmed and cut into
    2 cm (³/₄ inch) lengths
60 g (2¹/₄ oz/¹/₃ cup) risoni
2 tablespoons tomato paste (concentrated purée)
pesto (Favourites), to serve (optional)

Soak the dried cannellini beans overnight in plenty of water.

Melt the butter in a large saucepan over medium heat. Drain the cannellini beans and add them to the pan with the pancetta. Cook for 1 minute, then add the onion, carrot and celery. Sauté for 5 minutes, or until the onion is soft and transparent, then add the tomato, stock, bay leaf, rosemary sprig and 500 ml (17 fl oz/2 cups) water. Bring to the boil, then reduce the heat and gently simmer for 40 minutes, or until the cannellini beans are tender.

Add the zucchini, green beans, risoni and tomato paste and cook for a further 30 minutes, stirring frequently, until the risoni is al dente. Remove the bay leaf and rosemary sprig. Season to taste with sea salt and freshly ground black pepper and ladle into warmed deep bowls. Serve with a small bowl of pesto for stirring through, if desired. Serves 4–6

opposite: lentil and beetroot salad
over: beetroot and buffalo mozzarella salad, and minestrone

one-pot cooking

There's really something quite wonderful about throwing lots of ingredients into a pot, letting a little bit of slow cooking do the hard work and then lifting the lid and releasing all the wonderful aromas.

comforting chicken stew

Put 2 tablespoons plain (all-purpose) flour and 2 teaspoons sea salt in a bowl. Add 4 chicken leg quarters and toss to coat. Peel 1 carrot, 1 turnip, 1 parsnip and 4 boiling potatoes and cut into chunks. Toss in a large bowl with 2 sliced celery stalks and 1 sliced leek. Arrange half the vegetables in a large baking dish. Add the floured chicken, then the remaining vegetables. Pour in 500 ml (17 fl oz/2 cups) chicken stock (Favourites), then cover and bake in a moderate oven for 1 hour 20 minutes. Serve sprinkled with finely chopped parsley. Serves 4

lamb and quince tagine

Trim a 700 g (1 lb 9 oz) piece of boned lamb shoulder, cut it into bite-sized pieces and place in a large heavy-based saucepan. Add 8 peeled pickling onions, 1 crushed garlic clove, 1 cinnamon stick, 15 saffron threads, 1 teaspoon finely grated fresh ginger, 6 chopped dried apricots and 2 tablespoons butter. Toss together over medium heat, then pour in 600 ml (21 fl oz) water. Bring to the boil, reduce the heat, then cover and simmer for 1 hour. Peel and core 2 quinces and cut them into eighths. Add them to the tagine along with 1 teaspoon sea salt — you may also need to add a little more liquid at this point. Simmer for a further 30 minutes, then sprinkle with chopped coriander (cilantro) and toasted almond flakes. Serve with buttery couscous. Serves 4

spicy beef stew

Put a large heavy-based saucepan over medium heat. Add
2 tablespoons olive oil, 1 teaspoon ground cumin, 1 teaspoon
ground coriander, 1 teaspoon finely grated fresh ginger,
1/2 teaspoon ground cinnamon, 1/2 teaspoon red chilli flakes,
1/2 teaspoon ground turmeric and 4 finely sliced spring onions
(scallions). Stir until the spices are aromatic, then add 1 kg
(2 lb 4 oz) stewing beef that has been trimmed and cut into
chunks. Cook for several minutes, stirring to sear the beef on
all sides. Add 500 ml (17 fl oz/2 cups) water, then cover and
simmer over low heat for 40 minutes. Peel and thickly chop
2 carrots and 6 boiling potatoes and add to the stew. Cook
for 15 minutes, then add 200 g (7 oz) small trimmed green
beans and cook for a further 5 minutes. Serves 4–6

potato, capsicum and zucchini curry

Heat 3 tablespoons olive oil in a large heavy-based saucepan.
Add 2 crushed garlic cloves, 1 teaspoon ground turmeric,
1 teaspoon grated fresh ginger, 1 teaspoon fennel seeds,
2 large seeded and finely chopped red chillies and 2 roughly
chopped red onions. Sauté over medium heat for 5 minutes,
or until the onion is soft, then add 500 g (1 lb 2 oz) peeled and
sliced small boiling potatoes, 1 sliced red capsicum (pepper),
5 makrut (kaffir lime) leaves and 400 ml (14 fl oz) coconut milk.
Cover and simmer over low heat for 15 minutes. Add 500 g
(1 lb 2 oz) sliced zucchini (courgettes) and cook for a further
5 minutes. When ready to serve, add 4 tablespoons lime juice
and 2 tablespoons fish sauce and stir in a few handfuls of
coriander (cilantro) leaves. Serves 4

goat's cheese tart

300 g (10 1/2 oz) soft goat's cheese
3 eggs
5 egg yolks
375 ml (13 fl oz/1 1/2 cups) pouring (whipping) cream
25 cm (10 inch) pre-baked shortcrust pastry case (Favourites)
mixed leaf salad with walnut oil dressing (Favourites), to serve

Preheat the oven to 180°C (350°F/Gas 4). In a food processor, blend the goat's cheese, eggs and egg yolks to a smooth purée. Transfer to a bowl, then fold in the cream. Season with sea salt and some freshly ground black pepper.

Put the pastry case on a baking tray, then pour in the goat's cheese filling. Bake for 30 minutes, or until the top of the tart is lightly golden and the filling is firm. Remove from the oven and allow to cool a little.

When the tart is just warm, serve with a mixed leaf salad. Serves 8 as a starter or light meal

fish stew

3 tablespoons olive oil
500 g (1 lb 2 oz) snapper fillets, cut into 5 cm (2 inch) pieces
500 g (1 lb 2 oz) ling fillets, cut into 5 cm (2 inch) pieces
a pinch of saffron threads
2 spring onions (scallions), finely sliced
250 ml (9 fl oz/1 cup) dry white wine
1 litre (35 fl oz/4 cups) fish stock (Favourites)
2 celery stalks, finely sliced
400 g (14 oz) tin chopped tomatoes
100 g (3 1/2 oz/1/2 cup) long grain white rice
1 teaspoon dried oregano
1 bay leaf
a handful of parsley, roughly chopped
juice of 1 lemon
creamy mashed potato (Favourites), to serve (optional)

Heat the oil in a large heavy-based saucepan over medium heat. Working in batches, add the fish pieces and lightly cook them on all sides, removing the fish as it becomes opaque. Set aside.

Add the saffron and spring onion to the hot saucepan, stir once or twice in the warm oil, then stir in the wine. Allow to simmer for a minute before adding the stock, celery, tomato, rice, oregano and bay leaf. Bring to the boil, then reduce the heat and simmer for 20 minutes, or until the rice is cooked.

Just before serving, remove the bay leaf, then return the fish to the pan and add the parsley. Stir in the lemon juice and season to taste with sea salt and freshly ground black pepper. Serve on its own, or with creamy mashed potato. Serves 4–6

rice with tomatoes and spinach

1 tablespoon butter
500 g (1 lb 2 oz/1 large bunch) English spinach, washed, drained and finely chopped
400 g (14 oz/2 cups) basmati rice
3 tablespoons light olive oil
1/2 teaspoon ground turmeric
1 teaspoon ground cumin
1 red onion, finely sliced
2 vine-ripened tomatoes, finely chopped
750 ml (26 fl oz/3 cups) vegetable stock (Favourites)
plain yoghurt, to serve

Melt the butter in a frying pan over medium heat. Add the spinach, then cover and cook until the spinach is dark green and softly wilted. Remove from the heat and set aside. Wash the rice several times until the water runs clear.

In a large saucepan, heat the olive oil over medium heat and add the turmeric, cumin and onion. Sauté for 5–7 minutes, or until the onion is golden and slightly caramelized. Add the rice and stir together for 1 minute.

Squeeze any excess moisture from the spinach, then add it to the rice with the tomato and stock. Stir once, then bring to the boil. Cover, turn the heat down to the lowest setting, and cook for 25 minutes.

Serve topped with a dollop of yoghurt. Wonderful with chargrilled chicken or fish. Serves 6 as a side dish

opposite: goat's cheese tart
over: fish stew, and rice with tomatoes and spinach

snapper with lemony leeks and potatoes

3 boiling potatoes, such as long white, pink eye or
    kipfler (fingerling), peeled and finely sliced
juice of 1 lemon
250 ml (9 fl oz/1 cup) fish stock (Favourites)
2 leeks, white part only, rinsed and cut into 5 mm
    (1/4 inch) rounds
2 tablespoons butter
1 tablespoon salted capers, rinsed and drained
4 x 200 g (7 oz) snapper fillets
1 tablespoon light olive oil
a handful of flat-leaf (Italian) parsley, roughly chopped

Preheat the oven to 180°C (350°F/Gas 4). Arrange the potato
slices in a deep-sided baking dish, then pour the lemon juice
and stock over. Arrange the leek over the top, add the butter
in dabs and scatter with the capers. Season with a little
ground white pepper, cover with foil and bake for 50 minutes,
or until the leek and potato are soft and cooked through.

Rinse the snapper fillets and pat dry with paper towels.
Sprinkle with sea salt.

Heat the olive oil in a frying pan over high heat and add the
snapper, skin side down. Fry for several minutes until the
skin is lightly browned underneath, then flip the fish over and
cook the other side for 1 minute. Put the fish on a baking tray
and bake for 8 minutes. Remove from the oven and cover
loosely with foil.

Divide the baked leek and potato among four warmed plates.
Top with the snapper fillets, then spoon some of the cooking
juices over the top and scatter with the parsley. Serves 4

soupy mussels

1 kg (2 lb 4 oz) mussels
1 tablespoon butter
2 onions, diced
a pinch of saffron threads
400 g (14 oz) tin chopped tomatoes
4 tablespoons shaoxing rice wine
finely grated zest of 1 lemon
100 g (31/2 oz/1/2 cup) basmati rice
lemon wedges, to serve

Clean the mussels in the sink under cold running water,
scrubbing them to remove any barnacles or bits of hairy
'beard'. Throw away any broken mussels, or any open ones
that don't close when you tap them.

Melt the butter in a large saucepan over medium heat. Add the
onion and saffron and sauté for 5 minutes, or until the onion
is soft and transparent. Add the tomato, rice wine and lemon
zest and allow to simmer for a few minutes. Stir in 500 ml
(17 fl oz/2 cups) water and season to taste with sea salt.
Bring to the boil, stir in the rice, then cover and turn the heat
to low. Simmer for 20 minutes, or until the rice is just cooked.

Add the mussels and cover the pan. Turn the heat up and
stir the mussels occasionally. After a few minutes, check
that all the mussels have opened. If they haven't, toss them
once more and return to the heat for a further minute. After
that time, throw away any mussels that still haven't opened.
Ladle the mussels and soup into four warmed deep bowls.
Season with freshly ground black pepper and serve with
lemon wedges. Serves 4

blue-eye cod with fennel and tomato broth

1 small fennel bulb
1 tablespoon butter
1 small leek, white part only, rinsed and finely sliced
3 ripe tomatoes, finely chopped
1 litre (35 fl oz/4 cups) fish stock (Favourites)
2 tablespoons lemon juice
4 x 100 g (31/2 oz) blue-eye cod fillets
4 tablespoons aïoli (Favourites)
12 small basil leaves

Trim the fennel bulb, reserving the feathery fronds, then cut
the bulb in half and finely slice it.

Melt the butter in a large saucepan over medium heat,
add the leek and sauté for 5 minutes, or until soft. Add the
tomato, sliced fennel and stock. Bring to the boil, then reduce
the heat, cover and simmer for 15 minutes. Add the lemon
juice and blue-eye cod fillets and cover. Simmer for 7 minutes,
or until the fish is opaque and cooked through.

Lift the fish out with a spatula and divide among four warmed
pasta bowls. Ladle the broth over, top with a spoonful of aïoli,
then scatter with the fennel fronds and basil. Serves 4

opposite: snapper with lemony leeks and potatoes
over: soupy mussels, and blue-eye cod with
fennel and tomato broth

4 winter soups

jerusalem artichoke soup

1 tablespoon butter
2 onions, diced
500 g (1 lb 2 oz) Jerusalem artichokes, peeled and sliced
1 litre (35 fl oz/4 cups) chicken stock (Favourites)
100 g (3¹/2 oz) goat's curd
a generous pinch of ground nutmeg

Melt the butter in a saucepan. Add the onion and sauté over medium heat for 5 minutes, or until soft and transparent. Add the Jerusalem artichokes and stock and bring to the boil. Reduce the heat and simmer for 30 minutes, or until the artichoke is soft. Remove from the heat and allow to cool.

Purée the soup in a food processor or blender until smooth, then pour it back into the saucepan and gently reheat.

In a small bowl, mix together the goat's curd and nutmeg. Ladle the hot soup into four warmed bowls and add a spoonful of goat's curd to each. Sprinkle with freshly ground black pepper and nutmeg. Serves 4 as a starter

spiced carrot soup

2¹/2 tablespoons butter
1 red onion, diced
1 teaspoon ground cumin
3 tablespoons red lentils
500 g (1 lb 2 oz) carrots, peeled and finely chopped
1.5 litres (52 fl oz/6 cups) vegetable stock (Favourites)
ground cumin, extra, or thick (double/heavy) cream, to serve

Melt the butter in a saucepan over medium heat, then add the onion and cumin. Sauté for 5 minutes, or until the onion is soft and transparent. Add the lentils and carrot, then stir for a minute before pouring in the stock. Bring to the boil, then reduce the heat and slowly simmer for a further 40 minutes, or until the carrot is soft and beginning to fall apart.

Remove the pan from the heat and allow the soup to cool slightly. Transfer to a blender, a few ladlefuls at a time, and blend to a smooth purée. Pour the soup back into the saucepan and gently reheat. Season with sea salt and freshly ground black pepper and serve with a sprinkle of ground cumin or a dollop of cream. Serves 4 as a starter

chicken and corn soup

2 tablespoons butter
1 leek, white part only, rinsed and finely chopped
2 celery stalks, finely chopped
250 g (9 oz) chicken thigh meat, finely chopped
1 litre (35 fl oz/4 cups) chicken stock (favourites)
3 corn cobs, kernels removed
1 heaped tablespoon cornflour (cornstarch)
30 g (1 oz/1 bunch) chives, snipped

Heat a large saucepan over medium heat and add the butter and leek. Sauté for 5 minutes, or until the leek is soft and transparent. Reduce the heat to low and add the celery and chicken. Cover and allow to gently cook for 30 minutes.

Add the stock and corn kernels and bring to the boil. Cook for several minutes, or until the corn has turned golden yellow. Mix the cornflour with 4 tablespoons of water and pour it into the soup. Stir for several minutes, then remove from the heat. Ladle into four warmed bowls and sprinkle with the chives. Serves 4 as a starter

roast pumpkin and coconut soup

1 kg (2 lb 4 oz) jap or kent pumpkin, peeled and cut into chunks
2 tablespoons olive oil
1 garlic clove, finely sliced
2 leeks, rinsed and finely sliced
1 red chilli, seeded and finely chopped
500 ml (17 fl oz/2 cups) vegetable stock (Favourites)
200 ml (7 fl oz) coconut milk
a handful of coriander (cilantro) leaves

Preheat the oven to 180°C (350°F/Gas 4). Spread the pumpkin in a roasting tin and roast for 30 minutes, or until tender and golden brown.

Put the olive oil in a large saucepan over medium heat. Add the garlic and leek and sauté for 5 minutes, or until the leek is soft and transparent. Add the pumpkin, chilli and stock and simmer for 10 minutes. Remove from the heat and allow to cool slightly.

Transfer the soup to a blender and purée until smooth. Pour the soup into a clean saucepan and stir in the coconut milk. Gently reheat the soup, then ladle into four warmed bowls and scatter with coriander. Serves 4 as a starter

saffron, tomato and chicken risotto

1 litre (35 fl oz/4 cups) chicken stock (Favourites)
a generous pinch of saffron threads
2 tablespoons butter
2 garlic cloves, finely chopped
1 leek, white part only, rinsed and finely sliced
330 g (12 oz/1 1/2 cups) risotto rice
125 ml (4 fl oz/1/2 cup) white wine
300 g (10 1/2 oz) chicken thigh meat, diced
3 ripe roma (plum) tomatoes, diced
1 tablespoon finely grated lemon zest
4 tablespoons grated parmesan cheese
baby rocket (arugula) leaves, to serve
extra virgin olive oil, to serve

Bring the stock to the boil in a saucepan, then reduce the heat and keep at a low simmer. Put the saffron threads in a cup and cover with 125 ml (4 fl oz/1/2 cup) hot water.

Heat a large saucepan over medium heat. Add the butter, garlic and leek and sauté for 5 minutes, or until the leek is soft. Add the rice and stir for 1 minute, or until the rice is well coated and the grains are glossy. Stir once more, then add the wine.

Ladle 250 ml (9 fl oz/1 cup) of the hot stock into the pan and simmer, stirring occasionally until it has been completely absorbed. Add another 250 ml (9 fl oz/1 cup) stock, along with the chicken, tomato and saffron liquid. Stir for several minutes, until the stock is completely absorbed, then add another 250 ml (9 fl oz/1 cup) stock. Cook, stirring occasionally, until all the liquid has been absorbed, then test the rice to see if it is *al dente*. If it needs more cooking, stir in the remaining stock.

Fold the lemon zest and half the parmesan through the risotto. Spoon into tour warmed pasta bowls and sprinkle with the remaining parmesan. Scatter with a few rocket leaves and drizzle with a little olive oil. Serves 4

lemon risotto with seared prawns

1 litre (35 fl oz/4 cups) fish or vegetable stock (Favourites)
2 tablespoons butter
2 garlic cloves, finely chopped
2 leeks, white part only, rinsed and finely sliced
finely grated zest and juice of 1 lemon
330 g (12 oz/1 1/2 cups) risotto rice
4 tablespoons grated parmesan cheese
16 raw king prawns (shrimp), peeled and deveined, tails intact
extra virgin olive oil, to serve
flat-leaf (Italian) parsley, to serve

Bring the stock to the boil in a saucepan, then reduce the heat and keep at a low simmer.

Melt the butter in a large saucepan over medium heat. Add the garlic and leek and sauté for 5 minutes, or until the leek is soft and transparent. Add the lemon zest and rice and stir for 1 minute, or until the rice is well coated and the grains are glossy.

Ladle 250 ml (9 fl oz/1 cup) of the hot stock into the pan and simmer, stirring occasionally, until it has been completely absorbed. Add another 250 ml (9 fl oz/1 cup) stock and cook, stirring, for a further few minutes until the stock has been completely absorbed. Add another 250 ml (9 fl oz/1 cup) stock and cook, stirring occasionally, until all the liquid has been absorbed, then test the rice to see if it is *al dente*. If it needs more cooking, stir in the remaining stock. Lightly fold the parmesan and half the lemon juice through the risotto. Remove the pan from the heat while you cook the prawns.

Quickly heat a large frying pan over high heat and sear the prawns on both sides for a few minutes, until they turn pink and begin to curl up. Pour the remaining lemon juice over the prawns, then remove from the heat. Spoon the risotto into four warmed pasta bowls and top with the prawns. Serve with a drizzle of olive oil and a scattering of parsley. Serves 4

tagine of chicken, tomato and artichoke

3 tablespoons olive oil
2 red onions, finely sliced
2 garlic cloves, finely chopped
1 tablespoon finely grated fresh ginger
1 kg (2 lb 4 oz) chicken pieces, trimmed of fat
1 cinnamon stick
2 dried limes or 1 teaspoon finely chopped preserved lemon rind
juice of 1 lemon
400 g (14 oz) tin peeled tomatoes
4 bottled artichokes, drained
12 large green olives
steamed couscous (Favourites), to serve
a handful of flat-leaf (Italian) parsley, chopped

Heat the olive oil in a large heavy-based saucepan. Add the onion and sauté for 5 minutes, or until soft and transparent, then add the garlic and ginger. Cook for several minutes, then add the chicken, cinnamon stick, limes, lemon juice and tomato. Season with sea salt, cover with 250 ml (4 fl oz/1 cup) water and simmer, uncovered, for 30 minutes.

Add the artichokes and olives and cook for a further 10 minutes. Serve on a bed of steamed couscous, sprinkled with parsley. Serves 4

opposite: saffron, tomato and chicken risotto
over: lemon risotto with seared prawns, and
tagine of chicken, tomato and artichoke

roast tomato, salami and asparagus orzo

6 roma (plum) tomatoes
12 slices of salami, torn in half
350 g (12 oz/2 bunches) asparagus, trimmed
2 tablespoons olive oil
400 g (14 oz) orzo or risoni
70 g (2¹/₂ oz/³/₄ cup) shaved parmesan cheese
10 basil leaves, roughly torn
4 tablespoons extra virgin olive oil

Preheat the oven to 180°C (350°F/Gas 4). Line an ovenproof dish with baking paper, ensuring that the paper comes up the side of the dish.

Cut the tomatoes into quarters, place them in the baking dish and sprinkle with a little sea salt. Bake for 20 minutes, or until they are quite shrunken. Remove from the oven and cover each wedge of tomato with a slice of salami so that the oil from the salami will add fabulous flavour to the tomato.

Cut the asparagus spears in half crossways and add to the baking dish. Drizzle with the olive oil and bake for 10 minutes.

Bring a large pot of salted water to the boil and add the orzo. Cook until *al dente*, then drain and return to the warm pan. Add the tomato, salami, asparagus and the juices from the baking dish. Season with a little sea salt and freshly ground black pepper and gently toss to combine.

Pile into a serving dish, add the shaved parmesan and basil and drizzle with the extra virgin olive oil. Serves 4

seared beef with tomato butter

100 g (3¹/₂ oz) butter
50 g (1³/₄ oz/¹/₃ cup) semi-dried (sun-blushed) tomatoes
1 tablespoon finely chopped fresh tarragon
3 teaspoons wasabi paste
4 x 200 g (7 oz) sirloin steaks
steamed green beans, to serve

Put the butter, tomatoes, tarragon and wasabi paste in a food processor or blender and purée to a thick, chunky paste. Spoon onto a length of baking paper and roll up to form a log. Refrigerate until ready to use.

Heat a chargrill plate over medium–high heat and sear the steaks until the surface looks slightly bloody. Turn the steaks over and cook for 1 minute. Transfer to a warm plate, cover loosely with foil and allow to rest for a few minutes.

Serve with the tomato butter and steamed green beans. Serves 4

lamb shank and vegetable casserole

80 g (2³/₄ oz/²/₃ cup) plain (all-purpose) flour
4 lamb shanks (about 1.25 kg/2 lb 12 oz in total)
160 ml (5¹/₄ fl oz) olive oil
2 leeks, white part only, rinsed and sliced into rounds
2 garlic cloves, crushed
1 teaspoon rosemary
250 ml (9 fl oz/1 cup) dry sherry
400 g (14 oz) tin chopped tomatoes
2 carrots, peeled and sliced
500 ml (17 fl oz/2 cups) veal stock (Favourites)
4 desiree or other all-purpose potatoes, peeled and cut into chunks
gremolata (Favourites), to serve

Preheat the oven to 200°C (400°F/Gas 6). Put the flour in a plastic bag, add the lamb shanks and toss until well coated. Heat half the olive oil in a large heavy-based frying pan and add the lamb shanks. Cook, in batches if necessary, until the shanks are browned on all sides. Transfer to a casserole dish and wipe the frying pan clean with paper towels.

Add the remaining oil to the frying pan and sauté the leek, garlic and rosemary for 4 minutes, or until the leek is starting to soften. Add the sherry and cook for a few minutes before adding the tomato and carrot. Stir for 1 minute, then pour the sauce over the shanks. Add the stock and season with sea salt and freshly ground black pepper. Cover and bake for 1 hour.

Remove the casserole dish from the oven and turn the shanks around in the sauce. Add the potato, then cover and bake for a further 1 hour, or until the meat is tender and falling off the bone. Serve sprinkled with a little gremolata. Serves 4

opposite: roast tomato, salami and asparagus orzo
over: seared beef with tomato butter, and
lamb shank and vegetable casserole

Melt-in-the-mouth lamb shanks flavoured with herbs and winter vegetables

potatoes

I do love the humble spud. In the winter months there is nothing more comforting than potatoes, be they mashed, boiled, roasted or fried. Through the centuries, various regions have developed their own speciality dishes, from Italian gnocchi to Indian spiced potatoes, hefty Spanish omelettes, creamy French gratins, vinegary English chips and huge baked potatoes drowning in sour cream and cheese. Which only goes to prove that the potato is not so humble and is definitely our most popular vegetable.

- Toss warm boiled potatoes in a bowl with olive oil, sliced spring onions (scallions) and finely chopped mint and chives. Serve as a warm potato salad.

- Make a quick warm salad of rocket (arugula), boiled potatoes, Italian-style tinned tuna and mayonnaise.

- Toss boiled potatoes in a bowl with a handful of roughly chopped parsley and snipped chives. Season with sea salt and freshly ground black pepper and add lots of butter or olive oil. Smash the potatoes into roughly broken chunks and spoon into a warm serving bowl.

- Pan-fry onions and bacon in lots of butter and add some smashed boiled potatoes. Add finely chopped celery and chopped parsley. Makes a perfect TV dinner, especially when topped with sour cream!

- For a classic dish that always wins hearts, serve potato gratin (Favourites) with pan-seared steak and steamed green beans.

While some would argue that a roast potato (Favourites) needs no embellishment, try some of these classic flavours whenever you feel like a change.
- Toss potatoes in rosemary, whole garlic cloves and sea salt before roasting.
- Add some lemon juice to the basting oil and some slices of fresh lemon.
- Large green olives bring a wonderful flavour to roast potatoes, and the colours also work beautifully together.

For a Mediterranean twist add some roughly chopped tomato and fresh oregano prior to baking.
- If you like potatoes with a bit of spice, toss them in oil flavoured with a little ground cumin and paprika before roasting them.

Add a boost of flavour to simple baked potatoes (Favourites) with these serving ideas.
- Sour cream, grated gruyère cheese and fried prosciutto.
- Sour cream, smoked salmon and a scatter of capers.
- Grated cheddar cheese, oven-dried tomatoes and basil.
- Hummus, rocket (arugula) and tomato salad.
- Grated mozzarella cheese, tabouleh and chilli sauce.

chicken and vegetable pot roast

1.5 kg (3 lb 5 oz) whole organic chicken
1¹/2 tablespoons butter, softened
4 slices of prosciutto
2 onions, cut into eighths
2 large carrots, peeled and cut into chunks
1 celery stalk, cut into 2 cm (³/4 inch) lengths
1 turnip, peeled and cut into chunks
2 leeks, white part only, rinsed and sliced into 2 cm (³/4 inch)
    rounds
3 all-purpose potatoes, peeled and cut into chunks
1 rosemary sprig
250 ml (9 fl oz/1 cup) dry white wine
250 ml (9 fl oz/1 cup) chicken stock (Favourites)
a handful of flat-leaf (Italian) parsley, roughly chopped

Preheat the oven to 180°C (350°F/Gas 4). Sit the chicken in a 3 litre (104 fl oz/12 cup) casserole dish. Rub the butter over the breast of the chicken, then cover with the prosciutto slices. Arrange the vegetables and rosemary around the chicken, then pour the wine and stock over. Season well with sea salt and freshly ground black pepper. Cover and bake for 1 hour.

Remove the casserole dish from the oven and gently move the vegetables around. Using a large spoon, pour some of the juices over the chicken. Leave the lid off and roast for a further 30 minutes, or until the chicken is golden brown.

Place the chicken on a warm serving platter and arrange the vegetables around. Scatter with the parsley and drizzle with the sauces from the casserole dish. Serves 4–6

veal roll

500 g (1 lb 2 oz/1 large bunch) English spinach,
    washed and trimmed
8 slices of prosciutto
4 tablespoons green olive paste
2 x 270 g (9¹/2 oz) veal fillets
1 tablespoon olive oil
250 ml (9 fl oz/1 cup) veal stock (Favourites)
3 tablespoons butter
creamy polenta, to serve (Favourites)

Preheat the oven to 180°C (350°F/Gas 4).

Put the spinach in a saucepan, then cover and cook over low heat for a few minutes, or until the spinach has wilted. Drain the spinach in a colander and allow to cool. Squeeze to remove any excess liquid.

Lay a piece of plastic wrap on a work surface. Place four prosciutto slices on the plastic wrap, then cover with half the spinach. Rub 2 tablespoons of the olive paste over one of the veal fillets, then sit the fillet on the spinach and carefully roll it up in the prosciutto to make a neat parcel. (You can tie the roll up with kitchen string if needed.) Repeat with the remaining prosciutto, olive paste and veal fillet.

Heat the olive oil in a large non-stick frying pan and sear the veal rolls over high heat until golden brown all over. Place in a roasting tray and bake for 20 minutes. Remove from the oven, cover with foil and leave to rest in a warm place for 10 minutes.

Meanwhile, pour the stock into a saucepan and bring to the boil. Allow the stock to bubble away for 3 minutes, then reduce the heat to a simmer. Swirl the butter into the stock until it has melted, then remove from the heat.

Cut the veal rolls into several slices, and spoon the warm stock over. Serve with creamy polenta. Serves 4

honey roast chicken with couscous salad

1.8 kg (4 lb) whole organic chicken
35 g (1¹/4 oz/1 bunch) rosemary
1 lemon, cut into quarters
1 onion, cut into quarters
3 tablespoons butter, softened
90 g (3¹/4 oz/¹/4 cup) honey
185 g (6¹/2 oz/1 cup) couscous
1 tablespoon finely chopped lime pickle
a handful of flat-leaf (Italian) parsley, roughly chopped
a handful of coriander (cilantro) leaves, roughly chopped
2 tablespoons currants

Preheat the oven to 200°C (400°F/Gas 6). Rinse the chicken and pat dry with paper towels. Scatter some of the rosemary into a roasting tin, then generously rub the chicken skin with sea salt and sit it on top of the rosemary, breast side up.

Put the lemon, onion and some of the rosemary into the cavity of the chicken, then rub 2 tablespoons of the butter over the breast. Roast for 1 hour, then drizzle the honey over the chicken and roast for a further 20 minutes. To check that the chicken is cooked, pull a leg away from the body — the juices that run out should be clear. Remove from the oven, cover loosely with foil and allow to rest for 10 minutes before carving.

Meanwhile, put the couscous in a bowl with the remaining butter and pour 250 ml (9 fl oz/1 cup) boiling water over the top. Cover and allow to sit for 5 minutes, then fluff up the grains with a fork. Cover again and leave for a further 5 minutes. Rub the grains with your fingertips to remove any lumps, then stir the lime pickle, parsley, coriander and currants through.

Serve the carved chicken with the couscous and a spoonful of the roasting juices. Serves 4

opposite: chicken and vegetable pot roast
over: veal roll, and honey roast chicken with couscous salad

veal cutlets

6 anchovy fillets
2 egg yolks
juice of 1 lemon
3 tablespoons olive oil
185 g (6^1/$_2$ oz) tin tuna, drained
1 tablespoon small salted capers, rinsed, drained and chopped
4 frenched veal cutlets (French-trimmed rib chops)
500 g (1 lb 2 oz/1 bunch) English spinach, washed and trimmed
flat-leaf (Italian) parsley, to serve
lemon wedges, to serve

Preheat the oven to 180°C (350°F/Gas 4).

Put the anchovies, egg yolks, lemon juice, olive oil and tuna in a food processor or blender and purée to a thick sauce. Season with sea salt and freshly ground black pepper and stir in the capers.

Heat a large non-stick frying pan over high heat. Add the veal cutlets and sear for 2 minutes, then turn and sear for 1 minute. Place the cutlets on a baking tray and bake for 8–10 minutes. Remove from the oven, then cover loosely with foil and allow to rest for 5 minutes.

Meanwhile, put the spinach in the warm frying pan, then cover and cook over medium heat for 2 minutes, or until the spinach has turned emerald green.

Serve the cutlets scattered with parsley, with the spinach, a lemon wedge and anchovy mayonnaise on the side. Serves 4

pepper steaks with creamy mash

40 g (1^1/$_2$ oz) butter
2 garlic cloves, crushed
10 French shallots, cut in half
1 tablespoon green peppercorns
300 ml (10^1/$_2$ fl oz) veal stock (Favourites)
1 tablespoon olive oil
4 x 200 g (7 oz) fillet steaks
creamy mashed potato (Favourites) to serve

Heat the butter in a small saucepan. As it starts to froth, add the garlic, shallots and green peppercorns. Sauté over low heat for 10 minutes, or until the shallots are soft and turning lightly golden. Add the stock and keep at a low simmer.

Heat a non-stick frying pan over high heat. Rub the olive oil over the beef fillets and sear for 3 minutes, or until the surface looks slightly bloody. Turn the steaks over, reduce the heat and cook for a further 4–5 minutes. Transfer to a warm plate, cover loosely with foil and allow to rest for a few minutes.

Serve the steaks on a bed of creamy mashed potato and spoon the warm peppercorn sauce over the top. Serves 4

velvet pork belly

800 g (1 lb 12 oz) piece of pork belly
500 ml (17 fl oz/2 cups) chicken stock (Favourites)
250 ml (9 fl oz/1 cup) soy sauce
2 red chillies, cut in half and seeded
1 cinnamon stick
4 star anise
1 tablespoon finely grated fresh ginger
2 garlic cloves, crushed
1^1/$_2$ teaspoons Chinese five-spice
1 tablespoon grated palm sugar (jaggery) or soft brown sugar
12 fresh shiitake mushrooms
2 tablespoons vegetable oil
100 g (3^1/$_2$ oz) oyster mushrooms, cut in half
100 g (3^1/$_2$ oz) enoki mushrooms, trimmed
steamed Chinese greens, to serve
steamed white rice (Favourites), to serve

Preheat the oven to 180°C (350°F/Gas 4). Put the pork belly in a large pot and cover with cold water. Bring the water to the boil, then remove the pork and rinse under fresh water.

Put the stock, soy sauce, chillies, cinnamon, star anise, ginger, garlic and ^{1}/$_2$ teaspoon of the five-spice in a 2 litre (70 fl oz/8 cup) casserole dish. Add the pork, skin side up, and rub the skin with the remaining five-spice. Add enough water to ensure that most of the pork is sitting in liquid but the skin is dry. Cover and bake for 4 hours.

Remove the pork, place on a large tray, cover and refrigerate overnight. Strain the liquid, reserving 250 ml (9 fl oz/1 cup).

Pour the reserved cooking liquid into a saucepan and add the sugar, shiitake mushrooms and 125 ml (4 fl oz/^{1}/$_2$ cup) water. Bring to the boil, then reduce the heat and allow the sauce to simmer gently for 10 minutes.

Meanwhile, slice the pork belly into 3 x 8 cm (1^1/$_4$ x 3^1/$_4$ inch) strips. Heat the vegetable oil in a large non-stick frying pan and fry the pork belly strips on both sides until crisp and browned.

Just before serving, add the oyster and enoki mushrooms to the simmering sauce. Sit two pork belly strips on each warmed serving plate, then spoon the mushrooms and sauce over. Serve with steamed Chinese greens and steamed white rice. Serves 4

opposite: veal cutlets
over: pepper steaks with creamy mash, and velvet pork belly

A wintery treat of creamy mash and peppery steak

4 roast vegies

creamy baked onions

12 small pickling onions, peeled and trimmed
300 ml (10 1/2 fl oz) pouring (whipping) cream
1 garlic clove, crushed
1 fresh bay leaf
2 tablespoons finely chopped parsley

Preheat the oven to 200°C (400°F/Gas 6). Put the onions in a large oval baking dish. Add the cream, garlic and bay leaf and season lightly with sea salt and ground white pepper.

Bake for 1 hour, then remove from the oven and sprinkle with the parsley. Serve with roast beef, roast chicken or grilled sausages. Serves 4 as a side dish

spiced pumpkin

1 kg (2 lb 4 oz) jap or kent pumpkin
1 teaspoon ground cumin
1 teaspoon paprika
2 tablespoons olive oil

Preheat the oven to 180°C (350°F/Gas 4). Line a roasting tin with baking paper.

Peel the pumpkin, cut the flesh into bite-sized chunks and remove any seeds. Put the pumpkin pieces in a large bowl with the remaining ingredients and a generous sprinkle of sea salt and freshly ground black pepper. Toss to ensure the pumpkin pieces are well coated with the oil and spices, then spread them in the roasting tin.

Bake for 40 minutes, turning the pumpkin occasionally. Serve with roasted pork or grilled lamb cutlets. Serves 4 as a side dish

rosemary potatoes

1.2 kg (2 lb 10 oz) roasting potatoes, such as desiree, kipfler (fingerling) or Dutch cream
375 ml (13 fl oz/1 1/2 cups) chicken stock (Favourites) or water
1 1/2 tablespoons butter
1 tablespoon fresh rosemary

Preheat the oven to 200°C (400°F/Gas 6).

Peel the potatoes and cut them into quarters. Pour the stock into a roasting tin and add the potatoes. Dab the butter over the potatoes, then scatter with the rosemary and season with sea salt.

Bake for 30 minutes, then turn the potatoes over and bake for a further 30–35 minutes, or until golden and cooked through. Serves 4 as a side dish

tomato and eggplant bake

2 eggplants (aubergines)
4 tablespoons olive oil
1 teaspoon dried oregano
400 g (14 oz) tin chopped tomatoes
1 tablespoon pomegranate molasses (optional)
1 tablespoon soft brown sugar
12 cherry bocconcini (fresh baby mozzarella cheese)
a handful of basil

Preheat the oven to 180°C (350°F/Gas 4).

Slice the eggplants into thick rounds, cut the rounds into thick batons and put them in a bowl. Add the olive oil and oregano and season with sea salt and freshly ground black pepper. Toss several times to ensure the eggplant is well coated in the oil, then arrange in a large baking dish.

Bake for 20 minutes, then add the tomato, molasses and sugar. Toss to coat the eggplant in the tomato, then arrange the bocconcini over the top. Bake for a further 40 minutes.

Scatter with basil and serve with grilled sausages, veal cutlets or baked lamb. Serves 6 as a side dish

opposite: spiced pumpkin

corned beef with white sauce

1.5 kg (3 lb 5 oz) corned beef (silverside)
3 tablespoons soft brown sugar
2 fresh bay leaves
1 star anise
2 cloves
6 black peppercorns
2 tablespoons red wine vinegar
2 tablespoons port
8 baby carrots
8 baby onions or 4 onions
4 large cauliflower florets

white sauce
2 tablespoons butter
1 onion, finely diced
2 tablespoons plain (all-purpose) flour
500 ml (17 fl oz/2 cups) milk
1 teaspoon salted capers, rinsed and drained
2 tablespoons finely chopped parsley
1/4 teaspoon ground white pepper

Sit the corned beef in a large pot and add the sugar, bay leaves, star anise, cloves, peppercorns, vinegar and port. Fill the pot with water and place over high heat. Bring to the boil, reduce the heat and simmer for 2 1/2 hours, skimming off any debris and topping up with water to keep the meat fully submerged.

Trim and scrape the carrots. Remove the skin of the onions without trimming off the top and bottom. If you are using baby onions, leave them intact; if you are using large onions, slice them in half down the middle. Add the vegetables to the pot, then cover and allow to slowly simmer for 30 minutes.

Meanwhile, make the white sauce. Put the butter and onion in a saucepan and sauté over medium heat for 5 minutes, or until the onion is soft and lightly golden. Add the flour and cook for several minutes, stirring often, until the flour turns into a smooth paste that coats the onion. Add the milk a little at a time, working it into the flour, then continue to cook, stirring continuously, for 2–3 minutes, or until the sauce begins to thicken. Add the capers, parsley and white pepper and stir for a further minute before removing from the heat.

To serve, remove the vegetables from the pan with tongs and divide among four warmed plates. Remove the beef to a clean cutting board and slice thickly. Divide the slices among the plates and spoon over a little of the cooking liquid and several spoonfuls of white sauce. Serves 4

spiced lentils with lamb cutlets

2 tablespoons olive oil
2 garlic cloves, crushed
1 red onion, finely diced
1 teaspoon finely chopped tinned chipotle chilli
1 teaspoon ground turmeric
100 g (3 1/2 oz/1/2 cup) puy or tiny blue-green lentils
400 g (14 oz) tin chopped tomatoes
12 small frenched lamb cutlets (French-trimmed rib chops)
a handful of coriander (cilantro) leaves

Put the olive oil in a saucepan over medium heat. Add the garlic, onion, chilli and turmeric and sauté for 5 minutes, or until the onion is soft and transparent. Add the lentils and cook for 1 minute, stirring well. Stir in the tomato and 500 ml (17 fl oz/2 cups) water, then cover and simmer for 40 minutes, or until the lentils are tender. Season to taste with sea salt and freshly ground black pepper. Keep warm.

Heat a large non-stick frying pan over high heat. Add the lamb cutlets and sear until the surface looks slightly bloody. Turn the cutlets over and cook for 1–2 minutes. Transfer to a warm plate, cover loosely with foil and rest for a few minutes.

Spoon the lentils onto four warmed serving plates. Top with the cutlets and scatter with coriander. Serves 4

quince-glazed duck breast

4 boneless duck breasts, skin on
4 teaspoons quince paste
1 fennel bulb, trimmed and finely shaved or sliced
2 handfuls of picked watercress
2 ruby grapefruit

Preheat the oven to 180°C (350°F/Gas 4). Score the duck skin in a crisscross pattern, then rub some sea salt into the skin. Heat a frying pan over high heat and sear the duck breasts, skin side down, until lightly browned.

Sit the duck breasts, skin side up, on a rack set over a baking tray. Put a teaspoon of quince paste on each duck breast and bake for 5 minutes. Take the tray out of the oven and spread the softened quince paste over the duck. Bake for a further 10 minutes.

Meanwhile, put the fennel and watercress in a bowl. Using a sharp knife, remove the skin and all the pith from the grapefruit. Holding the grapefruit over the salad, remove the grapefruit segments by cutting between the membranes, and add them to the salad with any captured grapefruit juice. Season lightly with sea salt and freshly ground black pepper, then toss and divide among four plates.

Thinly slice the duck breasts on the diagonal and arrange over the salad. Serves 4

opposite: corned beef with white sauce
over: spiced lentils with lamb cutlets, and
quince-glazed duck breast

beef in red wine

1 kg (2 lb 4 oz) stewing beef
1 tablespoon plain (all-purpose) flour
350 g (12 oz) pork belly
3 tablespoons olive oil
2 garlic cloves, finely chopped
1 leek, white part only, rinsed and finely diced
1 carrot, peeled and diced
2 celery stalks, finely sliced
400 g (14 oz) tin chopped tomatoes
500 ml (17 fl oz/2 cups) red wine
2 bay leaves
500 g (1 lb 2 oz) small French shallots or baby onions,
    peeled but left whole
creamy mashed potato (Favourites), to serve

Preheat the oven to 180°C (350°F/Gas 4). Trim the beef,
cut it into bite-sized pieces and place in a large bowl. Add
the flour and a grind of black pepper, then rub the pepper
and flour into the beef. Set aside.

Remove the rind from the pork belly and finely chop the rind
and the flesh. Heat a 3 litre (104 fl oz/12 cup) flameproof
casserole dish over high heat. Add the oil and fry the pork
for a few minutes, then add the garlic, leek, carrot and celery.
Reduce the heat to low and sauté for 10 minutes, or until the
leek is soft. Remove all the ingredients with a slotted spoon,
ensuring that most of the oil remains in the dish.

Increase the heat and add the beef (in batches if necessary)
and cook until browned all over. Return the pork and
vegetable mixture and all the beef to the dish. Add the tomato,
wine, bay leaves and shallots, stir once or twice, then cover
and bake for 1 1/2 hours. Season to taste with sea salt and
freshly ground black pepper. If after this time the mixture is
quite wet, remove the lid, otherwise keep the lid on. Cook for
a further 30 minutes until the stew has a rich, thick sauce.
Serve with creamy mashed potato. Serves 4

lemon chicken with tomato salad

2 tablespoons olive oil
4 chicken leg quarters
2 tablespoons dry sherry
3 tablespoons lemon juice
2 tablespoons butter
6 lemon thyme sprigs
4 thin slices of lemon
150 g (5 1/2 oz/1 bunch) flat-leaf (Italian) parsley
250 g (9 oz) cherry tomatoes, cut in half
2 tablespoons salted capers, rinsed and drained
1 teaspoon red wine vinegar
3 teaspoons extra virgin olive oil
creamy mashed potato (Favourites), to serve (optional)

Preheat the oven to 200°C (400°F/Gas 6). Heat a non-stick
frying pan over high heat and add the olive oil. Sear the
chicken leg quarters on both sides until golden brown,
then transfer to a roasting tin. Season with a little sea salt.

Add 125 ml (4 fl oz/1/2 cup) water to the roasting tin, along
with the sherry, lemon juice, butter, thyme sprigs and lemon
slices. Bake for 35–40 minutes, or until the chicken is cooked
through. To test if the chicken is cooked, insert the point of a
sharp knife into the thickest part: the juices should run clear.
Remove from the oven, cover with foil and allow to rest while
making the salad.

Remove the leaves from the parsley and place in a bowl with
the tomato and capers. Add the vinegar and extra virgin olive
oil and toss to coat the salad with the dressing.

Serve the chicken drizzled with the roasting juices, with some
creamy mashed potato and the tomato salad. Serves 4

pork spare ribs

250 ml (9 fl oz/1 cup) soy sauce
175 g (6 oz/1/2 cup) golden syrup or maple syrup
4 tablespoons balsamic vinegar
4 tablespoons tomato paste (concentrated purée)
1 strip of orange zest
juice of 1 orange
1 tablespoon mustard powder
1 tablespoon finely grated fresh ginger
1 cinnamon stick
1/2 teaspoon ground cumin
1/2 teaspoon chilli powder
1 bay leaf
16–24 American style pork ribs, no thicker than 2 cm (3/4 inch)
creamy polenta (Favourites) or mashed pumpkin (Favourites),
    to serve

Put all the ingredients except the ribs in a small saucepan.
Mix well and bring to the boil, stirring to ensure that the
marinade does not catch on the base of the pan. Remove
the cinnamon stick and allow the marinade to cool a little.

Sit the ribs in a shallow dish and pour the marinade over them,
ensuring all the ribs are well coated in the marinade. Cover
and refrigerate for several hours, or preferably overnight.

Preheat the oven to 200°C (400°F/Gas 6). Line a ceramic
baking dish with baking paper and arrange the ribs so they
are lying flat. Pour any remaining marinade over the top.
Bake for 15 minutes, then turn the ribs over and bake for
a further 15 minutes.

Serve on a bed of creamy polenta or mashed pumpkin,
drizzled with the juices from the baking dish. Serves 4

opposite: beef in red wine
over: lemon chicken with tomato salad, and pork spare ribs

A finger-licking meal of hearty goodness

polenta and mash

One of the great things about chilly nights is being able to indulge in heart-warmingly thick and creamy mashes and polenta.

Polenta is incredibly easy to make, and as winter meals go it is the perfect complement to hearty stews, saucy meats and in fact anything that needs a gentle-flavoured base to soak up a serious sauce. Creamy polenta (Favourites) is a wonderful side dish, but can also be the main attraction in a simple meal. Spoon onto a warm plate and top with one of the following.
- Rich tomato sauce and fried chorizo sausage.
- Sliced bocconcini (fresh baby mozzarella cheese), crispy prosciutto and fried sage leaves.

- Gorgonzola cheese and baby English spinach leaves.
- Mascarpone cheese and chunky olive tapenade.

To make grilled polenta, follow the recipe for creamed polenta (Favourites) but do not add the butter and cheese. When it begins to pull away from the side of the saucepan, pour the polenta into a shallow lightly oiled baking tray, spread it around evenly and allow to cool. Cut the polenta into thick fingers or wedges and brush with a little olive oil before chargrilling or baking. Here are some terrific accompaniments.
- A salad of rocket (arugula), crispy prosciutto and parmesan cheese.
- Mushroom ragout (page 295).

- A salad of watercress, crumbled blue cheese and crispy bacon.
- Chilli tomato sauce.

Serve buttery mashed pumpkin (Favourites) with roast beef, pan-fried steak or grilled sausages. To the basic mix you can add snipped chives, crumbled crispy prosciutto or a few drops of Tabasco sauce for a chilli bite.

There's a recipe for a classic creamy mash in Favourites, but remember that mashed potato doesn't always have to play the straight-man to the main course. Pep up a bowl of mash with some finely chopped onion or sun-dried tomatoes.

Saffron threads or 2 fresh bay leaves added to the warm milk will add a subtle flavour, while a few drops of truffle oil will give the humble mash a real 'wow' factor. Or try a dash of colour and spice by mashing equal quantities of potatoes and pumpkin (winter squash) and adding a sprinkle of cumin.

And lastly, a few points to remember when making mash. Always mash the potatoes while they are still hot. If you wish to prepare them a little in advance, keep the mashed potato in the warm saucepan and heat over low heat when ready to serve. If you like your mash really smooth, invest in a simple potato ricer or mouli — and never blend in a food processor or you'll simply end up with a gluey mess.

roast beef with wild mushroom butter

2 tablespoons freshly ground black pepper
800 g (1 lb 12 oz) beef eye fillet, trimmed
10 g (1/4 oz) dried porcini mushrooms
2 1/2 tablespoons butter
1 tablespoon dijon mustard
creamy mashed potato (Favourites), to serve
steamed asparagus, to serve

Rub the pepper over the beef. Put the beef on a tray and leave it in the refrigerator, uncovered, overnight. Bring to room temperature before cooking.

Preheat the oven to 200°C (400°F/Gas 6). Put the mushrooms in a small bowl, cover with 125 ml (4 fl oz/1/2 cup) boiling water and soak for 10 minutes, or until soft. Drain, reserving the soaking liquid, then finely chop the mushrooms.

Heat 1 tablespoon of the butter in a small saucepan and add the mushrooms. Cook over medium heat for 5 minutes, then add the soaking liquid. Simmer for 10 minutes, or until most of the liquid has evaporated.

Roughly chop the remaining butter and put it in a bowl. Add the warm mushrooms and mustard and mix well.

Sit the beef in a roasting tin and roast for 10 minutes. Remove the roasting tin from the oven, turn the beef and roast for a further 5 minutes. Remove from the oven, season with sea salt, cover loosely with foil and allow to rest for 15 minutes.

Drain any juices from the roasting tin and stir them into the mushroom butter.

Roast the beef for a further 15 minutes. Slice thickly and serve topped with the mushroom butter, with some creamy mashed potato and steamed asparagus. Serves 4

lamb curry

3 tablespoons olive oil
juice of 2 lemons
1 tablespoon finely grated fresh ginger
2 teaspoons garam masala
1 kg (2 lb 4 oz) lamb shoulder, trimmed and cut into cubes
2 onions, finely sliced
400 g (14 oz) tin chopped tomatoes
2 tablespoons tomato paste (concentrated purée)
3 green chillies, seeded and cut into strips
250 ml (9 fl oz/1 cup) veal or beef stock (Favourites)
10 mint leaves, finely chopped
300 g (10 1/2 oz) plain yoghurt
steamed white rice (Favourites), to serve

In a small bowl, mix together 2 tablespoons of the oil, the lemon juice, ginger and garam masala. Put the lamb in a large ceramic dish and massage the oil mixture into the lamb to ensure it is well coated. Cover with plastic wrap and marinate in the refrigerator for 3 hours.

Heat the remaining oil in a large heavy-based saucepan. Add the onion and sauté over medium heat for a few minutes, or until the onion is soft. Add the lamb (in batches if necessary) and cook until browned all over. Return all the lamb to the pan, then add the tomato, tomato paste, chilli and stock. Reduce the heat and simmer, stirring occasionally, for 1 1/2 hours, or until the liquid has reduced and the lamb is coated in a rich, thick sauce.

Stir the mint into the yoghurt. Serve the lamb on a bed of steamed white rice with a dollop of minty yoghurt. Serves 4

bean and sausage stew

2 x 400 g (14 oz) tins cannellini beans, rinsed and drained
5 ripe roma (plum) tomatoes, roughly chopped
400 g (14 oz) tin chopped tomatoes
2 leeks, white part only, rinsed and roughly chopped
8 garlic cloves, peeled
2 bay leaves
250 ml (9 fl oz/1 cup) dry white wine
350 g (12 oz) good-quality spicy, thick sausages
a handful of parsley, roughly chopped
creamy mashed potato (Favourites) or warm crusty bread, to serve

Preheat the oven to 180°C (350°F/Gas 4). Put the beans, tomato, leek, garlic, bay leaves and wine in a 3 litre (104 fl oz/12 cup) casserole dish or ovenproof saucepan. Season with a little sea salt and freshly ground black pepper.

Prick the skin of the sausages with a fork, then sear them in a non-stick frying pan over high heat until browned on all sides. Cut the sausages into bite-sized chunks and add them to the casserole. Lightly stir everything together, then cover the dish with a lid or foil and bake for 1 1/2 hours.

Sprinkle with parsley and serve with creamy mashed potato or warm crusty bread. Serves 4

opposite: roast beef with wild mushroom butter
over: lamb curry, and bean and sausage stew

spiced orange salad with honeyed mascarpone

4 large oranges
230 g (8 oz/1 cup) caster (superfine) sugar
1 cinnamon stick
2 star anise
250 g (9 oz/scant 1¼ cups) mascarpone cheese
1 generous teaspoon honey

Remove the zest from two of the oranges and cut into very fine strips. Bring a small saucepan of water to the boil and add the zest strips. Boil for 1 minute, then drain.

Put the sugar, cinnamon stick, star anise and 170 ml (5½ fl oz/⅔ cup) water in a heavy-based saucepan and cook over low heat until the sugar melts into the water. Turn the heat up high and boil for 6–7 minutes, or until the syrup begins to colour. Add the blanched orange zest and cook for several minutes, then remove and reserve the zest and spices.

Cook the syrup for a further 5 minutes, or until it begins to turn golden caramel. Remove from the heat. Standing back from the saucepan, add 125 ml (4 fl oz/½ cup) water to the syrup to stop the syrup cooking. Allow to cool.

Remove the skin and pith from all the oranges. Thinly slice the oranges and remove any seeds, then arrange on a serving dish. Scatter with the reserved spices and orange zest strips. Pour the cooled syrup over, then cover and chill.

When ready to serve, fold the honey through the mascarpone and serve with the chilled oranges. Serves 4

chocolate and mascarpone parfait

125 g (4½ oz/scant ½ cup) caster (superfine) sugar
100 g (3½ oz) good-quality chocolate (70% cocoa)
4 egg yolks
2 tablespoons brandy
250 g (9 oz/scant 1¼ cups) mascarpone cheese

hazelnut crumbs
55 g (2 oz/½ cup) ground hazelnuts
165 g (5¾ oz/¾ cup) sugar

Line a 10 x 20 cm (4 x 8 inch) loaf (bar) tin with plastic wrap.

Put the sugar and 125 ml (4 fl oz/½ cup) water in a saucepan. Bring to the boil, stirring until the sugar has dissolved. Boil briskly for 3 minutes, then remove from the heat.

Break the chocolate into pieces and add them to the hot syrup, stirring until smooth.

Whisk the egg yolks until pale, then slowly add the hot chocolate sauce, beating until the mixture has cooled. Stir in the brandy, then whisk in the mascarpone. Spoon the mixture into the prepared tin and freeze overnight.

To make the hazelnut crumbs, line a baking tray with baking paper and scatter the ground hazelnuts over it. Put the sugar in a small saucepan over low heat. Slowly cook the sugar until it melts and begins to turn a toffee colour. Quickly remove from the heat and pour the toffee over the hazelnut — you may need to shuffle the baking paper a little to ensure that all the hazelnut is caught in the toffee. Allow to cool.

Break the cooled toffee into small pieces and blend to fine golden crumbs in a food processor or blender. Store in an airtight container until ready to serve. (The hazelnut crumbs can be made several days ahead.)

To serve, turn the parfait out onto a serving dish, sprinkle with hazelnut crumbs and cut into thick slices. Serves 6

treacle squares

350 g (12 oz/1 cup) golden syrup or treacle
100 g (3½ oz/1 heaped cup) desiccated coconut
grated zest and juice of 1 lemon
¼ teaspoon ground cardamom
1 egg
6 sheets of filo pastry
3 tablespoons butter, melted
icing (confectioners') sugar, to serve
vanilla ice cream, to serve

Preheat the oven to 180°C (350°F/Gas 4). Line a 20 x 30 cm (8 x 12 inch) baking tin with baking paper.

In a bowl, mix together the golden syrup, coconut, lemon zest, lemon juice, cardamom and egg.

Remove the filo pastry from the packet and cover with a slightly damp tea towel (dish towel). Place a sheet of pastry on the baking tray and brush with some melted butter. Repeat with two more layers of pastry. Now spread the filling over the pastry and top with another sheet of pastry. Brush with melted butter, then repeat with the remaining two pastry sheets. Generously brush the top sheet of pastry with butter, then bake for 30 minutes, or until golden brown.

Turn the pastry out onto a clean chopping board. Cut into large squares or triangles and dust generously with icing sugar. Serve warm, with a scoop of vanilla ice cream. Serves 6

opposite: spiced orange salad with honeyed mascarpone
over: chocolate and mascarpone parfait, and treacle squares

4 cream desserts

panettone trifle

2 eggs, separated
250 g (9 oz/heaped 1 cup) mascarpone cheese
3 tablespoons Tia Maria
3 tablespoons caster (superfine) sugar
4 tablespoons strong coffee
2 tablespoons marsala
200 g (7 oz) panettone
100 g (3¹/₂ oz/heaped 1 cup) flaked almonds, lightly toasted

Whisk the egg whites in a clean bowl using electric beaters until soft peaks form.

Put the egg yolks, mascarpone, Tia Maria and sugar in a separate bowl and stir to combine. Lightly fold the egg whites into the mascarpone mixture until well combined.

Pour the coffee and marsala into a bowl. Tear the panettone into bite-sized pieces and dip them in the coffee.

Layer the mascarpone, almonds and panettone in a large serving bowl or trifle dish or four parfait glasses, finishing with the mascarpone and a final sprinkle of almonds. Serves 4

eton mess

500 g (1 lb 2 oz/3¹/₃ cups) strawberries
1 tablespoon caster (superfine) sugar
4 meringues (Favourites)
300 ml (10¹/₂ fl oz) pouring (whipping) cream
1 teaspoon natural vanilla extract

Hull the strawberries, cut them in half and put them in a large bowl. Sprinkle with the sugar and lightly toss so all the fruit is coated. Set aside for 10 minutes.

Smash each meringue into several bits. Whip the cream in a separate bowl and fold in the vanilla.

Layer the strawberries, broken meringue and whipped cream into four bowls and serve immediately. Serves 4

cinnamon cream

3 tablespoons plain yoghurt
¹/₄ teaspoon ground cinnamon
¹/₂ teaspoon natural vanilla extract
1 teaspoon caster (superfine) sugar
150 ml (5 fl oz) pouring (whipping) cream, whipped
almond biscotti, to serve

Put the yoghurt in a bowl with the cinnamon, vanilla and sugar. Stir until the sugar has dissolved, then fold the whipped cream through. Cover with plastic wrap and refrigerate until needed. Serve with slow-poached quinces (page 361), poached pears or bottled preserved peaches, with some almond biscotti on the side. Serves 4

drunken chocolate mousse

150 g (5¹/₂ oz) chopped dark eating chocolate
4 tablespoons strong coffee
3 eggs, separated
1 teaspoon natural vanilla extract
3–4 tablespoons brandy
3 tablespoons soft brown sugar
100 ml (3¹/₂ fl oz) pouring (whipping) cream, whipped

Put the chocolate and coffee in a small heatproof bowl over a saucepan of simmering water, ensuring the base of the bowl does not touch the water. When the chocolate has melted, stir together, then remove the pan from the heat.

Whisk the egg yolks with the vanilla, then stir in the melted chocolate. When the mixture is smooth, stir in the brandy.

Whisk the egg whites in a separate bowl using electric beaters until quite firm peaks form, then add the sugar and whisk until stiff peaks form. Fold in the chocolate mixture and whipped cream. Cover and chill in the refrigerator for at least 1 hour. Serves 4

Quinces slow-cooked to a rosy richness

slow-poached quinces

110 g (3³/4 oz/¹/2 cup) sugar
2 tablespoons honey
2 fresh bay leaves
1 star anise
2 large quinces
thick (double/heavy) cream or vanilla ice cream, to serve

Put the sugar, honey, bay leaves and star anise in a saucepan and cover with 500 ml (17 fl oz/2 cups) water. Stir until the sugar has dissolved.

Peel the quinces, then cut them into eighths and remove the cores. Add the quince segments to the syrup and heat over medium heat until the syrup has come to a slow simmer. Reduce the heat to low, then cover and simmer gently for 3¹/2 hours, removing the bay leaves after the first hour. The quince segments should be soft and a wonderful rose colour.

Serve the quince with a drizzle of the syrup and some cream or vanilla ice cream. Serves 4

rhubarb sour cream cake

3 tablespoons unsalted butter, softened
380 g (13¹/2 oz/1²/3 cups firmly packed) soft brown sugar
2 eggs
1 teaspoon natural vanilla extract
300 g (10¹/2 oz) sour cream
300 g (10¹/2 oz/heaped 2¹/3 cups) plain (all-purpose) flour, sifted
1 teaspoon bicarbonate of soda (baking soda)
1 teaspoon baking powder
400 g (14 oz/1 bunch) rhubarb, roughly chopped
100 g (3¹/2 oz/scant ¹/2 cup) caster (superfine) sugar

Preheat the oven to 180°C (350°F/Gas 4). Grease and line a 25 cm (10 inch) spring-form cake tin.

Cream the butter and brown sugar using electric beaters, then add the eggs, vanilla and sour cream. Beat well, then sift in the flour, bicarbonate of soda and baking powder and fold together.

Spoon the batter into the prepared cake tin. Smooth the surface, then arrange the rhubarb over the top. Bake for 1¹/2 hours, or until a skewer inserted into the centre of the cake comes out clean. If the cake looks like it is browning too quickly, cover with foil for the last 30 minutes.

Remove the cake from the tin and allow to cool on a wire rack. When cool, lift the cake onto a serving plate.

Put the caster sugar in a small saucepan with 100 ml (3¹/2 fl oz) water. Heat over medium heat until the sugar has melted, then increase the heat to high. Boil until the sugar is starting to turn golden brown, occasionally swirling the pan, but not stirring the mixture. Quickly remove the toffee syrup from the heat and spoon over the rhubarb. Allow to cool before serving. Serves 10

madeira cupcakes

175 g (6 oz/heaped ³/4 cup) self-raising flour
1 teaspoon baking powder
100 g (3¹/2 oz/1 cup) ground almonds
175 g (6 oz) unsalted butter, softened
175 g (6 oz/³/4 cup) caster (superfine) sugar
3 eggs, beaten
finely grated zest and juice of 1 orange
3 tablespoons flaked almonds

orange mascarpone
160 ml (5¹/4 fl oz) orange juice
4 tablespoons sugar
250 g (9 oz/scant 1¹/4 cups) mascarpone cheese

Preheat the oven to 160°C (315°F/Gas 2–3). Line a 12-hole cupcake tin with paper cases.

Sift the flour and baking powder into a bowl and add the ground almonds. Using electric beaters, beat the butter and sugar until pale and creamy, then add the eggs, orange zest and orange juice. Beat until smooth, then fold the dry ingredients into the mixture.

Spoon the batter into the paper cases to about two-thirds full. Sprinkle with the flaked almonds. Bake for 15 minutes, or until a skewer inserted into the centre of a cupcake comes out clean. Remove from the oven and allow to cool.

Meanwhile, make the orange mascarpone. Put the orange juice and sugar in a small saucepan and bring to the boil. Reduce the heat to low and simmer until the orange syrup has reduced by half. Remove from the heat and allow to cool.

Stir 2 tablespoons of the orange syrup into the mascarpone. Using a sharp knife, neatly slice the cupcakes through the middle. Generously spread the orange mascarpone over the bottom half of each cupcake, then sit the tops back on the cupcakes. Drizzle with the remaining orange syrup and serve. Makes 12

opposite: slow-poached quinces
over: rhubarb sour cream cake, and madeira cupcakes

sultana cake

375 g (13 oz/3 cups) sultanas (golden raisins)
250 ml (9 fl oz/1 cup) hot Earl Grey tea
2 tablespoons brandy
350 g (12 oz/scant 1 1/2 cups) caster (superfine) sugar
250 g (9 oz) unsalted butter, softened
3 eggs, lightly beaten
310 g (11 oz/2 1/2 cups) plain (all-purpose) flour
3 1/2 teaspoons baking powder
1/2 teaspoon salt
100 g (3 1/2 oz/2/3 cup) blanched or flaked almonds

Preheat the oven to 180°C (350°F/Gas 4). Grease the base of a 20 cm (8 inch) spring-form cake tin. Line the side of the tin with a strip of baking paper that is 1 1/2 times the height of the tin. This will protect the cake as it rises.

Put the sultanas in a bowl and cover with the hot tea and the brandy. Allow to sit for 5 minutes.

Cream the sugar and butter using electric beaters, then fold in the eggs. Add the hot sultana mixture and stir to combine. Sift in the flour, baking powder and salt and lightly stir to combine.

Spoon the batter into the prepared tin and arrange the almonds over the top. Bake for 1 1/2 hours, or until a skewer inserted into the centre of the cake comes out clean. If the cake looks like it is browning too quickly, cover it with foil. Remove from the tin and allow to cool on a wire rack. Serves 10

baked apples

100 g (3 1/2 oz/1 cup) ground almonds
1/2 teaspoon mixed (pumpkin pie) spice
2 tablespoons butter, softened
2 tablespoons maple syrup
4 large green apples
thick (double/heavy) cream, vanilla ice cream or butterscotch
   ice cream, to serve

Preheat the oven to 160°C (315°F/Gas 2–3). Line a baking tray with baking paper.

Combine the ground almonds, mixed spice, butter and maple syrup in a small bowl.

Core the apples using an apple corer or a small sharp knife, ensuring that you remove all the tough core pieces. Using a sharp knife, make a shallow incision around the middle of each apple, just deep enough to cut through the skin.

Sit the apples on the baking tray and spoon the almond filling into the centre of each. Bake for 40 minutes, or until the apples are cooked through and slightly collapsed.

Serve warm with cream or ice cream. Serves 4

apple 'cake' with vanilla syrup

165 g (5 3/4 oz/3/4 cup) sugar
185 ml (6 fl oz/3/4 cup) apple juice
juice of 1 lemon
1 vanilla bean
10 green apples
thick (double/heavy) cream or vanilla ice cream, to serve

Preheat the oven to 120°C (235°F/Gas 1/2). Grease and line a 20 cm (8 inch) spring-form cake tin with baking paper. Sit the tin on a large sheet of foil and fold the foil up around the side of the tin — this should ensure the syrup doesn't escape during cooking. Sit the cake tin in a roasting tin.

Put the sugar, apple juice and lemon juice in a saucepan. Rub the vanilla bean between your fingertips to soften it, then use the tip of a sharp knife to split it along its length and scrape the seeds into the saucepan. Add the vanilla bean and bring to the boil, stirring until the sugar has dissolved. Reduce the heat to low and simmer for 10 minutes.

Peel the apples, then use an apple corer to remove the core, leaving the fruit in one piece. Finely slice the apples into thin circles. Layer the slices in the cake tin, lightly brushing each layer with some of the vanilla syrup.

Place the roasting tin in the oven and bake for 4 hours. The 'cake' will be lightly golden on top and will have shrunk quite considerably. Allow to cool, then turn out onto a plate and serve in thick wedges with cream or ice cream. Serves 6–8

seasonal ideas

- For simple apple turnovers, toss thin apple slices in a little sugar, cinnamon and lemon zest. Cut out 10 cm (4 inch) rounds of butter puff pastry and spoon a little of the mixture into the centre of each circle. Turn over half of each pastry circle to form a half-moon shape, then seal the edges. Put the turnovers on a baking tray lined with baking paper, sprinkle with sugar and prick the surface with a fork. Bake in a moderate oven until golden brown and serve hot.

- Fold thin sliced apple through a basic butter cake recipe (Favourites) and top with cinnamon sugar. Bake until golden brown.

opposite: sultana cake
over: baked apples, and apple 'cake' with vanilla syrup

deli desserts

Surprising everyone with a fantastic dessert at the end of an otherwise memorable meal shouldn't fill you with dread. Supermarket and delicatessen shelves are crammed with quick-fix dessert ideas. With a few twists on some old-time favourites you can still astonish all with an indulgent end to the meal.

- Wash and hull 250 g (9 oz/1²/₃ cups) strawberries and slice them in half. Sprinkle with icing (confectioners') sugar and a little dessert wine or berry liqueur. Toss gently, then leave to macerate for half an hour. Top with thick (double/heavy) cream and some Persian fairy floss.

- Nowadays you can find a wonderful selection of variously flavoured French nougats, from chocolate and almond through to cherry and pistachio. Cut a selection into cubes and pile onto a sharing plate. Serve with fresh cherries and coffee.

- Serve biscotti with sweet mascarpone (Favourites) and shot glasses of sweet liqueur.

- Slice a small panettone crossways into four circles. Pan-fry in a little butter until crisply golden, then top with a dollop of thick (double/heavy) cream and a big spoonful of bottled morello cherries.

- Serve shards of bitter dark chocolate with a fruit platter.

- Drizzle melted white chocolate over mixed frozen berries that have been dusted with icing (confectioners') sugar.

- Allow frozen blackberries to thaw, then sprinkle with icing (confectioners') sugar. Break coconut macaroons into small pieces and layer in trifle glasses with chocolate ice cream and the sweetened blackberries.

- Cut Turkish delight into tiny cubes and layer in tall glasses with strawberry coulis (Favourites) and vanilla ice cream.

- Buy some large meringues and gently break them open. Fill with whipped cream and bottled morello cherries. Decorate with grated dark chocolate.

- Lightly soak cubes of dark ginger cake in coffee liqueur and layer in small coffee glasses with mascarpone cheese or thick (double/heavy) cream. Scatter with grated dark chocolate.

- Smash toffee brittle into small pieces and sprinkle over rich chocolate ice cream.

- Serve amaretti biscuits with shot glasses of coffee liqueur.

berry meringue

4 egg whites
230 g (8 oz/1 cup) caster (superfine) sugar
1 teaspoon natural vanilla extract
500 g (1 lb 2 oz) frozen mixed berries
whipped cream or vanilla ice cream, to serve

Preheat the oven to 150°C (300/Gas 2).

Beat the egg whites using electric beaters until soft peaks form. Slowly add the sugar and beat until stiff and glossy. Beat in the vanilla.

Scatter the berries into a 25 cm (10 inch) oval ovenproof dish, then spoon the meringue over the top. Using a spoon, tease the surface into rough peaks. Bake for 45 minutes, or until the meringue is golden and cooked through. (Alternatively, the berries and meringue can be piled into 150 ml/5 fl oz ramekins and baked for about 20 minutes.)

Serve warm with whipped cream or vanilla ice cream. Serves 6

chocolate puddings

200 g (7 oz) good-quality dark chocolate (70% cocoa)
100 g (3¹/2 oz) unsalted butter
4 eggs, separated
80 g (2³/4 oz/scant ¹/2 cup) soft brown sugar
1 tablespoon plain (all-purpose) flour
1 tablespoon cornflour (cornstarch)
1 tablespoon cocoa powder
thick (double/heavy) cream, to serve

Thickly grease six 150 ml (5 fl oz) ramekins. Put them in the freezer to chill while you prepare the puddings.

Melt the chocolate and butter in a saucepan over low heat. Beat the egg yolks and sugar using electric beaters until thick and pale, then gradually stir in the melted chocolate mixture until well combined. Sift in the flour, cornflour and cocoa and fold through until smooth.

Whisk the egg whites using electric beaters until soft peaks form. Lightly fold one-third of the egg white through the chocolate mixture until lightly combined. Repeat this process twice with the remaining egg white. Spoon the mixture into the chilled ramekins and freeze until ready to cook.

Preheat the oven to 200°C (400°F/Gas 6). Bake the frozen puddings for 15 minutes, or until set on top. Remove from the oven and leave to sit for 10 minutes. Serve topped with a dollop of cream. Serves 4

chocolate mousse cake

400 g (14 oz) dark eating chocolate
170 ml (5¹/2 fl oz/²/3 cup) pouring (whipping) cream
3 tablespoons Grand Marnier
6 eggs, separated
¹/4 teaspoon ground cinnamon
100 g (3¹/2 oz/¹/2 cup) soft brown sugar
unsweetened cocoa powder, to serve
thick (double/heavy) cream or vanilla ice cream, to serve

Preheat the oven to 150°C (300°F/Gas 2). Grease and line a 23 cm (9 inch) spring-form cake tin with baking paper.

Put the chocolate and cream in a small heatproof bowl over a saucepan of simmering water, ensuring the base of the bowl does not touch the water. When the chocolate has melted, remove from the heat and stir in the Grand Marnier.

Beat the egg whites using electric beaters until stiff peaks form. In a separate bowl, beat the egg yolks, cinnamon and sugar until thick and fluffy. Fold the melted chocolate through the egg yolk mixture, then fold in the beaten egg white. Pour the batter into the prepared tin and bake for 45–50 minutes, or until a skewer inserted into the centre of the cake has some moist, but not wet, mixture on it.

Allow the cake to cool in the tin overnight. Just before serving, turn out onto a serving plate and dust with cocoa. Serve a thin wedge with a dollop of cream or vanilla ice cream. Serves 10

seasonal ideas
- Invest in some good-quality dark chocolate and break it up into rough pieces. Serve piled onto a platter with dried muscatel grapes, fresh strawberries and ripe figs and let everyone help themselves.
- Make a rich chocolate sauce (Favourites) and serve in small dipping bowls alongside shards of honeycomb or almond biscotti.

opposite: berry meringue
over: chocolate puddings, and chocolate mousse cake

A delicate spoonful of rich chocolate and sweet cream

favourites

savoury

citrus marinade

1 green chilli, seeded and finely chopped
1 garlic clove, finely chopped
1 teaspoon dried oregano
4 tablespoons olive oil
1/2 teaspoon ground cumin
grated zest and juice of 1 lime
juice of 1 orange
juice of 1 lemon

Put all the ingredients in a large non-metallic bowl and mix well.
Add 4–6 fish fillets or 1 kg (2 lb 4 oz) raw prawns (shrimp),
toss to coat, then cover and refrigerate for 30 minutes.

spicy marinade

2 garlic cloves, finely chopped
1 teaspoon chopped mint
1 teaspoon fresh thyme
1 tablespoon honey
4 tablespoons olive oil
1/2 teaspoon smoked paprika
1 teaspoon crushed, toasted cumin seeds
grated zest and juice of 1 lemon

Put all the ingredients in a large non-metallic bowl and mix well.
Add 6 boneless, skinless chicken breasts, 12 lamb cutlets or
4 lamb backstrap or loin fillets and toss to coat. Cover and
refrigerate for at least 1 hour, or longer if possible.

béchamel sauce

250 ml (9 fl oz/1 cup) milk
1 fresh bay leaf
6 black peppercorns
1 1/2 tablespoons butter
1 tablespoon plain (all-purpose) flour
freshly ground white pepper

Put the milk, bay leaf and peppercorns in a small saucepan.
Bring to the boil, then remove from the heat and set aside.

Melt the butter in a small saucepan. Add the flour and cook,
stirring, for 1 minute over medium heat. Remove from the heat
and gradually add the milk, whisking to make a smooth sauce.
Place back over medium heat and whisk until the sauce comes
to the boil and thickens. Remove the bay leaf and peppercorns
before using. Makes about 250 ml (9 fl oz/1 cup).

chilli mint sauce

1 tablespoon sugar
3 tablespoons rice vinegar
3 tablespoons vegetable oil
1 small red chilli, finely sliced
1 tablespoon fish sauce
1 tablespoon finely chopped mint

Put the sugar, vinegar, vegetable oil, chilli and fish sauce in
a small bowl and stir until the sugar has dissolved. Add the
mint, then drizzle over grilled fish, steamed greens or a
cucumber salad. Makes about 185 ml (6 fl oz/3/4 cup)

sweet chilli sauce

5 garlic cloves, peeled
2 large red chillies, chopped
10 cm (4 inch) piece of lemon grass, trimmed and finely chopped
6 cm (2 1/2 inch) knob of ginger, peeled and roughly chopped
5 cm (2 inch) knob of galangal, peeled and roughly chopped
10 makrut (kaffir lime) leaves, cut into thin strips
a handful of coriander (cilantro) leaves
100 ml (3 1/2 fl oz) Chinese black vinegar
2 tablespoons fish sauce
2 tablespoons soy sauce
345 g (12 oz/1 1/2 cups) caster (superfine) sugar

Blend the garlic, chill, lemon grass, ginger, galangal,
lime leaves and coriander to a rough paste in a mini food
processor. Mix the vinegar, fish sauce and soy sauce
together in a small bowl.

Put the sugar in a saucepan with 4 tablespoons of water
and stir over medium heat until the sugar has dissolved.
Turn the heat to high and cook for 4 minutes, or until the
sugar is beginning to colour. Keeping a constant watch,
continue boiling the sugar until it is almost burning and
has a wonderful toffee smell.

Quickly add the spice paste and stir for 1 minute. Stir in
the vinegar mixture and cook for a further 2 minutes, then
take the pan off the heat. Allow to cool, pour into a clean
glass jar, cover and refrigerate until ready to use. The
sauce will keep for several weeks in the refrigerator.
Makes 330 ml (11 1/4 fl oz/1 1/3 cups)

aïoli

2 egg yolks
1 large garlic clove, crushed
300 ml (10¹/2 fl oz) light olive oil
juice of 1 lemon
¹/4 teaspoon ground white pepper

Whisk together the egg yolks and garlic with a little sea salt.
Slowly start adding the oil in a thin stream, whisking all the
while. Add a little of the lemon juice, then continue slowly
adding the remaining oil. Gently fold in the remaining lemon
juice and season with the white pepper and some sea salt.
Makes about 375 ml (13 fl oz/1¹/2 cups)

gremolata

3 tablespoons finely chopped flat-leaf (Italian) parsley
1 tablespoon finely grated lemon zest
1 tablespoon finely grated fresh horseradish (optional)

Put all the ingredients on a chopping board. Using a large
sharp knife, chop them again, working all the ingredients
together as you chop. Serves 4

horseradish cream

2 tablespoons finely grated fresh horseradish
125 g (4¹/2 oz/¹/2 cup) sour cream
1 teaspoon lemon juice

Combine all the ingredients in a small bowl and season with
sea salt and freshly ground black pepper. Delicious with
roasted beetroot (beets), smoked salmon and roast beef.
Makes about 170 g (5³/4 oz/²/3 cup)

lemon mayonnaise

2 egg yolks
1 teaspoon mustard
1 tablespoon lemon juice
200 ml (7 fl oz) light olive oil

Whisk together the egg yolks, mustard and lemon juice
until light and creamy. Drizzle in the olive oil, a little at a time,
whisking continuously until a thick mayonnaise forms.
Season to taste. Makes about 250 ml (9 fl oz/1 cup)

lemon vinaigrette

1 tablespoon lemon juice
3 tablespoons extra virgin olive oil
1 garlic clove, bruised
¹/2 teaspoon honey

Put all the ingredients in a small screw-top jar and shake.
Season to taste and shake again just before drizzling over
salads. Makes about 80 ml (2¹/2 fl oz/¹/3 cup)

pesto

45 basil leaves (2 loosely packed cups)
a large handful of flat-leat (Italian) parsley, roughly chopped
4 tablespoons roughly grated parmesan cheese
3 tablespoons pine nuts, toasted
¹/2 garlic clove
150 ml (5 fl oz) olive oil

Put all the ingredients in a blender or food processor and
blend to a chunky paste. Makes about 250 g (9 oz/1 cup)

walnut oil dressing

1 tablespoon walnut oil
2 tablespoons olive oil
1 tablespoon red wine vinegar
¹/2 teaspoon honey

Whisk the ingredients together in a small bowl and season
to taste. Makes about 80 ml (2¹/2 fl oz/¹/3 cup)

onion jam

6 onions, finely sliced
2 tablespoons butter
1 tablespoon balsamic vinegar
1 tablespoon soft brown sugar

Put the onion in a saucepan with the butter and sauté over medium heat until the onion is soft and transparent. Stir in the vinegar and sugar, then cover and reduce the heat to low. Cook for 40 minutes, or until reduced to a sweet, jammy consistency. Makes about 300 g (10$^1/_2$ oz/1 cup)

bruschetta

Cut the required number of slices from a thick sourdough baguette or country-style loaf. Toast the bread on both sides, then rub a cut garlic clove over the surface. Drizzle with olive oil and season with a little sea salt and freshly ground black pepper.

scrambled eggs

2 organic eggs
4 tablespoons pouring (whipping) cream
1 teaspoon butter

There are a few points to remember when making perfect scrambled eggs. If you need to cook more than two serves, do it in batches — too much mixture in the pan will result in overcooked eggs and a frustrated cook!

For one serve, whisk together the eggs and cream. Heat the butter in a non-stick frying pan and pour in the eggs as the butter begins to sizzle. Cook on a low, even temperature and don't over-stir — slowly drag the cooked egg into the centre of the pan with a wooden spoon so that it softly folds together. The egg is ready when it is almost cooked through and appears soft, creamy and just a little loose in texture. Serves 1

roasted capsicums

2–3 red capsicums (peppers)
olive oil, for brushing

Preheat the oven to 200°C (400°F/Gas 6). Sit a small rack on or over a baking tray or roasting tin. Lightly rub the capsicums with olive oil and sit them on the rack.

Roast the capsicums for 8–10 minutes, or until the skins begin to blister and blacken — you may need to turn them several times so the skins blister all over. (If you have a gas stove you can also blister the skin by carefully putting the capsicums directly over the flame, turning them around as the skin blisters.) Put the roasted capsicums in a container, cover with plastic wrap and leave to cool — covering them will make them sweat and make them easier to peel.

Remove the blackened skin from the capsicums by gently rubbing it away with your fingertips — it should come away easily. Cut away the stems, and the seeds and membranes inside the capsicums. The flesh is now ready to eat or use.

roasted eggplants

1–2 large eggplants (aubergines)
oil, for brushing

Prick the eggplants all over with a skewer, then sit them directly on the naked flame of a gas burner or over a barbecue. Set the flames to low–medium and cook for 10 minutes, turning the eggplants occasionally, until they are blackened and blistered and beginning to collapse.

If you don't have a gas stove, lightly rub the eggplants in oil, then bake in a preheated 200°C (400°F/Gas 6) oven until the eggplants are cooked through — they will begin to collapse inwards and will feel soft and mushy when pressed with a finger.

Put the eggplants in a bowl and cover with plastic wrap. Allow to cool, then gently peel away the blackened skin.

steamed couscous

185 g (6¹/2 oz/1 cup) instant couscous
1 tablespoon butter

Put the couscous and butter in a large bowl and pour
250 ml (9 fl oz/1 cup) boiling water over the top. Cover and
allow to sit for 5 minutes, then fluff up the grains with a fork.
Cover again and leave for a further 5 minutes. Season with
a little sea salt and freshly ground black pepper, then rub
the grains with your fingertips to remove any lumps. Serve
warm or chilled. Serves 4 as a side dish

creamy polenta

200 g (7 oz/1¹/3 cups) polenta
1 teaspoon sea salt
2¹/2 tablespoons unsalted butter
75 g (2¹/2 oz/³/4 cup) grated parmesan cheese

Put the polenta in a jug to make it easy to pour. Bring 1 litre
(35 fl oz/4 cups) water to the boil in a large saucepan and
add the sea salt. Reduce the heat to a simmer and slowly
pour in the polenta. Stir with a whisk until well blended, then
reduce the heat to low and cook for 30 minutes, stirring
occasionally with a large wooden spoon. When the polenta
begins to pull away from the side of the pan, add the butter
and parmesan and stir to combine. Serves 4 as a side dish

saffron rice

750 ml (26 fl oz/3 cups) chicken stock (Favourites)
a generous pinch of saffron threads
3 tablespoons butter
1 onion, finely diced
500 g (1 lb 2 oz/2¹/2 cups) basmati rice

Bring the stock to the boil in a saucepan and add the saffron.
Remove from the heat and allow to infuse for 10 minutes.

Melt the butter in a large saucepan and add the onion.
Sauté over medium heat for 5 minutes, or until the onion is
soft and transparent. Add the rice, stir until the grains are
glossy, then pour in the stock. Bring to the boil, reduce the
heat to low, cover and cook for 15 minutes.

Remove the saucepan from the heat, keep covered and
allow to sit for 10 minutes. Serve with seafood or chicken.
Serves 6–8 as a side dish

steamed white rice

200 g (7 oz/1 cup) white long-grain rice
435 ml (15¹/4 oz/1³/4 cups) water

Put the rice in a saucepan with a tightly fitting lid. Cover
with the water and add a pinch of sea salt. Bring to the boil,
then stir once to ensure the grains have not stuck to the
base of the pan.

Cover the pan and turn the heat down to the lowest setting.
Cook the rice for 15 minutes, then take the pan off the heat and
allow the rice to sit for a further 10 minutes. Just before serving,
fluff up the grains with a fork. Serves 2–4 as a side dish

savoury shortcrust tart case

200 g (7 oz/heaped 1²/3 cups) plain (all-purpose) flour
100 g (3¹/2 oz) unsalted butter, chilled and cut into cubes
2 tablespoons chilled water

Put the flour, butter and a pinch of salt in a food processor
and process for 1 minute. Add the chilled water and process
until the mixture comes together. Wrap the dough in plastic
wrap and refrigerate for 30 minutes.

Grease a 25 cm (10 inch) tart tin or six 8 cm (3¹/4 inch) tartlet
tins. Roll the pastry out as thinly as possible between two
layers of plastic wrap, then use the plastic to help you line
the prepared tin or tins, removing the plastic wrap once the
pastry is in place. Put the tart tin or tins in the refrigerator and
chill for a further 30 minutes.

Preheat the oven to 180°C (350°F/Gas 4). Using a fork,
prick the pastry case(s) over the base, line with crumpled
baking paper and fill with rice or baking weights. Bake for
10–15 minutes, or until the pastry looks cooked and dry.
Remove from the oven and allow to cool. Makes 1 large
or 6 small cases

Note: The tart case will keep in the freezer for several weeks.
There is no need to thaw before using — simply put it in the
preheated oven directly from the freezer.

baked potatoes

4 large roasting potatoes, such as coliban or sebago

Preheat the oven to 200°C (400°F/Gas 6). Wash the potatoes well and sprinkle with sea salt while they are still damp. Place in a roasting tin and bake for 1 hour, or until they are well cooked — they should 'give' slightly when pressed with a finger and will have dry, crackly skin. Serves 4 as a side dish

creamy mashed potato

1 kg (2 lb 4 oz) all-purpose potatoes
125 ml (4 fl oz/1/2 cup) milk
100 g (31/2 oz) butter
pinch of ground white pepper

Peel the potatoes and cut them into chunks. Place in a large pot of cold water, bring to the boil and cook for 30 minutes, or until cooked through.

Meanwhile, put the milk and butter in a small saucepan. Warm over a low heat until the butter has melted.

Drain the potato and return to the warm pot. Mash the potato while it is still warm, then whisk in the buttery milk until the potato is soft and creamy. Season with sea salt and white pepper. Serves 4–6 as a side dish

mashed pumpkin

1 kg (2 lb 4 oz) pumpkin (winter squash)
100 g (31/2 oz) butter
1/4 teaspoon ground white pepper
1/4 teaspoon ground cumin

Peel the pumpkin, remove any seeds and cut the flesh into chunks. Place in a large pot of salted cold water and bring to the boil. Allow to boil for 10–12 minutes, or until tender.

Drain, return the warm pumpkin to the pot, then mash. Whisk in the butter, white pepper and cumin and season to taste with a little sea salt. Serves 4–6 as a side dish

potato gratin

1 whole garlic clove
250 ml (9 fl oz/1 cup) pouring (whipping) cream
2 tablespoons butter
500 g (1 lb 2 oz) boiling potatoes, such as desiree or Dutch
    cream, peeled and thinly sliced

Preheat the oven to 180°C (350°F/Gas 4). Put the garlic and cream in a small saucepan and heat slowly. Use 1 tablespoon of the butter to generously grease a gratin dish, then arrange the potato slices in layers, seasoning in between with sea salt and freshly ground black pepper. Remove the garlic from the cream, then pour the cream over the potatoes.

Dot the remaining butter over the gratin. Cover with foil and bake for 30 minutes, then remove the foil and bake for a further 30 minutes, or until the top is golden brown. Insert a skewer into the centre of the gratin to check that all the potatoes are cooked through. Serves 4–6 as a side dish

roast potatoes

8 roasting potatoes, such as coliban or sebago, peeled and
    cut into large chunks
olive oil, for drizzling

Preheat the oven to 200°C (400°F/Gas 6). Put the potatoes in a pot of cold salted water. Bring to the boil and cook the potatoes until they are almost cooked through, but still firm on the outside.

Drain and place in a roasting tin, then run the tines of a fork over the potato chunks to give the surface a little texture. Drizzle with olive oil, season with sea salt and bake for 1 hour, or until golden and crispy, turning the potatoes at least once during cooking. Serves 4 as a side dish

chicken stock

1 whole fresh organic chicken
1 onion, cut into quarters
2 celery stalks, roughly chopped
1 leek, white part only, rinsed and roughly chopped
1 bay leaf
a few flat-leaf (Italian) parsley stalks
6 black peppercorns

Rinse the chicken under cold running water and remove any fat from the cavity. Cut the chicken into several large pieces and place in a large heavy-based saucepan. Cover with 3 litres (105 fl oz/12 cups) cold water. Bring just to the boil, then reduce the heat to a simmer. Skim any fat from the surface, then add the remaining ingredients. Maintain the heat at a low simmer for 2 hours.

Strain the stock into a bowl and allow to cool. Using a large spoon, remove any fat that has risen to the surface. If a concentrated flavour is required, return the strained stock to a saucepan and simmer over low heat. If you are not using the stock immediately, cover and refrigerate or freeze. Makes about 2 litres (70 fl oz/8 cups)

vegetable stock

2 tablespoons unsalted butter
2 garlic cloves, crushed
2 onions, roughly chopped
4 leeks, white part only, rinsed and roughly chopped
3 carrots, peeled and roughly chopped
3 celery stalks, thickly sliced
1 fennel bulb, trimmed and roughly chopped
a handful of flat-leaf (Italian) parsley
2 thyme sprigs
2 black peppercorns

Melt the butter in a large heavy-based saucepan over medium heat. Add the garlic and onion and sauté for 5 minutes, or until the onion is soft and transparent. Add the remaining ingredients and 4 litres (140 fl oz/16 cups) cold water. Bring to the boil, then reduce the heat and simmer for 2 hours. Allow the stock to cool.

Strain the stock into a clean saucepan, using the back of a large spoon to press the liquid from the vegetables. Bring the stock to the boil, then reduce the heat to a rolling boil until the stock is reduced by half. If you are not using the stock immediately, cover and refrigerate or freeze. Makes about 2 litres (70 fl oz/8 cups)

fish stock

1 kg (2 lb 4 oz) fish bones
1 onion, roughly chopped
1 carrot, peeled and roughly chopped
1 fennel bulb, trimmed and sliced
2 celery stalks, roughly chopped
a few thyme sprigs
a few flat-leaf (Italian) parsley stalks
4 black peppercorns

Put the fish bones in a large saucepan with 3 litres (105 fl oz/12 cups) cold water. Bring just to the boil, then reduce the heat and simmer for 20 minutes. Strain the liquid through a fine sieve into another saucepan to remove the bones, then add the remaining ingredients. Return to the boil, then reduce the heat and simmer for a further 35 minutes.

Strain into a bowl. If you are not using the stock immediately, cover and refrigerate or freeze. Makes about 1.5 litres (52 fl oz/6 cups)

veal/beef stock

1 kg (2 lb 4 oz) veal or beef bones
2 tablespoons olive oil
2 onions, chopped
3 garlic cloves
2 leeks, white part only, rinsed and roughly chopped
2 celery stalks, roughly chopped
2 large tomatoes, roughly chopped
1 bay leaf
6 black peppercorns

Preheat the oven to 200°C (400°F/Gas 6). Put the veal or beef bones and olive oil in a large roasting tin, rub the oil over the bones and roast for 30 minutes. Add the onion, garlic, leek, celery and tomato to the roasting tin. Continue roasting for about 1 hour, or until the bones are well browned.

Put the roasted bones and vegetables in a large heavy-based saucepan and cover with 4 litres (140 fl oz/16 cups) cold water. Bring to the boil over medium heat, then reduce the heat to a simmer. Skim any fat from the surface, add the bay leaf and peppercorns and cook at a low simmer for 4 hours.

Strain the stock into a bowl and allow to cool. Using a large spoon, remove any fat from the surface. Return the stock to a clean saucepan and simmer over low heat to reduce and concentrate the flavour. If you are not using the stock immediately, cover and refrigerate or freeze. Makes about 2 litres (70 fl oz/8 cups)

sweet

scones

400 g (14 oz/3¹/₄ cups) plain (all-purpose) flour
3 teaspoons baking powder
2 tablespoons caster (superfine) sugar
85 g (3 oz) unsalted butter, chilled and diced
1 teaspoon lemon juice
200 ml (7 fl oz) milk
2 eggs

Preheat the oven to 200°C (400°F/Gas 6). Line a baking tray with baking paper. Sift the flour into a large bowl and add the baking powder, sugar, butter and a pinch of salt. Rub the butter into the flour until it resembles fine breadcrumbs.

In a separate bowl, stir the lemon juice into the milk, then whisk in the eggs.

Make a well in the centre of the dry ingredients and pour in the milk mixture. Stir until the ingredients just come together, then turn out onto a floured surface. Knead once or twice to just bring the dough together.

Press the dough out until it is 3–4 cm (1¹/₄–1¹/₂ inches) thick. Using a round cookie cutter, cut out rounds of dough and place them on the tray. Bake for 12 minutes, or until golden. Makes 15

cardamom almond bread

3 egg whites
80 g (2³/₄ oz/¹/₃ cup) caster (superfine) sugar
85 g (3 oz/²/₃ cup) plain (all-purpose) flour
zest of 2 oranges
90 g (3¹/₄ oz/¹/₂ cup) blanched almonds
¹/₄ teaspoon ground cardamom

Preheat the oven to 180°C (350°F/Gas 4). Grease an 8 x 22 cm (3¹/₄ x 8¹/₂ inch) loaf (bar) tin and line it with baking paper.

Beat the egg whites using electric beaters until they are stiff, then slowly whisk in the sugar. When the sugar has been fully incorporated and the whites are glossy, fold in the flour, orange zest, almonds and cardamom. Spoon the mixture into the prepared tin and bake for 40 minutes.

Cool the almond bread on a wire rack. When the loaf is cold, cut it into thin slices with a serrated knife and spread them out on a baking tray. Bake at 140°C (275°F/Gas 1) for 15 minutes, or until the slices are crisp. Allow to cool completely on a wire rack before storing in an airtight container. Makes about 30 slices

basic butter cake

250 g (9 oz) softened unsalted butter
230 g (8 oz/1 cup) caster (superfine) sugar
3 eggs
125 ml (4 fl oz/¹/₂ cup) milk
1 teaspoon natural vanilla extract
250 g (9 oz/2 cups) self-raising flour, sifted

Preheat the oven to 180°C (350°F/Gas 4). Grease and line a 23 cm (9 inch) spring-form cake tin.

Beat the butter and sugar until pale and creamy. Add the eggs, milk and vanilla and stir to combine. Fold in the flour, then spoon into the prepared tin. Bake for 1 hour, or until a skewer inserted into the centre of the cake comes out clean. Serves 8

sweet shortcrust tart case

200 g (7 oz/heaped 1²/₃ cups) plain (all-purpose) flour
100 g (3¹/₂ oz) unsalted butter, chilled and cut into cubes
1 tablespoon caster (superfine) sugar
2 tablespoons chilled water

Put the flour, butter, sugar and a pinch of salt in a food processor and process for 1 minute. Add the chilled water and process until the mixture comes together. Wrap the dough in plastic wrap and refrigerate for 30 minutes.

Grease a 25 cm (10 inch) tart tin or six 8 cm (3¹/₄ inch) tartlet tins. Roll the pastry out as thinly as possible between two layers of plastic wrap, then use it to line the prepared tin or tins, removing the plastic wrap once the pastry is in place. Chill for a further 30 minutes.

Preheat the oven to 180°C (350°F/Gas 4). Using a fork, prick the pastry over the base, line with crumpled baking paper and fill with rice or baking weights. Bake for 10–15 minutes, or until the pastry looks cooked and dry. Remove from the oven and allow to cool. Makes 1 large or 6 small cases

stewed apples

4 cooking apples, such as granny smith or golden delicious
juice of 1 orange
1 tablespoon butter

Peel and core the apples, chop into small pieces and place in a saucepan with the orange juice and butter. Cover and cook over low heat for 10–15 minutes, or until softly dissolved. Serve warm with custard, or use in a quick apple crumble. Serves 4

stewed rhubarb

500 g (1 lb 2 oz/1 bunch) rhubarb, washed and trimmed
80 g (2³/4 oz/¹/3 cup) caster (superfine) sugar

Roughly chop the rhubarb and place in a stainless steel
saucepan with the sugar. Cover and cook over low heat
for 10–15 minutes, or until the rhubarb has dissolved.
Serve warm with custard or rice pudding. Serves 4

berry coulis

300 g (10¹/2 oz) of your favourite fresh or frozen berries
1 tablespoon lemon juice
3 tablespoons caster (superfine) sugar, to taste

Put all the ingredients in a blender or food processor and
blend to a smooth sauce. Check the sweetness: add a little
more sugar if necessary. Strain through a fine sieve, then
store in a clean screw-top jar in the refrigerator for up to
1 week, or freeze until needed. Serves 8

dried fruit compote

a handful of each of the following dried fruits: figs, apricots,
    prunes, peaches and apples
3 tablespoons sugar
juice of 2 oranges
1 cinnamon stick

Chop the dried fruit into smallish pieces and place in a large
bowl. Put the remaining ingredients in a small saucepan with
250 ml (9 fl oz/1 cup) water. Bring to the boil over medium
heat, stirring to dissolve the sugar. Boil gently for 5–6 minutes,
then pour the hot syrup over the dried fruit. Cover and allow
to soak for several hours or overnight. Serves 8

sweet mascarpone

2 eggs, separated
250 g (9 oz/heaped 1 cup) mascarpone cheese
2–3 tablespoons caster (superfine) sugar
1 teaspoon finely grated orange zest
2 tablespoons Grand Marnier

Whisk the egg whites in a clean bowl until soft peaks form.
Combine the remaining ingredients in a separate bowl, then
lightly fold the egg white through until well combined.
Serves 4–6

meringues

2 egg whites
100 g (3¹/2 oz/scant ¹/2 cup) caster (superfine) sugar

Preheat the oven to 120°C (235°F/Gas ¹/2). Line a baking tray
with baking paper. Beat the egg whites using electric beaters
until soft peaks form, then gradually add half the sugar, beating
quite fast for 2 minutes until stiff peaks form. Remove the
beaters and lightly fold the remaining sugar through.

Spoon the mixture into large dollops on the baking tray, then
bake for 1¹/2 hours. Turn the oven off, leaving the door open,
and allow the meringues to cool in the oven. Store in an
airtight container until ready to use. Makes 8

passionfruit syrup

230 g (8 oz/1 cup) caster (superfine) sugar
1 vanilla bean, split lengthways
1 large red chilli, seeded and finely chopped (optional)
pulp of 3 passionfruit
juice of 1 lime

Put the sugar, vanilla bean, chilli, passionfruit pulp and
500 ml (17 fl oz/2 cups) water in a small saucepan. Bring
to the boil, then reduce the heat and simmer for 15 minutes.
Allow to cool, then stir in the lime juice. Pour into a clean
glass screw-top jar and refrigerate until ready to use.
Makes about 350 ml (12 fl oz)

chocolate sauce

185 g (6¹/2 oz/1 cup) soft brown sugar
3 tablespoons butter
185 ml (6 fl oz/³/4 cup) whipping (pouring) cream
60 g (2¹/2 oz/generous ¹/3 cup) chopped dark chocolate

Put the sugar, butter and cream in a small saucepan. Bring
to the boil, stirring, then reduce the heat and simmer for a
few minutes. Remove from the heat, add the chocolate and
stir until melted. Allow to cool before serving. Serves 8

glossary

american-style pork ribs

These are pork ribs that are trimmed from the inside of the belly and still have quite a bit of meat attached. They generally come as a rack, but often butchers will trim them into pairs.

balsamic vinegar

Balsamic vinegar is a dark, fragrant, sweetish aged vinegar made from grape juice. The production of authentic balsamic vinegar is carefully controlled. Bottles of the real thing are labelled *Aceto Balsamico Tradizionale de Modena*, while commercial varieties simply have *Aceto Balsamico de Modena*. Caramelized balsamic vinegar is a sweetened reduction that is thicker, sweeter and less acidic than regular balsamic vinegar and is available from most speciality food stores.

betel leaf

This delicate green leaf, also known as wild betel leaf or *char plu*, is commonly eaten raw in Thai cuisine, where it is often used as a base or a wrapping for the small appetizers known as *miang*. The leaves are sold in bunches in Thai or Asian speciality shops.

black rice

This form of glutinous rice owes its colour to the layer of bran left intact on the grain which colours the rice as it cooks, resulting in a uniformly purplish-black rice. Predominantly used for sweet dishes in Thailand and the Philippines, it is available from Asian food stores.

black sesame seeds

Mainly used in Asian cooking, black sesame seeds add colour, crunch and a distinct nuttiness to whatever dish they garnish. They can be found in most Asian grocery stores. Purchase the seeds regularly, as they can become rancid with age.

bocconcini cheese

These are small balls of fresh mozzarella cheese, often sold sitting in their own whey. When fresh they are soft and springy to the touch and have a milky taste. They are available from delicatessens.

brioche

Brioche is a light, sweet French-style bread flavoured with eggs and butter. Its rich colouring and fine texture make it ideal for breakfast dishes and for desserts. It is sold in bakeries and some large supermarkets.

broad beans

Broad or fava beans can be eaten whole when they are very young, but are more commonly sold as large, flat beans which need to be shelled like peas, then cooked and peeled of the outer tough skin to reveal delicate bright-green beans. When fresh beans are not in season, look for the shelled frozen beans sold in most large supermarkets.

buffalo mozzarella

A soft, creamy white mozzarella cheese traditionally made in southern Italy. It is considered to be the best-quality mozzarella due to its texture and flavour.

burghul

Popular in the Middle East, burghul (bulgur) is the key ingredient in tabouleh and pilaff. You can buy these wheat kernels either whole or cracked into fine, medium or coarse grains. They are pre-steamed and pre-baked to minimize cooking time.

butter puff pastry

This is puff pastry made with butter rather than vegetable fat, which gives it a much more buttery flavour than standard puff pastry. If you can't find any, use ordinary puff pastry and brush it with melted butter to add flavour.

buttermilk

This low-fat dairy product is made from skim milk and milk powder, with a culture similar to yoghurt introduced. It is often used in baking (as a raising agent) and can be found in the refrigerated section of most supermarkets. It has a tart taste.

cannellini beans

These small white beans are most commonly used in soups, stews and salads. They can be bought dried, or pre-cooked in tins.

casareccia

These short lengths of rolled and twisted Italian pasta are traditionally served with a meat sauce. This style of pasta is now commercially produced and is available in most large supermarkets.

chinese black vinegar

This rice vinegar is sharper than white rice varieties and is traditionally used in stir-fries, soups and dipping sauces. The Chinese province of Chekiang has the reputation for producing the best black vinegars.

chinese roasted duck

These whole ducks are rubbed with Chinese spices, then roasted until the skin is crispy and a glossy, golden brown. You can buy them freshly cooked from speciality Chinese stores and butchers.

chinese salted black beans

These black beans are sold vacuum-packed or in tins in Asian food stores. Their strong flavour brings a rich saltiness to stir-fries and sauces for beef dishes.

chipotle chillies

Large jalapeño chillies that have been smoked and dried are known as chipotle chillies. They are sold in delicatessens in tins, preserved in a smoky rich sauce, or can be bought in dried form, in which case they must be reconstituted in warm water before use.

chocolate

Couverture is the best-quality chocolate. This bittersweet chocolate contains the highest percentage of cocoa butter and is sold in good delicatessens and food stores. If you are unable to obtain chocolate of this standard, then it is preferable to use a good-quality eating chocolate rather than a cheap cooking chocolate. Cooking chocolates, on the whole, do not have a good flavour and tend to result in an oily rather than buttery texture.

chorizo sausage

A spicy, coarse-textured Spanish-style sausage which is normally sliced and then cooked. It lends a wonderful flavour to soups, stews and salads.

coconut

The coconut is a common cooking ingredient in the Pacific, South-East Asia and India. The flesh is often grated or shredded and then dried. Shredding coconut produces small thin strips of dried coconut which are often used decoratively in desserts. Desiccated coconut is finely grated coconut which has been dried. It can be used in savoury as well as sweet dishes.

coconut cream/milk

Coconut milk is sold in tins in most supermarkets and is made from freshly grated coconut. Slightly thicker than coconut milk, coconut cream is also sold in tins alongside coconut milk. If you can't obtain coconut cream, use the thick cream off the top of several tins of coconut milk instead. Pour the milk into a jug and leave it to settle — the cream will separate out at the top.

couscous

Couscous is the favoured dish of North Africa. It is made from a flour-coated granular semolina and traditionally steamed in a *couscousiere*. Nowadays, instant couscous is available in most large supermarkets.

crème fraîche

A naturally soured cream that is lighter than sour cream, sold in gourmet food stores and some large supermarkets.

daikon

Daikon is a large white radish. Its flavour varies from mild to surprisingly spicy, depending on the season and variety. Daikon contains an enzyme that aids digestion. It can be freshly grated or slow-cooked in broths, and is sold in large supermarkets or Asian grocery stores. Select firm, shiny vegetables with unscarred skins.

dashi granules

A common ingredient in Japanese cooking, dashi is a stock base made from dried kelp and flakes of dried bonito (a type of fish). Instant dashi can be bought from Asian food stores. Follow the manufacturer's instructions and simply add water to make an easy stock.

dried asian fried shallots

Crisp-fried shallots or onions are available from most Asian grocery stores and are normally packaged in plastic tubs or bags. They are used as a flavour enhancer, scattered over rice and savoury dishes.

dried barberries

Small elongated red berries used in Middle Eastern desserts. They have a slight acid bite that balances fruity or sugary desserts.

dried chinese egg vermicelli

These very thin noodles are made from wheat flour, water and egg. They are normally sold in small neat bundles of dried yellow noodles.

dried limes

Traditionally used in Persian cuisine, dried limes are small, black and withered-looking and feel hard and almost hollow. They add an exquisite flavour and are sold by Middle Eastern grocers.

fish sauce

This pungent, salty liquid made from fermented fish is widely used in South-East Asian cooking to add a salty, savoury flavour. Buy a small bottle and store it in the fridge.

french or red asian shallots

These small onions have a thin, papery skin and grow in bunches. They are also sometimes referred to as eschallots.

furikake seasoning

A Japanese seasoning made from dried flakes of seaweed combined with salt, sesame seeds and flakes of bonito (a type of fish). Usually used as a flavouring shaken over rice and noodles.

garam masala

An Indian spice blend featuring ground cumin, coriander, cardamom, cloves and nutmeg.

gelatine

Leaf gelatine is available in sheets of varying sizes. Be careful to check the manufacturer's instructions regarding which ratio of liquid to gelatine sheet to use. If leaves are unavailable, use gelatine powder instead, making sure it is well dissolved in warm liquid before using in recipes. Again, refer to the manufacturer's instructions.

golden syrup

A light golden-coloured syrup that has a thick consistency similar to honey. It is used to flavour puddings and other sweet recipes.

gruyère cheese

This firm cow's milk cheese has a smooth texture and natural rind. It has a nutty flavour and melts easily, making it perfect for use in tarts and gratins.

hoisin sauce

A Chinese sauce made from a base of fermented soya beans. Hoisin has a distinctive salty, sweet flavour with a hint of garlic and Chinese five-spice.

horseradish

Horseradish is the pungent root of the mustard family. Large and white, it has a knobbly brown skin and a very spicy, hot flavour. It is usually freshly grated as a condiment for roast beef and smoked fish. When commercially produced, horseradish is often blended with cream to give it a smoother texture. Dollop on roast beef or smoked salmon.

jerusalem artichoke

No relation to the globe artichoke, these small tubers are in fact a cousin of the sunflower. Their sweet, earthy flavour makes them ideal for soups and purées.

kecap manis

This is a thick, sweet-flavoured soy sauce used in Indonesian cooking.

lemon grass

These long, fragrant stems are very popular in Thai cuisine. The tough outer layers should be stripped off first, and the white stem can then be used either finely chopped or whole in soups. Lemon grass will keep refrigerated for up to 2 weeks.

lime pickle

Jars of lime pickle are available from Indian grocery stores and large supermarkets. It is usually served as a side dish in Indian cooking.

makrut leaves

Also known as kaffir lime, the glossy leaves of this South-East Asian tree impart a wonderful citrusy aroma to stir-fries, soups and curries. Where possible, always use fresh rather than dried leaves as they are far more fragrant.

marsala

Perhaps Italy's most famous fortified wine, marsala is available in sweet and dry varieties. Often used in desserts such as zabaglione, it is superb with eggs, cream and almonds.

mascarpone cheese

This heavy, Italian-style set cream is used as a base in many sweet and savoury dishes. It is made from cream rather than milk, so is high in fat. A popular use is in the Italian dessert tiramisu. It is sold in delicatessens and supermarkets.

mirin

Mirin is a rice wine used in Japanese cooking. It adds sweetness to many sauces and dressings, and is used for marinating and glazing dishes such as teriyaki. It is available from Asian grocery stores and most supermarkets.

miso paste

An important ingredient in Japanese cooking, miso paste is made of fermented soya beans and other flavourings such as wheat, rice or barley. It is used as a flavouring and a condiment.

natural vanilla extract

When using vanilla essence, always ensure it is made from real vanilla and is not labelled 'imitation' vanilla extract or essence. The flavours are quite different, with the imitation being almost acrid in its aftertaste. See also vanilla bean.

niçoise olives

Niçoise or Ligurian olives are small black olives that are commonly used in salads or scattered over prepared dishes. They are not suitable for making into pastes (tapenades).

nori

Nori is an edible seaweed sold in paper-thin sheets. To concentrate the flavour, lightly roast the shiny side of the sheets over a low flame. Nori sheets are available from most large supermarkets and Asian grocery stores.

orange flower water

This perfumed distillation of bitter-orange blossoms is mostly used as a flavouring in baked goods and drinks. It is readily available from large supermarkets and delicatessens.

orzo

A small rice-shaped pasta often used in soups.

palm sugar

Palm sugar, also known as jaggery, is obtained from the sap of various palm trees and is sold as hard cakes, or in cylinders and in plastic jars. If it is very hard it will need to be grated. It can be found in Asian grocery stores or large supermarkets. Substitute dark brown sugar when palm sugar is unavailable.

pancetta

This is the salted belly of pork, somewhat like streaky bacon. It is available from delicatessens and some supermarkets. Pancetta is available either rolled and finely sliced, or in large pieces ready to be diced or roughly cut.

panettone

An aromatic northern Italian yeast bread made with raisins and candied peel, panettone is traditionally eaten at Christmas, when it is sold in Italian delicatessens or large supermarkets. It is available in large and small sizes.

papaya

This large tropical fruit can be red, orange or yellow. It contains an enzyme that stops gelatine setting, so avoid using it in jellies. It is sometimes called a pawpaw, but is really part of the custard apple family.

passata

A rich, thick tomato purée made from sieved tomatoes. It can be used as a base in sauces and soups.

pecorino cheese

A strong-flavoured, hard cheese made from sheep's milk. It is quite similar to parmesan cheese in flavour.

peppercorns

Pink and green peppercorns are the unripe berries of pepper trees and are pickled in vinegar. They add a peppery, piquant flavour to rich dishes such as buttery sauces or terrines.

pickled ginger

Japanese pickled ginger is available from most large supermarkets. The thin slivers of young ginger root are pickled in sweet vinegar and turn a distinctive salmon-pink colour in the process. This soft pink colour is often exaggerated to a hot pink colour in commercially produced ginger, which has had food colouring added. The vinegar is an ideal additive to sauces where a sweet, gingery bite is called for.

polenta

Polenta is a yellow, grainy cornmeal that is slowly cooked in boiling water to form a thick, savoury porridge.

pomegranate molasses

This is a thick syrup made from the reduction of pomegranate juice. It has a bittersweet flavour, which adds a sour bite to many Middle Eastern dishes. It is available from Middle Eastern speciality stores. The closest substitute is sweetened tamarind.

porcini mushrooms

Porcini mushrooms, which are also known as ceps in France, are highly prized as a flavouring agent in European cooking. In appearance they are creamy brown with thick rounded caps. They are more commonly available dried and are sold in most delicatessens and speciality food stores.

pork belly

A cut of meat taken from the underside of a pig. This particular section is commonly used for streaky bacon and pancetta, but pieces can also be slow-cooked, providing a rich and very succulent meat.

preserved lemon

These are whole lemons preserved in salt or brine, which turns their rind soft and pliable. Only the rind is used in cooking — the pulp should be scraped out and discarded. The lemons are available from delicatessens.

prosciutto

Prosciutto is a lightly salted, air-dried ham. It is commonly sold in paper-thin slices, and can be found in most large supermarkets. Parma ham and San Daniele are two types of prosciutto.

puy lentils

Originally grown in the volcanic soils of the Puy region in France, these lentils are highly prized for their flavour and the fact that they hold their shape during cooking.

quince paste

Quinces are large, aromatic fruits with a high pectin content. When cooked and reduced, the resulting paste is of a jelly-like consistency and has a rich pink colour. Quince paste can be purchased at most delicatessens.

quinoa

A grain native to South America, quinoa is high in protein and very nourishing as it contains all eight essential amino acids. A wonderful base for salads and hearty sauces, quinoa is an ideal substitute for brown rice and has a similar nutty flavour. It is available from health food stores.

raw caster sugar

Also known as superfine sugar, this is a finer form of raw (demerara) sugar. Its colouring brings a lovely brown tone to the food it is sweetening and a slightly caramel flavour.

rice wine vinegar

Made from fermented rice, this vinegar comes in clear, red and black versions. If no colour is specified in a recipe, use the clear vinegar. The clear rice wine vinegar is sweeter and milder than its European counterparts or the darker and sharper-flavoured Chinese black vinegar.

risoni

Risoni are small rice-shaped pasta. They are ideal for use in soups or salads where their small shape is able to absorb the other flavours in the dish.

risotto rice

Three well-known varieties of risotto rice are widely available today: arborio, a large plump grain that makes a sticky risotto; vialone nano, a shorter grain that produces a loose consistency and maintains more of a bite in the middle; and carnaroli, which is similar in size to vialone nano, and makes a good, firm risotto. All varieties are interchangeable, although cooking times may vary by five minutes or so.

rosewater

The distilled essence of rose petals, rosewater is used in small quantities to impart a perfumed flavour to pastries, fruit salads and sweet puddings. It is available from delicatessens and large supermarkets.

saffron threads

The orange-red stigmas from one species of crocus plant, saffron threads are the most expensive spice in the world. Each flower consists of three stigmas, which are hand-picked, then dried — a very labour-intensive process. Saffron should be bought in small quantities and used sparingly as it has a very strong flavour. Beware of inexpensive brands when buying saffron, as cheap 'real' saffron does not exist!

sansho pepper

A hot Japanese spice with a slightly numbing, peppery flavour.

sashimi-grade fish

Fish sold for making sushi and sashimi is intended to be eaten raw, and so is usually the freshest fish at the markets. Buy a thick piece cut from the centre rather than the narrower tail end.

semolina

Semolina is made of coarse granules of durum wheat. Fine semolina has smaller grains and is available from gourmet food stores.

shaoxing rice wine

This Chinese rice wine is used to add flavour to braised dishes and sauces. It takes its name from Shaoxing or Shao Hsing, a provincial town in northern China which has been producing rice wine for centuries. Shaoxing rice wine is similar to a fine sherry and is made from glutinous rice.

shiitake mushrooms

These Asian mushrooms have white gills and a brown cap. Meaty in texture, they keep their shape well when cooked. Dried shiitake are often sold as dried Chinese mushrooms.

sichuan peppercorns

Dried red berries of the prickly ash tree, native to Sichuan in China. Their flavour is spicy-hot and leaves a numbing aftertaste, which can linger for some time. Dry-fry and crush the berries for the best flavour. Japanese sancho pepper is a close relative and may be used instead.

smoked paprika

Paprika is commonly sold as a dried, rich-red powder made from a member of the chilli family. It is sold in many grades, from delicate through to sweet and finally hot. Smoked paprika from Spain adds a distinct rich, smoky flavour to recipes and is well worth looking for if you enjoy introducing these flavours into your favourite dishes.

soba noodles

These thin buckwheat noodles make an ideal base for many Asian-style noodle salads or soups. They are usually sold dried and are sometimes flavoured with green tea.

somen noodles

These thin, wheat-based Japanese noodles are commonly sold dried and in bundles. They are available from Japanese speciality stores, large supermarkets and health food shops.

sour cherries

Sour or morello cherries are most commonly sold bottled in sweet juice. They have a slightly tart flavour, making them ideal for baking.

sourdough bread

Sourdough is a French-style bread that uses a fermented dough as its raising agent. It is commonly sold as a thick-textured country-style loaf.

star anise

This is a pretty, star-shaped dried fruit containing small, oval, brown seeds. Star anise has a flavour similar to anise, but is more liquorice-like. It is commonly used whole because of its decorative shape.

sterilizing jars

Sterilize your jars or bottles before filling them with food you intend to keep for a while. Wash them in hot soapy water, boil for 10 minutes in a saucepan large enough to completely submerge them, then drain on a clean tea towel (dish towel). Dry in a 130°C (250°F/Gas 1) oven and then remove and fill while the jars are still hot.

sumac

Sumac is a peppery, sour spice made from dried and ground sumac berries. The fruit of a shrub found in the northern hemisphere, it is widely used in Middle Eastern cookery. Sumac is available from most large supermarkets and Middle Eastern speciality stores.

tahini

This thick, creamy paste is made from husked and ground white sesame seeds. It is used to give a strong nutty flavour to Middle Eastern salads or sauces. Tahini is available in jars from health food stores and most supermarkets.

tamarind

Tamarind is the sour pulp of an Asian fruit. It is most commonly available compressed into cakes or refined as tamarind concentrate in jars. Tamarind concentrate is widely available; the pulp can be found in Asian food shops.

tofu

This white curd is made from soya beans and is a great source of protein. Bland in taste, it takes on the flavour of other ingredients. Tofu is usually sold in blocks and comes in several different grades - soft (silken), firm, sheets and deep-fried. Refrigerate fresh tofu covered in water for up to five days, changing the water daily.

vanilla bean

The long, slim black vanilla bean has a wonderful caramel aroma which synthetic vanillas can never capture. Good-quality beans are soft and not too dry. Store unused vanilla pods in a full jar of castor (superfine) sugar — this will help keep the vanilla fresh, and the aroma of the bean will also quickly infuse the sugar, making it a wonderful addition to desserts and baking.

vine leaves

The large, green leaves of the grapevine are sold packed in tins, jars or plastic packs or in brine. They are used in Greek and Middle Eastern cookery to wrap foods for cooking. Vine leaves in brine should be rinsed before use to remove some of the salty flavour. Before using fresh young vine leaves, simmer them in water for 10 minutes to soften them.

wasabi

Mostly sold in tubes or in a powdered dried form (mixed to a paste with a little water), wasabi comes from the dark green root of a Japanese aquatic plant and has a very hot flavour. It is used to flavour sushi, sashimi and some sauces.

water chestnuts

The edible white tubers of an aquatic plant, water chestnuts add a delicate, crunchy texture to South-East Asian dishes. Fresh water chestnuts are sold in Asian grocers, or you can buy them whole or sliced in tins from supermarkets.

index